The People's Car Book

Also by Sal Fariello:

- **Automotive Service Marketing**

- **Fathers & Grandfathers Under Siege**

- **Father's Guide to Child Support, Custody and Visitation**

- **Mother's Guide to Child Support, Custody and Visitation**

- and -

- **Mugged By Mr. Badwrench**

The People's Car Book

The One Essential Handbook for People

Who Don't Trust Mechanics,

Car Salesmen, or Car Manufacturers

Sal Fariello

St. Martin's Press   New York

Design by Vera Guagliata-Fariello

Library of Congress Cataloging-in-Publication Data

Fariello, Sal.
　　The people's car book : the one essential handbook for people who don't trust mechanics, car salesmen, or car manufacturers / Sal Fariello.
　　　　p.　cm.
　　"A Thomas Dunne book."
　　ISBN 0-312-08278-9
　　1. Automobiles—Purchasing.　2. Automobiles—Maintenance and repair.　3. Consumer education.　I. Title.
　　TL162.F37　1992
　　629.222'029'7—dc20

92-26608
CIP

First Edition: February 1993

10 9 8 7 6 5 4 3 2 1

MONEY-BACK GUARANTEE

If you are not completely satisfied with *The People's Car Book*, we will be happy to refund your purchase price.

To receive a refund, you must return the book (which must be undamaged) with a copy of the sales receipt and a self-addressed stamped envelope to:

Thomas Dunne Books
℅ St. Martin's Press, Inc.
175 Fifth Avenue
New York, NY 10010

This offer is good for returns received within 30 days after purchase.

Here's what you'll find in The People's Car Book

Contents

Contents

Part I

How to Save Money When You Buy or Lease a Car

What You Will Find in Part I

EVERY CAR manufacturer loves a *prospective* customer. Car companies spend millions of dollars trying to make prospective customers actual car buyers. Unfortunately, after you have made a purchase, the same carmakers that wooed you to make a sale sometimes treat you like you don't exist if you happen to have bought a lemon. Assuming the relative quality of the car you intend to buy is not an issue (every company builds some lemons), how can you judge the quality of the company responsible for backing up its warranty? In Part I we'll look at data that shed light on which carmakers do a good job caring for their customers and which ones just do a lot of talking.

Most consumers think getting the best price on a new car simply involves shopping at several dealers and buying from the one that offers the lowest figure. Not true. This strategy can cost you hundreds or even thousands of dollars. Nowadays many consumers are turning to leasing to avoid a large down payment on a new car. Most people pay far too much for their lease because they don't know a few tricks of the trade. Part I will show you how to avoid many of the traps that await the unwary shopper who wants to buy or lease a new car, or buy a used car.

Here's what you'll find in Part I

Contents

Chapter 1: Buying a New Car

Chapter 2: Leasing a New Car

3

Contents

Chapter 1

Buying a New Car

Import or Domestic: Which Should You Choose?

MANY CONSUMERS believe that cars made by U.S. manufacturers are inferior to those made in Japan or Europe. This is absolutely untrue. U.S. carmakers have solved most of their major quality problems. The quality of many American-made cars is on par with or better than Japanese, European, or Korean products. Unfortunately, most potential car buyers are unaware of this. The American philosophy of car manufacturing used to consist of allowing many cars to leave the factory with defects and letting the dealers' service departments fix problems that should have been corrected on the assembly line. But many car dealers were too busy or too inept to get the job done. Nightmares involving aggrieved consumers who made endless visits to the service department for warranty repairs became legendary. Many of these disgruntled American car buyers said, "Never again," and turned to imported products.

Those who switched to cars made in Europe often found themselves no better off. Most cars coming from European factories in the 1970s and early 1980s were just as defect ridden and unreliable as their American counterparts. In addition, the cost of maintenance and repairs to these European models was (and generally still is) much higher than that for equivalent work done on an American car.

Japanese cars were another story. Although generally more costly to repair (this is still true), they were assembled with fewer defects. Dealers liked selling them because they didn't break down a lot and didn't create a lot of headaches for the service department. This is not to say that Japanese cars did not have serious problems in the 1970s and early 1980s. Industry insiders know full well the horrors of Japanese cars that turned to buckets of rust after only a few years on the road. And then there were the endless valve jobs, blown cylinder engine head gaskets, and broken cam belts that plagued some cars made in Japan. Nevertheless, consumers liked them. They were relatively cheap. Window handles and other hardware didn't come off in your hand. Doors fit. Trunks closed tight. Paint jobs looked nice. And most important, shrewd and progressive companies such as Toyota were smart enough to make sure their dealers took good care of customers who did have problems.

All this made for a good reputation for the Japanese carmakers. They well deserve it. But are the cars still better in quality than their American-made counterparts? It depends on the model. There are some models of Japanese cars that are not all that great. Minivans are good examples. As of this writing, Chrysler builds some of the best minivans. Nissan has turned to Ford Motor Company for help in building a world class minivan. This sort of collaboration suggests the Japanese understand that U.S. carmakers certainly know how to do some things right.

Presently the best models produced by all major automobile manufacturers are roughly equal in quality. With this in mind, you should choose a new car based on the following guidelines:

1. Your personal transportation needs and budget.

2. The performance record of the model you are considering.

3. The Customer Satisfaction Index (CSI) and reputation of the selling dealer.

4. The customer service record of the manufacturer.

Can You Trust the J.D. Power Surveys?

Automobile advertisers often boast about being number one in one or more surveys conducted by the J.D. Power company. This company conducts three surveys that should be of interest to consumers and can help you determine which make of car to buy. The surveys are:

1. Initial quality.

2. Customer satisfaction index.

3. Vehicle dependability index.

Initial Quality

There is no longer a major difference in overall product quality among most major automobile nameplates. The much touted J.D. Power annual Initial Quality Survey

(IQS) places a certain make of car in first place. If there is a first place, of course there has to be a fifth place, a tenth place, and so forth. But just how significant is the difference in quality between first and tenth place, for example?

Not significant at all! The tenth-place model is only a few tenths of a defect (Power prefers to call defects "problems") per car worse than the first-place model. A few tenths of a defect is meaningless. Therefore, you should not assume that you are buying the best car because it rates near the top of the J.D. Power IQS.

The survey itself derives information about product quality by polling about 70,000 people who bought new cars in November or December. The following February, questionnaires are sent to the car buyers. The questions seek to determine overall satisfaction with the quality of the car purchased during the initial 90 days of ownership. Questions target 12 major areas where there can be problems: paint job, brakes, transmission, etc. The results are tabulated into defects per 100 cars. To obtain defects per individual car divide by 100. For example, a car having 100 defects per 100 cars averages 1 defect per car. One hundred fifty defects per 100 cars means there are 1.5 defects per car. To obtain a copy of the latest J. D. Power IQS, visit a public library that carries *Automotive News* (an auto industry weekly tabloid) and review the June issues, one of which will probably contain the IQS results. You can also call the *Automotive News* editorial offices at (313) 446-0361. Speak to any editor and

explain that you want the IQS results. Be polite and you'll likely get the information you need. You can also contact J.D. Power and Associates at (818) 889-3719.

Before you make the mistake of only buying cars in the top ten slots in the Power IQS, you must consider what the survey results really mean. The survey clearly shows that you can expect fewer problems with Japanese-built autos than those made in America or Europe. However, many American cars demonstrate only a reported four- or five-tenths of a defect per car more than their Japanese counterparts. So small a difference is not significant.

The 1991 Power IQS Survey

In 1991, the industry average number of defects per car was 1.4, (whereas in 1992 the average was 1.25, so quality is improving). Overall, Toyota averaged 0.9 defects per car, whereas Honda averaged 1.1. Nissan averaged 1.6. America's new entry, Saturn, came in at a respectable 1.5 defects per car—better than Nissan but worse than Toyota and Honda. So if you are considering the purchase of a new car, use the Power IQS only if buying the highest *initial* quality available is important to you. Other issues you should weigh such as a car's long-term reliability and the level of customer service provided by the dealer and manufacturer give more importance to ownership of a car over time.

Remember that the Power survey is a survey of *initial* quality. It reflects owner experiences with their cars over the first three months of driving. Some cars, particularly

those made in America, have a habit of manifesting all sorts of minor problems when they are new, but work fine afterwards and last longer than average. Another point you must not forget is that the IQS considers a minor defect as having the same weight as a major one. Here's where American cars are at a disadvantage. As I implied, American cars, compared with Japanese models, are generally built with less attention to detail where fit and finish are concerned. Nevertheless, domestic cars have excellent major mechanical systems. The minor initial complaints consumers may have about American cars can distort the results of the Power survey in favor of Japanese makes.

The important point to keep in mind is that in general, American cars are fast closing the quality gap separating them from Japanese autos. In 1980 most American cars averaged about eight defects per car, whereas Japanese units averaged just two. Presently, Japanese autos have a small advantage—about one-half of a defect per car. This slight upper hand is demonstrated by the 1991 IQS. The top 23 models and their number of problems per car as reported in New York *Newsday* (taken from the Power survey) are as follows:

Lexus LS400 0.47	Toyota Camry 0.79
Acura NSX 0.71	Toyota Cressida 0.80
BMW 750iL 0.74	Mercedes-Benz 190E 0.89
Lexus ES250 0.76	Honda CRX 0.89
Mercedes-Benz S-Class 0.77	Plymouth Colt 0.90
Pontiac 6000 0.78	Buick Century 0.91
Infinity Q45 0.78	

Toyota Corolla 0.91	Oldsmobile Cierra 0.97
Mercury Grand Marquis 0.91	Geo Prizm 0.98
Dodge Colt 0.96	Buick LeSabre 0.99
BMW 735i/iL 0.97	Infinity G20 0.99
Toyota Tercel 0.97	Mercury Topaz 0.99

Keep in mind that the average number of defects per car reported in the Power IQS for 1991 was 1.4. Lexus LS400 led the pack with a paltry 0.47 defect per car. The twenty-third car on the list, Mercury Topaz, had a reported 0.99 defect per car, a mere 0.52 defect more than the Lexus. That's only one-half defect more per car; not a bad figure when you consider that the Lexus costs over *three times more* than the Topaz.

When it comes to the quality of domestically built cars, the 1991 IQS results speak for themselves. You'll see several U.S. nameplates high on the lists and all of them cost just a fraction of the sticker price you'll find glued to a Lexus LS400. There's no knocking the quality of the Lexus LS400—the car is superb. But you can get one that is for all *practical* purposes just as good for a lot less money. You don't have to buy Japanese makes anymore to get a good car.

The 1992 Power IQS Survey

The 1992 Power IQS survey indicates that vehicle quality is improving, with Japanese-built cars still leading the pack. The average number of defects reported for 1992 American-made cars was 1.36. Asian cars were a bit more impressive with 1.05 defects, whereas European-built cars had 1.58 defects per car. Once again, keep in mind that a little

annoyance such as a squeak in a glove box door can be considered a "problem" having as much weight in the survey as a burned out transmission.

The top 10 models and their number of problems per car as reported in the June 1, 1992 edition of *Automotive News* (taken from the Power survey) are as follows:

Lexus LS 400 0.46	Toyota Corolla 0.76
Toyota Cressida 0.49	Buick Regal (sedan) 0.78
Infinity Q45 0.53	Toyota Camry 0.84
Olds Cutlass Ciera 0.70	Acura Legend 0.85
Lexus SC300/SC400 0.72	Buick Century 0.85

The top 1992 makes in the Power IQS survey as reported in *Automotive News* were:

Infinity 0.70	Lincoln 1.14
Lexus 0.73	Acura 1.15
Toyota 0.85	Oldsmobile 1.21
Honda 1.05	Subaru 1.22
Nissan 1.08	Audi 1.24
Saturn 1.09	Buick 1.25

Clearly, the quality of cars overall is getting better. Doubtlessly, of delight to the "buy-American" advocates is the fact that domestic cars are finding their way into the upper levels of the quality surveys as they approach parity with their Asian counterparts. Nevertheless a stampede back to American cars by car buyers is not likely. Too many domestic car companies have let their customers down with poor product quality in the past and ever worse service. It would be overly optimistic to expect consumers to forget this overnight just because the Big Three automakers have finally learned how to build high quality cars. The quest for greater market share by Detroit carmakers is going to be a long, hard fight.

J.D. Power Customer Satisfaction Index

Not to be confused with car dealer customer satisfaction index (CSI) reports, the J.D. Power CSI survey evaluates consumer satisfaction with their cars. Dealer CSI scores are compiled by car manufacturers, while the Power CSI survey is the product of independent research. Another distinguishing feature is that the CSI surveys done by car manufacturers factor in service department performance as a significant variable in generating the CSI score, whereas the Power survey is more product dependent.

The Power satisfaction index attempts to measure the consumer's overall satisfaction with his or her car after one year of ownership. Survey questions address satisfaction with the selling dealer, the manufacturers and the reliability of the car. The average CSI score for all manufacturers in the 1991 model year was 127 (127 defects per one hundred cars). Most makes improved their scores compared to the previous two years, indicating that, overall, cars are getting better.

Of the 38 nameplates surveyed in 1991, Japanese brands claimed five of the top ten spots for customer satisfaction. The top ten were as follows:

Infiniti	Honda	Cadillac
Lexus	Toyota	Buick
Mercedes-Benz	Audi	BMW
Acura		

In 1992 the top ten models were:

Lexus	Mercedes-Benz	Cadillac
Infinity	Toyota	Honda
Saturn	Audi	Jaguar
Acura		

While the top four models in the 1991 survey are unquestionably excellent cars, they should be, considering their price. Virtually everything Honda and Toyota do is a class act, so their presence in the 1991 top ten is no surprise. Interestingly, Cadillac and Buick rank high, even above Nissan, Mazda, Suburu, Mitsubishi, and other Japanese makes. And although Oldsmobile didn't make it into the top ten in 1991, its rank of fourteenth put it above Volvo, Saab, Jaguar, Porsche, and other high-prestige European makes. Clearly, many American cars, particularly those built by General Motors, have made great leaps forward in quality and customer satisfaction. Note particularly that Saturn, an offshoot of General Motors, rated third in the 1992 CSI survey.

The results of the J.D. Power CSI survey for 1991 are listed below. An AA after the make indicates that make was above average in the survey. A BA indicates the nameplate rated below average. Car makes appear in descending order of customer satisfaction.

Infiniti (AA)	Audi (AA)
Lexus (AA)	Cadillac (AA)
Mercedes-Benz (AA)	Buick (AA)
Acura (AA)	BMW (AA)
Honda (AA)	Suburu (AA)
Toyota (AA)	Mazda (AA)

Nissan (AA)	Jaguar (BA)
Oldsmobile (AA)	Suzuki (BA)
Plymouth (BA)	Pontiac (BA)
Lincoln (BA)	Daihatsu (BA)
Mercury (BA)	Eagle (BA)
Volvo (BA)	Peugeot (BA)
Dodge (BA)	Alfa Romeo (BA)
Saab (BA)	Isuzu (BA)
Volkswagen (BA)	Porsche (BA)
Mitsubishi (BA)	Geo (BA)
Chevrolet (BA)	Hyundai (BA)
Chrysler (BA)	Sterling (BA)
Ford (BA)	Yugo (BA)

When you look at the results, you must remember that a manufacturer may have an overall low CSI rating even though it makes certain models that consumers are generally satisfied with. For example, Chrysler's CSI performance in 1991 was rather poor. However, the Plymouth Acclaim and Dodge Spirit, both built by Chrysler, are excellent cars that owners generally love and rate highly. Yet dissatisfaction with other models built by Chrysler were responsible for depressing its overall scores. You must also keep in mind that the Power CSI survey takes into account customer satisfaction with quality of service received from the dealer and the manufacturer, as well as the quality of the car. There is evidence that Chrysler and its dealers have not been doing a good job handling customer complaints. The same holds true for Ford. Corroboration of this is found in the lemon law surveys performed in various states and discussed later in this book. A poor dealer record may have brought about the relatively low CSI standings of Ford and Chrysler despite the fact that both build some excellent cars.

The standings in the Power CSI survey clearly show that service is a major part of a consumer's overall satisfaction with a particular car. Even though a company builds some good cars, it can engender consumer dissatisfaction by failing to offer good customer service. In the section of this book entitled, Which Car Companies Treat Their Customers Best, we'll see that the Power CSI ratings corroborate other data suggesting that companies such as Chrysler, Ford, Hyundai, and Yugo have not been resolving customer complaints effectively.

Now that you know the Power CSI survey includes an evaluation of customer satisfaction with both the actual car and the servicing offered, how can you separate the two? Can you use the Power survey to help you judge which car to buy? The answer is yes. Here's a rule of thumb you can follow. If a car is rated worse than average according to *Consumer Reports* frequency of repair data (see next section), and if the company that builds it scores below average in the Power CSI survey, don't buy the car. If you do, you may wind up with a poor car backed up by a poor service organization.

Vehicle Dependability Index

Many consumers have come to believe that all American-made cars are unreliable. A little known J.D. Power survey suggests otherwise. Dubbed the Power Vehicle Dependability Index (VDI), this survey tracks the reliability of past models. A recent VDI survey of 1985 cars ranked the top makes in descending order as follows:

Mercedes-Benz	Lincoln
Toyota	Oldsmobile
Honda	Mercury
Buick	Mazda
Cadillac	Pontiac
BMW and Porsche (tied)	

Not surprisingly, Mercedes-Benz took top honors for the reliability of its 1985 cars. For the prices they charge, Mercedes should build reliable cars! And of course Toyota and Honda are right up there near the top.

But what many may find startling is the presence of four General Motors car lines in a list of the top twelve most reliable 1985 cars. There is a lesson here about cars that few consumers really understand—there is a big difference between quality and reliability.

I have already pointed out that American cars tend to have more minor nuisance problems than their Japanese counterparts. By nuisance problems I mean doors that come from the factory improperly adjusted, minor squeaks and rattles, and so forth. These are *quality* problems. Generally, a quality problem involves something the factory did not assemble correctly. Quality problems often do not affect long-term *reliability*. In other words, once the dealer gets all the little bugs out under warranty, the car will run year after year without serious breakdowns. Reliability in essence is the ability of a car to operate without breakdowns.

The Power VDI for 1985 cars indicates that General Motors has been building reliable cars even though the average quality of its fleet may not have been the best. Like other domestic carmakers, General Motors has cleaned up its act as far as quality is concerned. Considering that on average, domestic cars are reliable and of good quality, there is no reason not to consider them when purchasing a new car.

Consumer Reports Repair Data—How Reliable?

Although every major carmaker generally builds excellent vehicles, some models produced by a particular manufacturer may be unsatisfactory. When you are considering the purchase of a particular model, it is worth the effort to study the repair data provided by *Consumer Reports* magazine in the annual auto issue released every April. Those models with a consistently worse than average repair history have the greatest likelihood of giving you trouble. Car models rated much worse than average in several categories in the frequency of repair tables may be mechanical dogs that will come back to bite your pocketbook. If you see a lot of solid black dots in the tables for a particular model, consider a different car.

Some critics of *Consumer Reports'* frequency of repair data argue that the facts are not representative of the general population because only *Consumer Reports* subscribers are surveyed. While I don't agree with all that *Consumer Reports* recommends when it comes to automotive matters, I fully support the magazine's repair surveys. If *Consumer Reports* repair tables indicate a car model is a mechanical monster, it probably is. One caveat, though—many car models do improve from model year to model year. Fre-

quency of repair data may condemn a 1991 model, but the same model can improve the next year and become an average or better than average car. Should you take a chance that this will happen? Your safest strategy is to wait until a favorable verdict comes in and then take the plunge with the previously doubtful model.

Which Car Companies Treat Their Customers Best?

Every car manufacturer promises you the world before you buy a car. How a manufacturer performs when you need help after you have bought a lemon can be quite another story. Part of the decision to buy a particular nameplate should be based on the quality of the customer service provided by the manufacturer and its dealers. Since all manufacturers and their dealers make claims of excellent customer service, how can you tell who can really deliver what they promise from those whose assertions are empty advertising? The data accumulated by the attorneys general of Florida and New York in connection with their respective lemon law programs provide objective information about which car companies provide the best customer service.

In Florida or New York a car owner who cannot get satisfaction from the dealer or manufacturer can make use of a state-run arbitration program. An arbitrator can award the consumer a replacement car, cash, or nothing depending on the facts of the case. Many car companies try especially hard to resolve customer complaints before they go to arbitration. These companies do an admirable job of discovering what it is that makes the customer unhappy and rectifying the situation before the drastic step of arbitration becomes necessary. Other car companies appear less able to satisfy their customers.

In Florida, the state attorney general's office compiles statistics that strongly suggest which car companies are doing a good job, and those that are doing a not so good job, of handling customer complaints. Florida looks at a carmaker's percentage of sales in the state and projects the expected percentage of lemons (a car that winds up in arbitration is considered a lemon if an award is made in the consumer's favor) based on sales.

For example, if Acme Motors sells 5 percent of all cars sold in Florida, it should not generate more than 5 percent of the lemons. Let's suppose that Acme does sell 5 percent of the cars sold in Florida but generates 15 percent of the lemons. What might we conclude from this? We might surmise that either Acme builds a lot of lemons or that Acme itself is a lemon of a company—that is, when customers experience problems, Acme doesn't do enough to solve them. Keep in mind that Acme might build really good cars. Their high lemon percentage might just be the result of poor handling of customer complaints, which inevitably occur in connection with some cars sold by every manufacturer.

Florida publishes a lemon index of carmakers that sell more than 4000 cars in the state. A lemon index of 1 means the car company generates a number of lemons in proportion to its percentage of sales in Florida. An index greater than 1 means a company generates more lemons than it should considering its sales. A number under 1 means a company appears to be doing a better than average job of solving customer complaints. Florida's 1990 lemon index is as follows:

Hyundai 10.45	Ford 1.01
Suburu 3.12	Mazda 1.0
BMW 2.86	Mitsubishi 0.68
Chrysler 1.71	Toyota 0.57
Mercedes-Benz 1.67	Honda 0.53
Isuzu 1.58	General Motors 0.37
Volvo 1.47	Volkswagen 0.0
Nissan 1.43	

In 1990 Hyundai generated more than ten times its expected share of lemons, hardly a performance to be proud of. Toyota and Honda generated much less than their share of lemons (naturally). But look at General Motors! Here's a company that sold more cars than any other manufacturer in Florida in 1990, yet generated the fewest lemons, except for Volkswagen. This does not necessarily mean that General Motors builds better cars than the other companies. It does suggest, however, that the people at GM are trying real hard to satisfy their customers when they do have problems. Kudos to GM— it's about time American carmakers put their money where their mouths are when it comes to getting problems solved before consumers decide to go to court.

If we consider the Florida data all by itself, GM comes out smelling like roses, Hyundai smells like rotten fish, and the rest are somewhere in between. But what about the New York data? Does the New York data corroborate what Florida discovered about the customer handling performance of particular carmakers?

New York computes its lemon data in a method similar to Florida's. The New York attorney general's office derives the manufacturers' share of the national market from data published in *Automotive News,* an auto industry publication. According to administrators of the New York lemon law program, the manufacturers' percentage of the national market is approximately the same as their percentage of the New York market. Although New York does not publish anything analogous to Florida's lemon index, its data can be converted to an index similar to Florida's. The list that follows shows the results for 1990 and 1991. Each carmaker's market share was averaged over two years, and the lemon index for the two years was averaged to arrive at the figure listed. Keep in mind that the larger the number, the worse the carmaker's performance.

Jaguar 7.2	BMW 0.96
Porsche 4.0	Volvo 0.72
Saab 3.12	General Motors 0.66
Chrysler 2.22	Nissan 0.46
Yugo 2.0	Mazda 0.43
Hyundai 1.92	Toyota 0.28
Volkswagen 1.56	Suburu 0.18
Ford 1.54	Mercedes-Benz 0.13
Mitsubishi 1.23	Honda 0.07

Now let's look at the New York lemon data for 1990 with the Florida lemon index number in parenthesis. A N/A means the car make was not included in the 1990 Florida report because fewer than 4000 of that make were sold in Florida in that year.

Jaguar 7.2 (N/A)	BMW 0.96 (2.86)
Porsche 4.0 (N/A)	Volvo 0.72 (1.47)
Saab 3.12 (N/A)	General Motors 0.66 (0.37)
Chrysler 2.22 (1.71)	Nissan 0.46 (1.43)
Yugo 2.0 (N/A)	Mazda 0.43 (1.0)
Hyundai 1.92 (10.45)	Toyota 0.28 (0.57)
Volkswagen 1.56 (0.0)	Suburu 0.18 (3.12)
Ford 1.54 (1.01)	Mercedes-Benz 0.13 (1.67)
Mitsubishi 1.23 (0.68)	Honda 0.07 (0.53)

You will notice that some car models that generated more than their expected share of lemons in Florida generated fewer than their expected share in New York. There are a number of variables that can account for this discrepancy. One important reason is the structure of the carmaker's service organization. Manufacturers have zone offices all over the country. Some zones may do a better job of resolving customer complaints than others.

Despite the variables, some patterns seem to emerge. Toyota and Honda always appear to generate fewer lemons and always rate high in every customer satisfaction survey done by J.D. Power. Also, their cars always rate high in *Consumer Reports'* frequency of repair surveys. Give Toyota and Honda credit for consistency! General Motors looks good in the Florida lemon report as well as the New York report. Not coincidentally, many of its cars have been improving in other industry surveys.

For additional insight into how the carmakers take care of their customers I looked at lemon law data compiled by the state of Washington, although in a somewhat different context. If a manufacturer is doing a good job of backing its dealers and making its customers happy, it should not generate an inordinately high number of requests for arbitration. Why should a consumer have to take this drastic step to get satisfaction? Buying the customer off once he or she has filed for arbitration is one thing, but keeping the customer from filing a complaint to begin with is quite another. In my opinion, any manufacturer that consistently generates more than its share of arbitration requests is doing a lousy job of resolving customer complaints.

My objective in examining the Washington state data was to find out which carmakers generated more than their expected share of arbitration requests. For 1988, 1989, 1990 and 1991 the Washington attorney general's office received 1295 requests for arbitration from vehicle owners. I determined the percentage of arbitration requests each manufacturer generated and compared that with the manufacturer's average national market share over the three-year period. I then arrived at an arbitration request index. An index of 1.0 is normal. In other words, a carmaker with an index of 1.0 generated a percentage of arbitration requests equal to its market share. A value below 1.0 is good. A value above 1.0 means the carmaker generated more arbitration requests than it should have.

Here's a list of the carmakers that appeared to do a good job of making their customers happy, with the best performers at the top of the list. The number adjacent to the manufacturer is the arbitration index. An

index of 0.19, for example, means the company only generated 19 percent of the arbitration requests it would have been expected to generate. On the other hand, the figure 30.8 means the company generated over 30 times the expected number of arbitration requests.

Mercedes-Benz 0.19	Nissan 0.52
BMW 0.22	Mitsubishi 0.53
Honda 0.23	Hyundai 0.65
Toyota 0.37	Mazda 0.90
Volvo 0.52	

Here is a list of the companies that appear to have done a worse job, according to the Washington data:

Peugeot 30.8	Audi 1.5
Yugo 12.0	Ford 1.42
Saab 3.44	Volkswagen 1.15
Chrysler 2.85	General Motors 1.06 (Chevrolet Division 1.70)

If we look at the best performers, not surprisingly Honda, Toyota, and Mercedes-Benz rank very high. Hyundai seems to have been doing something right in Washington state that it has had trouble doing elsewhere in the country. General Motors is the only domestic manufacturer that generated fewer arbitration requests than it might have been expected to, based on its market share. This is a credit to a company that has gone a long way toward improving its tarnished image.

Now let's look at the worst performers. Peugeot and Yugo are an abomination.

Chrysler is an abomination. Ford, as usual, stands a few steps below mediocrity on the ladder of customer service.

Recommended Car Manufacturers

Considering the J.D. Power surveys, the lemon reports of the states of Florida, New York, and Washington, and the *Consumer Reports* frequency of repair data, I believe the following carmakers are well above average in customer service and/or product reliability:

Saturn	Honda
Lexus	Toyota
Infinity	Mercedes-Benz
Acura	General Motors

                               * Except for GM's
                                Chevrolet Division

Saturn Saturn is new, but the company has shown real class and concern in taking care of its customers. In the first year of production, Saturn received a bad batch of antifreeze from a supplier. Rather than risk customer dissatisfaction with the repairs that could have been done to correct the problem, Saturn replaced more than 1800 cars already purchased by customers. Incredible! Saturn builds nice cars and the company takes good care of its customers—the perfect combination. Give Saturn a careful look before you buy a Japanese-built car. Saturn came in third in the 1991 J.D. Power Customer Satisfaction Index and deserved its fine standing. American car companies can do something right after all!

Lexus, Infinity, Acura, Honda, Toyota

What can you say about companies that build good cars and provide good service to their customers? Buy them if you like Japanese cars (and if you can afford them—they're not cheap!)

Mercedes-Benz The car is overpriced. Way overpriced. The maintenance is overpriced. Way overpriced. But the car is very high in quality and reliability and reflects excellent engineering. The company generally makes its customers happy when they have a problem. Should you buy a Mercedes for the quality? Some Japanese and American cars are just as good for a lot less money. If you enjoy bleeding financially for the sake of status, buy a Mercedes.

Car Manufacturers Not Recommended

The following carmakers are in my opinion below average in product quality and/or customer service:

Alfa Romeo	Hyundai	Sterling
Chevrolet	Peugeot	Yugo
Chrysler	Saab	

Alfa Romeo Even with my Italian last name I can't find anything positive to say about this make. The J.D. Power CSI results are not good. Alfa ranked fifth in the 1991 J.D. Power worst nameplates in terms of CSI. Alfa dealers tend not to keep the franchise as long as dealers of other makes. Consequently, they probably don't care as much about their customers and treat them accordingly. Alfas have improved in recent years due to a cash infusion from Fiat. But I consider Fiat a schlock outfit (they bombed in this country due to pathetic product quality), so I don't expect them to work miracles with Alfa Romeo. Alfas are at home in the U.S. only in places like Southampton, Long Island, and Beverly Hills, California. Otherwise they would be unmissed if they stayed in Milan, where they come from.

Chevrolet I don't like anybody or anything whose name begins with general, but I generally do like General Motors' cars and the job its divisions are doing caring for their customers—with the exception of Chevrolet. In my opinion Chevrolet has been a festering sore marring GM's corporate image. Why does the Chevrolet division and its dealers rank as the kings and queens of schlock? Because many of Chevrolet's products suffer from assembly problems (a downgrading of initial quality), and their dealers can certainly do a better job of satisfying customers. No wonder Chevrolet ranked eighth in the 1991 J.D. Power worst nameplates in terms of CSI. And to make matters worse, *Consumer Reports* April, 1992 survey of owner satisfaction with 1989 and 1990 models reveals that much of Chevrolet's product lineup failed to please people who bought a Chevrolet car or light truck, with the S10 series being a major offender.

From 1988 through 1990 Chevrolet generated over 18 percent of the arbitration requests received by the attorney general's office in Washington state, even though Chevrolet commanded 13.7 percent of the national market. This gives Chevrolet an arbitration request index of 1.34 for those years, a lousy track record. When 1991 Washington data is considered, Chevrolet's

arbitration index is 1.70. In other words, Chevrolet generated 170 percent of the arbitration requests it should have in proportion to its market share. This compares with an arbitration request record of 1.06 overall in Washington state for all General Motors cars during the years 1988 through 1991, which is respectable. I don't recommend Chevrolet's Geo line of cars because they are sold by Chevrolet dealers, who generally do not appear to back the product up adequately. This appears to be corroborated by the 1991 J.D. Power CSI data which place Geo sixth in the list of worst nameplates. Only Chevrolet can take a Japanese quality car and drive it into the cesspool of customer satisfaction ratings!

Chrysler Although Chrysler builds a few really excellent cars and a great minivan, I cannot recommend the company's products at this time. When you buy a Chrysler product, if you get a good one you'll be delighted. If you get one with problems, you may go through hell trying to get it fixed. The company does not do a good job proactively resolving consumer complaints. Too many Chrysler product owners wind up in lemon law arbitrations. Chrysler tends to wait for disasters to happen and then attempts to do something about them *after* the damage has been done. Case in point: the A604 Ultradrive automatic transmission fiasco. These transmissions failed at an alarming rate in 1989 and 1990 vehicles. When *Consumer Reports* tested a 1991 model with a bad transmission, they blew the whistle on Chrysler. The company then went into a panic to resolve the problems it created. It was too little too late. Now the A604 is a good transmission (or at least no worse than the average automatic transmission), but it would have been good earlier had Chrysler recalled vehicles equipped with A604s and fixed them before customers were inconvenienced by mechanical failure. So the bottom line on Chrysler is that it makes some great products but gives lousy customer satisfaction. Chrysler will be the company to watch if it improves its handling of customer complaints, and if its new generation of products dubbed the L/H model line are successful in the marketplace. The L/H models look great on paper, and look even better on display at auto shows. But can Chrysler convince its legions of disgruntled customers that it now takes service seriously? In July 1992 Chrysler committed $30 million to retraining its dealer personnel in the fine of art of delivering good customer service. The program better work or Chrysler will join Henry J., Packard, Studebaker, et. al. in the graveyard of U.S. auto companies that couldn't cut it in the tough American market.

If Chrysler's demise becomes imminent, I firmly endorse another government bail-out, not because America needs Chrysler's cars, but because America needs Lee Iacocca at the helm of a major car company. We'd miss his flamboyant style. We'd miss his swaggering TV commercials. And we'd miss the only car company chief executive who can appear on "Night Line" without boring the viewer to sleep. Iacocca is the only car executive in Detroit's history to come off looking like something other than a forked-tongue, cut-throat, back-stabbing creep.

America loves Lee Iacocca. He has to be worth a few billion of the taxpayers' dollars to hold onto, isn't he?

Hyundai Hyundai needs to go a long way toward improving its ability to respond to customer complaints. *Consumer Reports* April 1992 owner satisfaction surveys paint a bleak picture of customer satisfaction with 1989 and 1990 Hundai products. The same magazine stated that the 1991 Excel would have made the worst list too if 1991 cars had been included in the April 1992 report.

Until Hyundai demonstrates that it can resolve a greater percentage of consumer complaints without going into arbitration, I cannot recommend their cars. Furthermore, Hyundai has not offered cars on a par with Japanese car quality and reliability. If you want a Japanese car, buy a Japanese car—Hyundai in my opinion is just a cheap knockoff. The Koreans have not yet arrived when it comes to building top-notch cars.

Peugeot I don't like the car. I don't like the company. I don't like their dealers. Why would anybody want to pay so much money for a supposedly prestigious car actually used as a taxicab in Paris? Buy French wine—not French cars. The French car worth owning has yet to be imported into the United States and it probably never will be. Besides, soon you won't be able to buy a new Peugeot. The manufacturer has announced that it will pull out of the U.S. market. Good riddance! Anybody intent on buying a new Peugeot will soon have to find another form of self-flagellation.

Saab Saab's sales in the United States have fallen steadily over the last few years. I think Americans are catching on that buying a Saab can amount to buying a lot of headaches. The cars are a pain in the neck to fix. They cost too much. They are excellent choices for masochists and yuppie holdouts who haven't woken up to the realities of the new decade—status and contentment don't always go hand in hand.

Sterling I wish this car on all my enemies. The British, once a powerful force in both the U.S. and the world auto markets, were blown out of here by shoddy quality and Japanese competition. Sterling, in my opinion, provides solid evidence that the sun has set on the British empire. Some nice mechanical features exist thanks to collaboration with Honda, and a few nice cosmetic touches in the interior—but there are the same old British quality lapses elsewhere, especially in its electrical systems. Mazda, with their Miata sports car, has shown how wonderfully a British car can be built when it isn't built by the British. If you love old things British as I do, find a good used MGB or a Triumph for fun and buy something other than a Sterling for basic transportation.

Yugo In the past—trash, pure trash. Yugo has had quality and reliability problems since its introduction in the U.S. market. Who designed this turkey, Marshall Tito (may he rest in peace)? Although the manufacturer has been making substantial product improvements, the stability and viability of Yugo's business operations in the U.S. is doubtful. Coupled with the political unrest in Yugoslavia and the financial troubles of the parent company, the stability of Yugo's dealer network and warranty support remains questionable. My recommendation—make Yugo the last car on your shopping list. Or buy it only as a step up from roller skates. If you do buy one, don't let the salesperson talk you into a burglar alarm. The market for stolen Yugos isn't too strong.

Ooops, just before we go to press, Yugo folds in the U.S., packs its bags and goes home. Oh well, there are always used Yugos for inveterate masochists.

Carmakers I Don't Trust (And Maybe You Shouldn't Either)

BMW Just a bunch of Mercedes wannabes. You have to desire status desperately to buy a BMW. Although BMW generally gets some good customer satisfaction scores, lemon law statistics in Florida don't make the BMW people look too saintly when it comes to resolving complaints. Why do I distrust BMW? Too much advertising hype and not enough substance. Lately they have been touting a so-called nearly maintenance-free engine. Under the pompous veneer of all the puffery lies a lot of technology that has been available on Chevrolets for several years. Ordinary, very very ordinary. You want to pay $50,000 for hype? You're better off with a Lexus or an Infinity. Lower price, better cars.

Ford Ford says quality is job number 1. Maybe! Sure, they build some nice cars. They also build some turkeys. And their track record for customer satisfaction seems always to linger a notch or two below mediocrity. If you buy a Ford, be especially careful about the dealer you buy from. Ford has some great dealers. They also have some monsters. Some Ford dealers are unhappy about the way the company pays warranty claims—they say Ford is cheap and does not want to pay a fair rate for parts and labor. I think this is at the root of Ford's lackluster customer satisfaction performance.

Mitsubishi   Toyota or Honda Mitsubishi is not! Mitsubishi is proof that even a Japanese company can wallow in mediocrity. The cars are pretty good. A lot of their dealers are not. Mitsubishi is aware that they have some second-rate dealers, and the factory has expressed a desire to clean up the act. Be very careful about the dealer you buy from.

Volvo   Overrated and overpriced. Strictly for die-hard yuppies and egotists who believe they know something about cars that nobody else knows. Volvos break down as much as other cars. They cost a bundle to fix. The company occasionally uses advertising characterized by dubious ethics. For example, Volvo got caught by the Texas state attorney general falsifying advertisements that grossly misrepresented the strength of their cars. Competitors' cars had their roof pillars sawed through while Volvo's were reinforced. When driven over by a truck, Volvos appeared stronger, because the other cars' roofs collapsed. Of course they collapsed— the pillars were cut! In addition to this kind of sleaze, Volvos seem archaic and boring. I'd rather have a Buick any day.

How to Select a Car Dealer

If you buy your new car from the wrong car dealer, you can run into trouble getting it repaired under warranty. Many instances of consumer dissatisfaction with a car arise from poor service at the dealer. This trauma can be avoided if you know how to distinguish the competent, consumer-oriented dealers from those who have little interest in helping.

What is the Customer Satisfaction Index?

I have already talked about the J.D. Power Customer Satisfaction Index (CSI) as a barometer of consumer satisfaction with various makes of cars. The carmakers do a similar survey in connection with their dealers. Before you consider buying a car from a particular dealership, you should determine the dealership's customer satisfaction index. The CSI is a rating assigned to the dealership by the manufacturer based on surveys of the dealership's customers. The surveys determine the level of customer satisfaction with the sales and service departments. Some very small volume dealerships might not have CSI ratings assigned to them for all makes they sell.

Because the ratings are assigned by the manufacturers, you might assume they are inaccurate and self-serving. Not so! In the fiercely competitive automotive marketplace, every customer counts. Manufacturers are now very sensitive to customer-relations problems created by their dealerships, so the surveys are designed to accumulate meaningful data. CSI ratings provide a good indication of what you can expect from a dealership in terms of customer service. There are plenty of dealerships with very poor ratings—you should not buy a car from one of these.

To find out what a dealership's CSI ratings are, ask the salesperson. Dealerships with good scores will be happy to show you what they are. Those with substandard scores will evade the issue. So that you can understand how to interpret CSI data, let's consider a CSI report that a typical General Motors dealership would show you. Other manufacturers use different report nomenclature, but their reports contain essentially the same information. For example, Ford Motor Company has what they call the QC-P program. QC-P, which stands for Quality Commitment-Performance, is Ford's proprietary customer-satisfaction rating system. Unlike GM's system, which rates dealer performance in percentages up to 100 percent, Ford's system assigns a point rating with a maximum of ten points.

The first page of a GM CSI report contains the title "Dealer Report of Customer Satisfaction" along with the issue date. Make sure the report you are shown is recent. The next page, labeled A, is titled "Key Measures of Customer Satisfaction." The following page, labeled 1, is the page containing the data you need. There are two columns on the page. Each column contains CSI average percentages: one column indicates the last twelve months and the other lists the percentages for the last three months. Basically, the three-month column reveals short-term

trends in the dealership's performance. You should pay attention to the twelve-month CSI scores.

The only CSI score you have to worry about is called "Overall Satisfaction with Selling Dealer." There are three CSI scores listed for overall satisfaction. A separate overall satisfaction score is found in each of three columns labeled YOUR AVERAGE (meaning the dealer's average), ZONE AVERAGE, and DIVISION AVERAGE. The important numbers are the dealer's average (YOUR AVERAGE) compared with the zone average.

DIVISION AVERAGE refers to the nationwide performance of an entire division of the parent corporation, for example, Pontiac Division or Buick Division of General Motors Corporation. This number is meaningful to the manufacturer but not to the average customer. ZONE AVERAGE is important because it measures the performance of dealers in a limited geographical area or "zone." This figure tells you how other similar dealerships in your area are performing in terms of customer satisfaction. YOUR AVERAGE is the dealership's absolute performance and must be compared to the zone average to be meaningful.

The dealership's absolute average by itself is not important. Suppose, for example, that a dealership has an overall satisfaction of 80 percent. If the zone average is 78 percent, the dealership score of 80 percent is quite good. On the other hand, if the zone average is 85 percent, the dealership's average of 80 percent is not good at all. You should buy your car from a dealer whose overall CSI rating is at or above zone average.

The reason a dealership's score relative to its zone is important is because high-zone customer satisfaction ratings are more difficult to achieve in some areas of the country. In the New York metropolitan area, for example, a zone average of 80 percent might be excellent, whereas in a rural zone in the Midwest 80 percent could be low. Consumers in the major metropolitan areas are typically harder to please than those in small towns. Also, small town dealers generally take better care of their customers.

You should, however, not let dealership CSI ratings absolutely influence your decision about the car you want to buy. For example, suppose you want to purchase a Buick and discover that the zone CSI average is 80 percent. Then you discover later on that the zone CSI rating for Oldsmobile is 85 percent. It would be a mistake to alter your decision and opt for an Oldsmobile because of the difference in zone CSI ratings. CSI ratings for a car line can be influenced by various demographic factors, including the age group of the people who typically buy a certain make. Age can affect product expectations and overall satisfaction. Therefore, you first should decide on the kind of car you want, then you should select a dealership with a good CSI score.

How to Negotiate the Best Price

Before I let you in on some car buying tricks that can save you hundreds or even thousands of dollars, I'd like to give you a warning: don't be penny-wise but dollar-foolish as many car buyers are. There is little wisdom in buying a new car from a dealership with a low CSI rating just to save $50 or $100. Smart car buying means getting the best price from a reputable dealer with a good service department, not chiseling some high-volume discounter down to a bare bones profit. Such a dealer might sell you the car, but heaven help you when you need service under warranty!

Okay, so you have an answer to that—you'll save fifty bucks at Schlocko Motors and have warranty service done at Integrity Motors five miles away. Keep in mind, however, that Integrity Motors knows you didn't buy the car from them, and they're not too happy about that. They have their own customers to worry about, so why should they care about you?

Technically, Integrity Motors might have to honor your warranty; at least on paper they'll have to. And they will—in three or four weeks, which is how long they'll make you wait every time you need warranty work. And when your car finally gets into the shop, oops—the part you need isn't in stock. They'll have to order it. That will take another two weeks. But don't call them, they'll call you. And on and on it goes until they wear you down and make you go back to Schlocko Motors where the baboons in the service department will butcher your car and make you wish you had bought a horse. In *Mugged by Mr. Badwrench* I explain the many techniques a consumer can use to distinguish the decent car dealers from the creeps. The book also explains how to deal with the crooks in the auto business if you made the mistake of buying a car from one of them.

But it's best to avoid the deadbeats and buy from reputable dealers.

If you want to avoid warranty hassles and save money, here are car-buying steps you can take:

Step 1. Try to buy the car you really want. Select a car that best suits your wants, your needs, your ego, and your budget. Few people buy a car strictly for utilitarian reasons. If luxury, style, and prestige are important to you, indulge yourself if you can afford it.

Step 2. Don't buy a lemon. Check *Consumer Reports'* frequency of repair data for the model you have chosen. Steer clear of cars with worse than average repair histories. Also review the material in the section entitled, Which Car Companies Treat Their Customers Best?

Step 3. Determine the dealer's cost for the car you want. Buy a copy of *Edmund's New Car Prices* in your local bookstore. For about five bucks this guide will give you the dealer's cost plus destination charges of just about any car, including options and special "packages" you may want to purchase. Add to the *Edmund's* dealer cost-figure the dealer's co-operative advertising and marketing association charges for the car you want. The dealer has to pay the factory for these items so you have to pay the dealer. Typically, these costs can amount to $100 to $300. Ask the salesman to show you the factory invoice to determine the exact price for the car you are buying.

Sometimes prices can change after *Edmund's* went to press for a particular model year. Always check the dealer's invoice to see if prices have gone up or down.

Step 4. Find out the wholesale value of your used car if you are going to trade it in. Stop by your local bank and ask the loan officer to quote you its approximate value from the National Automobile Dealers Association (NADA) used car guide. The guide is also available in many libraries. This guide, published monthly for various regions of the country, reports on the price of used cars selling in the wholesale market. Used car values differ regionally and from month to month. The wholesale value of your old car is listed in the far left column under the heading "Av'g Trd-In." You add or subtract a certain amount of money for options and excess mileage and arrive at the wholesale value. The dealer must give you at least the wholesale value if the car is in good condition.

Another way to estimate the value of your used car is to visit a few used car lots. Ask the proprietor of each lot how much he or she would pay for your car if you were willing to sell it immediately. Sometimes a used car lot will offer you a better price than would a dealer basing his offer on the NADA used car guide. Used car values can vary from region to region. What a used car dealer is willing to pay may reflect a higher demand for your car than may exist in some other area of the country.

Another way to determine the value of your used car is to obtain a copy of *Edmund's Used Car Prices*, which are published quarterly. You can pick one up at your local bookstore.

Step 5. Visit the dealer closest to where you live. Tell the salesperson you are interested in buying a new car. Ask to see the dealer's CSI report. If the dealer's CSI is below zone average, consider another dealer or possibly another make of car. If the dealer will not show you the CSI report, do not buy your car there.

Step 6. Make the salesperson an offer. Do not allow the salesperson to quote you a price. I'll tell you how to make an offer shortly. Right now, it is important that you understand why you and not the salesperson must make the offer. Most people get price quotes from two or three dealers and buy from the one that offers the lowest price. This is not the way to get the best deal on a new car.

All dealers want to get as much profit from a new car as possible. This is only fair. As businessmen they are entitled to the manufacturer's suggested retail price (MSRP) if they can get it. Your objective is to pay as much under MSRP as you can. If you buy on the basis of the lowest quoted price, that may still not be the best possible deal you could have negotiated because every dealer is seeking maximum profit. Working one dealer's quote against the other's is not desirable either; it is time-consuming and frustrating. This gimmick forces you to bounce from dealer to dealer haggling over a few bucks, with the net result something like the dealer saying, "I'll beat the other guy's price by $50 if you buy from me." Using the right strategy, you might be able to beat the other guy's price by several hundred dollars without wasting time traveling from dealer to dealer.

The right strategy entails maintaining some control over the transaction. When you allow the salesperson to quote you a price, you have surrendered control. If you maintain control as the buyer, you can bargain from a position of strength. The way to do this is to make a preemptive offer.

Here's how to make the offer. Start with a lowball offer—a figure less than that which the dealer is likely to accept. Do not sound arrogant. Don't make the salesperson feel that you are trying to be deliberately manipulative. Don't denigrate the product. Nobody likes a wise guy. Just politely say, "This seems like a real nice car you are trying to sell me. Unfortunately, all I can afford to pay for it right now is _____, and I'll need at least $_____ for my trade-in." The figure you offer should be the dealer's cost as found in *Edmund's*, plus $150. This amount will not reflect dealer advertising costs, which you will have to pay. That's okay, for now you're just lowballing the salesperson. The amount you ask for your trade-in should be based on the NADA used-car guide, an offer made to you by a used car dealer, or a figure obtained from *Edmund's Used Car Prices.*

Naturally, the salesperson will become indignant at your offer, insisting that such a selling price is impossible. It is, and you know it. Your objective is to get the salesperson to invest energy and emotion in closing a sale. The more energy and emotion the salesperson invests, the greater the desire to make a deal with you, any deal, to get you to buy the car. That's the way most salespeople are. Closing the sale almost becomes more important psychologically than making a profit once there has been an investment of energy and emotion.

At this stage, you can tell the salesperson that you will try to find more money in your budget if the salesperson could justify a higher price by showing you the factory invoice. Mention that you obtained a dealer's cost figure from *Edmund's*. Now the salesperson will show you the advertising costs that have to be tacked onto the selling price. You must be willing to pay these costs. The question now is, Even if you were willing to pay the advertising costs, would the dealer accept a profit of just $150 over cost? It depends. If the model you want to buy is in demand and selling—well, he will not be interested in your offer. If the model is not selling well, or if the dealer has a cash flow problem, your offer may be accepted. Many dealers will accept a profit of $150 on some models; on others, $500, $1000, or more is the minimum they'll accept.

Set an objective in your mind, say, a maximum of $300 over dealer's cost including advertising. If you can't get the salesperson to accept the $150 deal, offer another $150. If the new offer goes unaccepted, write your name and telephone number on a piece of paper. Politely excuse yourself on the pretext that you have another appointment. Leave your name and phone number with the salesperson, along with the invitation to call if there is any way your deal can be accepted. You will probably get a call. The dealer will try to sell you a car one way or another.

Try the same approach on one or two other dealers. If one accepts your offer (assuming the dealer also has a high CSI score),

you win. If no dealer accepts your offer, you'll have to come up with more money.

Step 7. Inspect the new car thoroughly for damage before you sign for it. Read Pitfalls to Avoid When You Take Delivery of Your Car.

Step 8. Avoid getting ripped off in the business office when you sign for the car. Even though you may have negotiated a great deal, your hard bargaining can could have been in vain if you are not careful when you sign for the car. Read How to Avoid Getting Gypped When You Sign on the Dotted Line for details.

You'll have to sign an odometer statement if you trade in a used car. Make sure you fill in the mileage. Do not sign a blank statement! If the dealer or wholesaler rolls back the odometer, it is possible for you to get involved in a legal mess if the true mileage was not recorded on the statement.

Pitfalls to Avoid When You Take Delivery of Your Car

Don't sign for your new car until you have had a chance to inspect it thoroughly. Take delivery during daylight so you can examine the paint job and the body for scratches and dents. Scrutinize the paint carefully. Look for sanding marks in the paint. This is evidence of a prior repair. Look for undulations (waviness) in the sheet metal. These irregularities can indicate the presence of body filler used to repair large dents.

Make the dealer fix serious cosmetic problems in a body shop before you accept the car. Otherwise, you can simply refuse to accept the car if you believe the problems are extensive and serious. Minor blemishes requiring only a little touch-up paint can be noted on the delivery papers. Check the carpeting and upholstery for tears or punctures. Insist that problems be described in writing so that they can be corrected for free under warranty.

Try all accessories. Make sure they work properly. Start the engine. Drive the car around the dealer's lot. I have seen more than a few new cars with serious defects in major mechanical systems. Often you can detect these during a short spin around the lot. Don't accept the car if it does not feel right to you, or if the engine does not run properly. Make the dealer fix these problems before you sign for the car. Check the trunk for a spare tire, and make sure your car has a jack.

How to Avoid Getting Gypped When You Sign on the Dotted Line

If the salesperson can't get a good profit from you, the F&I man will. At least he will try. Who is the F&I man? The finance and insurance man, now more commonly referred to as the business manager. The business manager will often try to sell you extras that you don't need, such as extended warranties, service contracts, credit life insurance, and other goodies. You made the deal. Now make the dealer stick to it. And read the papers you sign carefully! Often, unwary consumers sign for a loan at a higher interest rate than they bargained for. Don't fall into this trap. Read, read, read before you sign.

Extended Warranties and Options

Extended Warranties (Service Contracts)

Extended warranties, which are really service contracts, are very lucrative for car dealers. They are a lousy investment, though, for the new car buyer. These days car quality is better than ever, and new car warranties are extensive. Chances are the investment in an extended warranty will never pay off. All an extended warranty amounts to is an insurance policy with a ridiculously high premium. If you have the extra money available, don't spend it on an extended warranty. Put it in an interest-bearing account, and self-insure against breakdowns that may occur after the warranty expires.

If you absolutely insist on making your car dealer richer by buying an extended warranty, purchase only the one underwritten by the vehicle manufacturer. Extended warranties provided by insurance companies through contract administrators are generally a bad bet. In the last few years several service contract administrators have gone out of business, leaving the contract holders with a lot of worthless paper. Many of those which have stayed in business have a nasty reputation for evading payment on repair claims with one flimsy excuse or another.

Never, never buy a service contract underwritten by a car dealer. Many car dealers in the United States are shakier financially than service contract administrators. You would be better off taking your money to a casino than betting it on the future solvency of any car dealer.

Options

Air Bags A life-saving device for sure—if used with safety belts. Don't assume you can buy a car with an air bag to avoid the necessity of using your three-point belt system. Air bags complement seat belts; they don't replace them.

Antilock Brakes Carmakers are touting this option as though it were the greatest safety invention since the rear-view mirror. Don't be deceived. There is no evidence that antilock brakes prevent accidents. In fact, there are people in the automotive industry who are concerned that antilock brakes may have been oversold as a safety benefit. Some drivers can become overconfident, thinking antilock brakes will compensate for bad driving judgment. This misconception could potentially cause accidents.

Antilock brakes will prevent loss of steering control due to locked wheels. However, there is no convincing evidence available to indicate that a substantial number of accidents are caused by loss of steering control due to locked wheels. Additionally, although this kind of brake system can help a vehicle stop in less time and distance under certain conditions, under other conditions it can actually increase stopping distance. If you are braking in powder snow or sand, locked wheels are actually a benefit.

Drawbacks associated with antilock brakes are added initial cost, repair complexity, and additional cost of repair. Typically, antilock brakes have added nearly a thousand dollars to the cost of a new car. If a car manufac-

turer could figure out a way to make them standard equipment (or optional) for about $200, I'd consider the small added safety of antilock brakes well worth the money.

Burglar Alarm You'll only annoy your neighbors with this one, not the burglars. The pros can steal a car before a police officer can appear on the scene. Car burglar alarms always seem to sound off at the wrong time, and don't scare away talented car thieves. Anybody who wastes money on this gadget deserves to be ticketed for noise pollution when a false alarm sounds.

Paint Sealant An absolute joke—on you! Dealers make a ton of money on this garbage. Buy a can of good wax; it's all your car's paint will ever need.

Rustproofing Save your money. Cars don't need extra rustproofing anymore. Some manufacturers will void their rust warranty if rustproofing is incorrectly applied, which it often is. Too much rustproofing can clog the moisture drain holes in body panels. This problem results in an accumulation of water and corrosion.

Sound System Many audio specialty shops can install a better sound system than you can get from the car manufacturer, and for a lot less money. Of course, it means you have to make an additional purchase not included in your lease or finance agreement. Some consumers find this inconvenient and opt for the factory audio system. That's okay, most of them are pretty good now, but they're still a shade short of the deluxe quality you'll get at an audio shop.

Turbocharger   Turbochargers are generally a pain in the neck. If you want more power than the standard engine offers, get an optional bigger engine, one that is naturally aspirated (non-turbocharged).

Undercoating   Undercoating is as archaic as ignition points. Modern cars don't need extra undercoating. Your dealer needs undercoating to make extra profit on each new car sold. If you still believe in undercoating, become a dealer.

How to Get the Most Out of Your Warranty

You pay for the warranty that comes with your new car. The car manufacturer anticipates a certain cost of repairing every vehicle under warranty and factors that cost into the suggested retail price. Since you pay for a warranty, you should know how to get all the value out of it that you can.

Here are seven strategies for maximizing the value of your new car warranty:

1. Put all your complaints in writing. Make a written list of any problems you want corrected. Record the mileage and date on the list. Give a copy of the list to the service department, and keep a copy in your records.

2. Always demand a copy of the warranty repair order. Even if you do not pay for re-

pairs you are entitled to a copy of the repair order showing what work was done.

3. Review each warranty repair order carefully. Make sure all your complaints were recorded. It doesn't matter if the shop could not find a problem. You have a complaint, and that's what counts. If there is no record of your complaint on the repair order, send a certified letter to the service department and the dealer's owner or general manager registering your complaint. Keep a copy of the letter and the return receipt. This will make it impossible for the dealer to deny you ever voiced the complaint.

4. If the dealer cannot or will not resolve your complaints in a reasonable time, send a certified letter to the manufacturer. State your complaint, the vehicle's identification number, where it was purchased, date of purchase, current mileage, and how you can be contacted by a manufacturer's representative to arrange for resolution of your complaint.

5. Have your car thoroughly inspected before the warranty expires. Take the car to a qualified independent repair shop. Ask for a written report of the condition of struts, shocks, power steering seals, transmission seals, CV joint boots, engine gaskets and seals, charging system, air conditioning system, and so forth. Also, ask the mechanic to road test the vehicle and check brake rotors, transmission operation, engine performance, handling, etc. A

good mechanic can inspect a vehicle in about thirty minutes. Make sure any problems found are put in writing. You'll be surprised at how many problems can be found that can be nipped in the bud before your warranty expires.

Take the list of problems with you to your dealer, and request repairs under warranty. If the dealer refuses, send a copy of the list to the manufacturer as described in item 4.

6. If both the dealer and manufacturer refuse to correct the problems, send a certified letter to both, advising them they are in breach of warranty. Tell them you will arrange to have the repairs done elsewhere and will reserve the option to sue in small claims court to recover expenses. Carbon copy your letter to your state attorney general's office. Chances are your dealer will contact you to get the dispute resolved.

7. If your car's engine does not run correctly, always try to have repairs done free under the terms of your car's emissions warranty. See to Part III of this book for details about this warranty.

Chapter 2

Leasing a New Car

Is Leasing Right for You?

LEASING A new car may be better than buying one. Leasing may be desirable under the following conditions:

- You drive less than 15,000 miles per year.

- You don't have a lot of cash as a down payment on a new car.

- You don't like keeping a car more than four years.

- You don't want to tie up a large down payment in a non-appreciating asset.

- You own a business or you are self-employed.

- You think of a car payment as a necessary evil, in the same context as a utility bill.

How to Negotiate the Best Lease

The monthly payment you are required to make on a lease is based on the following simplified computations. The simple equations underscore one important point: when you lease a car, you pay for the depreciation of the car over the term of the lease plus a certain amount of interest. Note that depreciation is the difference between capitalization cost and residual value. Obviously, you want to keep the capitalization cost low and the residual high to hold down monthly payments. Later we'll look into how this works in detail.

$$\frac{\text{Capitalization Cost} - \text{Residual}}{\text{Number of Months of Lease}} = \text{Monthly Depreciation}$$

$$\text{Monthly Interest} + \text{Monthly Depreciation} = \text{Monthly Lease Payment}$$

Most people pay too much for a lease because they don't know how a lease works. When you lease a car, you are really acting as a purchasing agent for the leasing company, so you have to negotiate the best *selling price,* just as though you were buying the car. The leasing company buys the car from the dealer and then rents it to you. Don't lease a car based on monthly payment. Establish the selling price and the value of your trade-in, then negotiate other terms of the lease.

Suppose, for example, you want to lease an Oldsmobile through GMAC, the finance arm of General Motors. The dealer will sell the car you choose to GMAC, the leasing company. Regardless of the price for which the dealer sells the car, GMAC will pass the costs on to you so they make a profit. You must keep the selling cost to GMAC low so that your monthly payments are low.

How do you know if your monthly payments are the lowest possible? There are three details you must determine:

1. Capitalization cost.

2. Residual.

3. Lease rate (finance charge or interest).

To keep your monthly payments low, you must get the following:

- Low capitalization cost.

- High residual.

- Low lease rate.

Capitalization Cost

The capitalization cost is the selling price of the car plus lease origination fees, minus applied rebates and the trade-in value of your used car. Let's consider an example without origination fees, rebates, and trade-in. Suppose the car you want has a retail price of $20,000. You negotiate a selling price of $17,000. This is the price you would pay if you were buying the car outright. Instead of making monthly lease payments based on a $20,000 purchase price less residual, your payments will be based on a $17,000 purchase price less residual. Instinct tells you you'll probably have a much lower monthly payment, and you're right!

Never fall for a monthly payment lease offer without determining the capitalization cost. Except in some factory lease deals (we'll discuss this later), you can almost always negotiate a lower capitalization cost by being a hard bargainer.

Residual

The residual is how much the car is worth at the end of the lease. The projected end of lease value is based on the *Automotive Leasing Guide (ALG)*, *Kelly Blue Book, Black Book,* or some other lease guide. Some manufacturers use a fixed percentage of the manufacturer's suggested retail price (MSRP) as a residual value in factory leases; 29 percent is a common residual value on 48-month leases. On a car with an MSRP of $20,000 the predetermined residual would be $5800 after 48 months. Sometimes you can negotiate residual value. This is true when you use an independent leasing company. If you are getting a manufacturer's lease, for example, through Ford Credit, GMAC, or Chrysler Credit, the residual will be predetermined. Most manufacturers are so desperate to lease cars that they assign an artificially high residual value to their cars to keep monthly payments low.

Whatever residual you are quoted, ask the salesperson to explain where the figure came from. Compare the quoted residuals offered by a few dealers to determine who is offering the best deal.

Lease Rate

Lease rate is a finance charge. This is the interest the leasing company charges you for the use of their money. Most consumers have no idea how much interest they are paying when they lease a car. There are two commonly used methods of computing interest on a car lease:

1. Cap cost method.

2. Money factor.

Cap Cost Using this method, interest is computed based on depreciation. Let's look at an example. The MSRP on a car is $20,000. You negotiate a $17,000 selling price (capitalization cost). The residual value after 48 months is $5800 (29 percent of MSRP). Let's assume the lease rate is 7.5 percent. First we calculate depreciation:

$$\text{depreciation} = \text{capitalization cost} - \text{residual}$$
$$\text{depreciation} = \$17,000 - \$5800$$
$$\text{depreciation} = \$11,200$$

Next we calculate monthly interest:

$$\text{Monthly Interest} = \frac{\text{annual percentage (converted to decimal)}}{12} \times \text{depreciation}$$

$$\text{Monthly Interest} = \frac{0.075}{12} = 0.0063 \times \$11,200 = \$70.56$$

In this case the monthly interest payment is $70.56. Notice that you have to convert the lease rate to a decimal. To do this, move the decimal point two places to the left. For example, a lease rate of 7.5 percent is 0.075. A rate of 10.5 percent is 0.105. A rate of 12.4 percent is 0.124. After the decimal is moved to the left, you divide by 12 and then multiply by the depreciation to get the monthly interest.

Money Factor This is also called the constant yield method. With this method, capitalization cost and residual are added together. The sum is multiplied by a money factor, with the result being the monthly interest.

$$\text{Monthly Interest} = (\text{capitalization cost} + \text{residual}) \times \text{money factor}$$

Note: In computing the interest on an actual lease, lease origination fees and sometimes sales tax are added to the sum of the capitalization cost and residual, and then multiplied by the money factor. The origination fee and sales tax are not considered now for simplicity. Refer to "Sales Tax" in the section entitled Extra Leasing Fees for an example of how sales tax and origination fees are used to calculate monthly interest when sales tax is capitalized.

Let's use the same capitalization cost and residual we used for the cap cost method and see how the results compare. We'll set the money factor at 0.003125, which corresponds to an interest rate of 7.5 percent.

$$\begin{aligned}\text{Monthly Interest} &= \$17,000 + \$5800 \times 0.003125 \\ &= \$22,800 \times 0.003125 \\ &= \$71.25\end{aligned}$$

This is slightly higher than the $70.56 interest computed using the cap cost method. Always ask your salesperson to give you a written quote confirming the money factor used to compute the interest on your lease.

Converting the Money Factor to an Interest Rate

A money factor can be converted to an interest rate very simply. Just multiply the money factor by 24 and move the decimal two places to the right. For example, let's convert a money factor of 0.003125 to an interest rate.

$$0.003125 \times 24 = 0.075$$

Now we move the decimal two places to the right and arrive at 7.5 percent.

Let's try another example. We'll convert a quoted money factor of 0.006458 to an interest rate.

$$0.006458 \times 24 = 0.155$$

Moving the decimal two places to the right, we get 15.5 percent. That's a pretty high rate by today's standards. If the money factor converts to an interest rate higher than banks are charging for auto loans, you're being charged too much.

Rebates

If the car you want to lease has a rebate, apply the rebate to the capitalization cost. This will lower the amount capitalized. Sometimes consumers are told that rebates cannot be applied to a lease. Don't believe it.

Used Car Trade-In

If you have a car you want to trade in, you can apply its value toward a reduction of the capitalization cost of the new car. You can determine the trade-in value of your old car by going to a library and checking the NADA used car guide.

This guide is published monthly for various regions of the country. Used car values differ regionally and from month to month. The wholesale value of your old car is listed in the far left column under the heading "Av'g Trd-In." You add or subtract a certain amount of money for options and excess mileage and arrive at the wholesale value. The dealer must give you at least the wholesale value if the car is in good condition.

Extra Leasing Fees You'll Have to Pay

So far we've looked at the capitalization cost as the selling price of the vehicle. Actually there are other charges you can expect to pay when you lease a car. These charges are generally added to the capitalization cost of the car. Here are the most common:

Security Deposit

Most leases require a one-month security deposit. This is refunded to you when the lease terminates. Some manufacturers' leases waive the security deposit for prior leasing customers. One example is GM's Smart Lease program. The security deposit is not added to the capitalization cost. It is generally paid separately.

Lease Origination Fee

This fee is roughly analogous to paying points on a new mortgage. The origination fee is usually not more than one month's

lease payment. Some manufacturers' leases waive the lease origination fee. The lease origination fee can be added to the capitalization cost and spread out over the term of the lease.

Registration and Title

This fee covers the cost of having the dealer process the vehicle's registration. Fifty to one hundred dollars is a typical amount.

Sales Tax

Sales tax on a leased car is collected in three ways:

- The tax is capitalized.

- The tax is added to the monthly cost of the lease and separately itemized on your monthly statement.

- You pay the tax separately in one lump sum when you sign the lease.

Paying the tax in a lump sum up front is not a good idea. It will cost you more to capitalize sales tax, but you won't be tying up a lot of money. Remember, one of the advantages of leasing is that you don't have to tie up a lot of cash. Let's look at the first two possibilities in detail:

The Sales Tax is Capitalized You don't actually pay a separate lump sum tax charge. Sales tax becomes part of the capital cost of the car. The sales tax is used to compute the depreciation amount and the interest. The tax becomes a portion of the total monthly lease payment. Here's an example of how this works.

Origination fee	$300
Capitalization cost	+ $17,000
	$17,300
Less residual	− $5,800
Taxable amount	$11,500

Assuming a tax rate of 7 percent let's figure the sales tax:

$$\$11,500 \times 7\% = \$805$$

Now let's compute a monthly payment using this amount of tax. First we add the total tax to the amount to be depreciated:

Compute Monthly Depreciation Charge

Origination fee	$300
Capitalization cost	$17,000
Tax	$805
	$18,105
Less residual	− $5,800
Depreciation amount	$12,305

Assuming the lease is 48 months, we divide the depreciation by 48 to arrive at the monthly cost of depreciation:

$$\$12,305 \div 48 = \$256.35 \text{ Monthly Cost of Depreciation}$$

Now we figure the monthly interest charge. Tax is added to make the calculation:

Compute Monthly Interest Charge

Origination fee	$300
Capitalization cost	$17,000
Tax	$805
Residual	$5,800
	$23,905

The interest is computed using the money factor method, with a money factor of 0.003125 (7.5 percent):

$$\text{Interest} = \left(\begin{matrix}\text{Cap.}\\\text{Cost}\end{matrix} + \text{Residual} + \begin{matrix}\text{Orig.}\\\text{Fee}\end{matrix} + \text{Tax}\right) \times \begin{matrix}\text{Money}\\\text{Factor}\end{matrix}$$

$$\$23,905 \times 0.003125 = \$74.70 \text{ Total Monthly Interest}$$

$$\begin{matrix}\text{Total}\\\text{Monthly}\\\text{Payment}\end{matrix} = \text{Depreciation} + \text{Interest}$$
$$= \$256.35 + \$74.70$$

Tax Assessment Against Monthly Cost of Lease When tax is computed this way, the tax rate is applied to the monthly lease payment and added as a monthly tax payment. Here's an example using a tax rate of 7 percent and a monthly lease payment of $300:

Compute Monthly Tax Payment

$$\text{Monthly Tax} = \text{Lease Payment} \times \text{Tax Rate}$$
$$\text{Monthly Tax} = \$300 \times 7\% = \$21$$

The monthly tax on the lease is $21.

Will it Cost You More to Lease Than to Buy?

Sometimes leasing can be cheaper than buying. This is especially true if you own a business or you are self-employed and can legally write off a large portion of the car's use as a business expense.

Keep in mind that leasing a car is just another way to finance it. Many manufacturers are desperate to lease new cars to move excess inventory. Consequently, they offer incredibly low lease rates. The cost of using the leasing company's money to finance depreciation can be lower than the rate you would pay at a bank to borrow money to buy a car.

Now you may argue that when the lease is over, you don't own anything, whereas when you are through paying a loan you own the car. If you reason this way, you are missing an important point about leasing. When you lease, you don't pay for the entire value of the car. You only pay for the depreciation of the car over the period of the lease.

When you buy a car, you pay the entire purchase price. When the loan is paid off, you are left with a vehicle that has depreciated and has limited resale value. How much could you sell your car for after the loan is paid off? That's what counts. If you add up what it cost you to buy the car and finance it and subtract the resale value, that's the true cost of using the car over the life of the loan.

Now compare what it would cost you to use the same car over the life of a lease of equal duration. If you get a low enough lease rate as well as some of the concessions available through manufacturers' lease plans such as waiver of origination fee, the lease could be cheaper.

Another thing to consider is the large down payment you have to make on a new car when you buy instead of lease. Having that money tied up in an asset that does not appreciate represents what finance experts call an opportunity cost. Let's say you place a down payment of $5000 on a $20,000 car. If you leased, you could invest that money in a mutual fund or some other interest-bearing instrument. When you compare the cost of leasing with the cost of buying, you have to factor in the loss of income on the down payment.

Total cost per mile for use of your vehicle is important in weighing leasing versus buying. If you like to drive a car 150,000 miles and usually do so with few major repairs before you scrap it, you are way ahead of the game. Kudos to you! Your cost per mile is comparatively minuscule. Carmakers hate people like you because you are beating the system.

There is no point in your even considering a lease. If you tire of a car every few years and want "fresh wheels" from time to time, your cost per mile of ownership goes up, but you enjoy a new car more often. Leasing may be the solution. You'll have a nice new car every few years. And you'll be doing your patriotic duty by staying in hock forever and stimulating the economy while you drive your nice new car.

Lease Ripoffs

There are three common pitfalls unwary consumers fall into when they lease a car:

1. Open-ended leases.

2. Cap cost reductions.

3. Failure to itemize capitalization cost, residual, and lease rate.

Open-ended Leases

In this kind of lease you are responsible for the resale value at the end of the lease. You can really get clobbered if the actual resale value is way below the residual.

Since an open-ended lease is a gamble on the car's resale value, you should pay a lower monthly payment than you would for a closed-end lease, where you are only responsible for excess wear and tear but not the book value of the car. Some dealers (lessors) lure customers into leases having a low advertised monthly fee without advising the customer (lessee) that the lease is open-ended. When the customer turns in the car at the lease termination, shock sets in once the financial hammer falls. Don't let it fall on you.

Stick with closed-end leases. You only pay extra at lease termination if you exceed the mileage limit or if you beat the car up severely. If the car is in reasonably good condition, there will be no penalties. Read the lease termination clause for excess wear and tear for a definition of what constitutes greater than normal wear. Reputable lessors do not place onerous terms on their lessees as far as wear and tear are concerned.

Cap Cost Reductions

You see an advertisement for a lease deal with a payment so low it sounds unbelievable.

It probably is. The fine print usually calls for a hefty cap cost reduction. This stands for capitalization cost reduction which is a euphemism for a down payment! Give the leasing company more money up front and your monthly payments will be lower.

One of the best inducements to lease is to avoid tying up capital in a non-appreciating asset—a car. If to afford a lease you have to make a cap cost reduction, lease a cheaper car. If that's not acceptable, keep the car you have and invest in something that will yield dividends—psychoanalysis! You've got to be nuts if you want to tie up a bundle of cash in a lease deal.

Failure to Itemize Capitalization Cost, Residual, and Lease Rate

These items are not normally itemized on a lease contract. Nevertheless, you can insist that they be itemized on the dealer's vehicle order. This is the order you sign when you leave a deposit to hold the vehicle as you would do if you were buying it.

Make sure you get a copy of the vehicle order. You must absolutely insist that the basic terms of the lease are spelled out. This includes the monthly payment *including* tax, refundable security deposit, origination fee, registration fee, term of the lease, yearly mileage allowance, capitalization cost, residual, and lease rate. Also, make sure the order indicates that you intend to sign a closed-end lease.

When you sign the lease contract, make sure the monthly payment matches the amount indicated on the vehicle order. Also, check that the mileage allowance and term of the lease are as agreed.

Manufacturers' Leases

Many carmakers subsidize leases through their own captive leasing arms. They do this by grossly overestimating the residual value of the car at the end of the lease. The residual allowed is usually far higher than what the car will be worth when wholesaled at the end of the lease. In addition to very high residuals, manufacturers' leases often include very low lease rates. Considering the goodies many car companies are throwing in to induce you to lease, there is very little reason any more to lease from an independent leasing company if you are sure you will not have to break a lease early.

There is one potential drawback to a manufacturers' lease program. The residual is so high that if you want to terminate the lease early you can get clobbered financially. This happens because the early termination fee is based partly on the surplus available after the vehicle is sold. Surplus is the difference between residual and the actual wholesale price recovered. If the residual is very high, there will be no surplus, and you'll get stuck paying a bundle to bail out of the lease.

With this in mind, the best strategy is to make sure that you carry a manufacturer's lease to the end of the term. This kind of lease is a real bargain going in, but it is very costly if you want to get out early.

Capitalization Cost in a Manufacturer's Lease

Some manufacturers' leases do not allow you to negotiate the selling price of the car.

The lease payment is computed from a selling price (capitalization cost) of the full sticker (MSRP). The monthly lease payment is kept low by artificially inflating the residual value, which reduces the amount depreciated.

This tactic makes the manufacturer look good because it creates the illusion of a high resale value. High resale value adds prestige to a nameplate. Of course, the resale value as reflected in the residual can be pure fiction. Another benefit to the manufacturer is that this kind of lease deal eliminates haggling over selling price, something that a few of the more arrogant car companies like to avoid because it supposedly demeans their marque.

So how do you know if you are getting a good deal if you can't negotiate the selling price? Find out what the fair residual value should be by checking the NADA used car guide, *Automotive Leasing Guide, Black Book, Kelly's Blue Book*, or similar publication. Your bank's loan officer will have one of them. The amount that the residual has been inflated is approximately the amount the selling price has been discounted for the purpose of arriving at the low monthly lease payment. If the discount off the MSRP is not enough to make you happy, don't execute the lease. Remember, many dealers will sell and lease cars for $250 or less over their cost. Why should you pay more if you can avoid it?

Any time a manufacturer's lease is nationally advertised at a fixed monthly payment, try to haggle for a lower capitalization cost (selling price) to further reduce the monthly lease fee. Every car company is boosting residuals to help move inventory. Your objective is to find the lessor with the highest residual and the lowest capitalization cost.

Terminating the Lease Early

You may want to get out of your lease early. Expect to pay some big penalties if you decide to do this. One way to avoid a cash payout of these penalties is to roll over the amount owed into a lease on another new car. Of course this will result in much higher monthly lease payments.

The early termination clause of a lease should include a provision that gives you credit for unearned interest. Make sure you do not sign an agreement requiring you to pay the balance of all interest that would be due if the lease ran to the end of the term.

Early termination penalties may include:

1. Excess mileage charge.

2. Depreciation fee. This is computed as the sum of all monthly payments not yet due minus unearned lease charges (interest) minus the surplus on the sale of the car. The surplus is the difference between residual value and wholesale price of the car.

Excess Mileage Charge

The termination clause must define how much you will have to pay for mileage over the monthly limit. If the yearly limit is 15,000 miles, the monthly limit should be 1250. The charge per mile should not be more than the charge per mile for exceeding the maximum

mileage allowance over the entire term of the lease. A charge of eight or ten cents per mile is typical. Do not sign a contract that requires more.

Depreciation Fee

When you terminate a lease early you'll be charged for depreciation. Here's how the depreciation charge typically works. You will be required to pay all the remaining monthly payments on the lease. An interest credit will be subtracted. This interest is called unearned lease charges; they are "unearned" because the leasing company does not deserve all the interest because the lease is ending early. Make sure the termination agreement defines the total interest (lease charges) payable over the entire course of the lease. Part of the interest will be credited to your account when you terminate. You will not receive a credit for the monthly interest times the number of unused months of the lease. Instead, you will get less based on a formula that only an accountant or a computer could ever make sense of. Make sure the contract defines how the interest credit is computed.

Besides unearned lease charges, another amount is subtracted. It is called the surplus. This amount is the difference between the wholesale value of the car at the time the lease is terminated and the residual. If the residual is very high, as it is in manufacturers' leases, there will be no surplus and you'll have to pay a bundle!

Let's look at an example of what happens when a 48-month lease at $300 per month is terminated early with 36 months left to go on the lease. Let's assume the vehicle has 20,000 miles on the odometer (5000 miles over the yearly allowance). We'll assume a residual of $5000 and a wholesale value of $11,000.

Excess mileage penalty @ 10¢ per mile	$500
36 payments × $300	+ $10,800
	$ 11,300
Less unearned interest	– $1980
Balance of payments due	$9320
Wholesale	$11,000
Less residual	– $5000
Surplus	$6000
Balance of payments due	$9320
Surplus	– $6000
Balance owed the leasing company	$3320

In this example, you would owe the leasing company $3320 to bail out of the lease early. Actually, you would owe more because they would hit you for auction fees to get rid of your car at a wholesale auction. Notice that in this case a surplus reduced the balance owed the leasing company. If the residual were very high, there would be less surplus and more owed to the leasing company. Very often the residual is high because manufacturers' leases have grossly inflated residual values. Don't go into a manufacturers' lease expecting to get out of it early with your hide intact!

When the Lease is Over

If you maintain the lease to the end of the term, all you have to do is return it to the leasing company's agent (usually the selling dealer). If there is no excess mileage, extraordinary wear and tear will be your only concern.

Make sure you get a vehicle condition report and odometer statement signed by the leasing agent. Take a series of dated photographs of the entire car before you turn it in. These pictures are your record of the condition it was in when you returned it. Reputable lessors will not split hairs about minor dents and dings, but serious body damage and upholstery damage will go against you.

You must not forget to obtain a filled-in copy of the odometer statement. It is the only record you have of the mileage at the time you returned the vehicle. Assuming there is no unusual wear and tear, you'll get your security deposit back in a few weeks. If there is a dispute, your copy of the vehicle condition report and your photographs can help you avoid unnecessary penalties.

Chapter 3

Buying a Used Car

How to Determine a Fair Price for a Used Car

WHETHER YOU buy a used car from its owner or from a dealer, you should know what the vehicle is really worth. Most people shop for prices at used car lots. They also compare advertised prices found in newspapers. These tactics are no way to set a price for a used car. You could think you are getting a great deal when in fact you are getting fleeced.

To establish the value of a used car, you have to determine its worth in the wholesale market. The wholesale market is fundamentally a system of used car auctions where dealers buy and sell used cars. The value of a used car is what it will fetch at an auction.

The NADA used car guide reports on how much used cars are selling for at these auctions. The guide is published monthly in regional editions because used car values fluctuate monthly and regionally (convertibles are not as popular in Alaska as they are in Florida!). You can get an NADA guide at your local library. If your bank makes auto loans, the loan officer will have a copy. The wholesale value of a used car is listed in the far left column under the heading "Av'g Trd-In." You add or subtract a certain amount of money for options and excess mileage and arrive at the wholesale value. This figure is the maximum amount a dealer would pay to obtain the car in trade.

Your objective is to obtain the used car you want for no more than wholesale if you are buying it privately from the owner, or as little above wholesale as you can if you are buying it from a dealer. The NADA guide lists the average retail price of each car in the far right column. This figure gives you an idea of the average list price of the used car you are interested in. Never pay the retail price. Another source of used car prices is *Edmund's Used Car Prices*, available in most bookstores.

How to Check the Car Mechanically

Is the car you want to buy a lemon? Used car dealers will tell you not to worry. They'll try to sell you a service contract for the "peace of mind" it will assure you. Baloney! A service contract on a mechanical bomb won't offer you much solace if you are in and out of the repair shop every other day. Forget service contracts; they are a waste of money.

Instead, spend a few bucks on a thorough mechanical inspection by a competent mechanic. If the car checks out okay buy it, assuming the price is right. Most sellers will not allow you to take a car to your mechanic. You'll have to bring your mechanic with you. A company called Auto Critic has started a franchise operation that specializes in used car inspections at the car's location. They dispatch a well-equipped van and a certified technician to evaluate the car. Check the *Yellow Pages* for used car evaluation services.

Many mechanics will inspect a used car for $75. I think a truly thorough inspection is well worth an investment of $150. This small amount of money can spare you many times as much in grief and subsequent repairs. Here are some of the items that should be checked:

Interior

Headliner Look for water stains, especially near the windshield. Stains indicate water leaks.

Upholstery and Carpets Look for tears.

Floor Panels Lift the floor mats or carpeting, and look for rust or corrosion. Water leaks into the car can cause severe rust problems on the floor panels.

Odometer Look for greasy fingerprints on odometer. This could mean the odometer was turned back. Make sure the speedometer works.

Accessories Make sure they all work. Don't forget to check the heated rear window and the emergency flashers. These are often overlooked.

Windows Make sure all of them work properly.

Exterior

Vinyl Top Check for bubbles. Bubbles indicate rust under the vinyl.

Paint Look for mismatched color from panel to panel. This discrepancy indicates prior body work. Look for evidence of body filler used to correct accident damage. Waviness in the sheet metal or sanding marks under the paint are giveaways.

Door Gaskets and Weather Strips Check for damage.

Undercoating Check for recent undercoating. This is maneuver usually done to hide chassis damage.

Chassis Check for damage or welds that indicate prior body work.

Tires Check for sidewall damage and tread depth. Make sure there is a matched set on the car.

CV Joints Check for torn boots.

Transmission Seals Check for transmission leaks.

Exhaust System Check for rotted muffler or pipes. Check for catalytic converter corrosion.

Engine

Dynamic Compression and Power Balance
This assessment is done with an engine analyzer. The test will help isolate one or more bad cylinders.

Computer Check for stored trouble codes. Have your mechanic clear all codes, road test the car, and see which codes return. The

trouble must be fixed before you buy the car. Trouble codes can be quickly obtained using a device called a scanner.

Oil Seals, Belts, Hoses Check for oil leaks, cracked belts, and cracked or leaking hoses.

Blue Smoke from Exhaust With the engine running, snap throttle sharply. Blue smoke from exhaust indicates bad valve stem seals or bad piston rings.

Engine Knocks Raise engine rpm. Listen for engine knocks indicating excessive wear.

Emissions Check exhaust gas for excessive carbon monoxide or hydrocarbons. If carbon monoxide levels are too high, the catalytic converter could be bad.

Charging System Check alternator output and battery condition.

Cooling System Pressurize system to check for leaks.

Brakes

Master Cylinder Check fluid in master cylinder. If fluid is milky the brake system is contaminated with moisture. If fluid is dark the system is dirty.

Brake Hoses and Tubing Check for cracked hoses. Check for rusted steel brake tubing.

Brake Linings Check the front brake pads

for adequate thickness. Check rear linings similarly.

Calipers and Wheel Cylinders Check for leaking calipers and/or wheel cylinders.

Drums and Rotors Measure thickness of rotors. If below manufacturer's suggested minimum thickness, the rotors must be replaced in matched sets. Check inside diameter of drums. Diameter must not exceed suggested maximum.

Road Test

Starting Make sure the engine starts easily when it is cold.

Warning Lights Check all instrument cluster warning lights to make sure they work.

Engine Performance Engine should accelerate and idle smoothly without pinging. Make sure engine does not overheat.

Steering Car should not pull to one side. Power steering should work smoothly. Be especially suspicious of some GM cars manufactured before the 1988 model year. Many had defective power steering racks that malfunction only in very cold weather. When conditions are warm, the steering system seems to work fine. Cost of repair is about $300.

Brakes Make sure there is no brake pulsation or pulling. Make sure the emergency brake works. Make sure the brake pedal does not slowly descend to the floor when light, steady pressure is placed on it. Check for air in the brake system. If the pedal has to be pumped to bring it to a normal height, there is air in the system.

Speedometer Does it work? Don't buy the car if it doesn't. The odometer might not reflect the true mileage.

Odometer Statement

If you are buying the car from a dealer, ask to see the odometer statement signed by the previous owner. This will give you some assurance that the "clock" was not "kicked back."

Recalls

Make sure that all safety recalls have been taken care of. Call the National Highway Traffic Safety Administration recall hotline at 1 (800) 424-9393. Give them the vehicle identification number, make, and model year, and they'll tell you if there were any safety recalls on the car. Ask the dealer or owner of the car to prove that the recalls were done.

Maintenance Records

Ask for maintenance records to verify that the required maintenance was performed at the recommended intervals.

Buying a Used Car from the Owner

Get the car inspected. If it is fine, offer the wholesale price. Show the owner the wholesale value from the NADA guide. Chances are the owner is anxious to get rid of the car and will take an offer of wholesale or slightly above. If there are problems with the car, deduct the estimated repair cost from your offer or ask the owner to fix them before you buy.

When you conclude the purchase, make sure you get a bill of sale indicating the mileage indicated on the odometer. If you subsequently discover that the odometer was rolled back, you'll have stronger legal recourse with the mileage indicated on the bill of sale.

Buying a Used Car from a Dealer

Make sure you check the car just as you would if you were buying it privately from the owner. Do not buy a service contract. Service contracts do not make good financial sense. Get a clearly written used car warranty instead.

Some used car lots do not have a service department. I don't like these operations because their ability to honor the warranty is suspect. If you buy from a new car dealer, at least you'll be assured of the existence of a service department. How do you know if they will take good care of you if you have problems with your used car? Simple. Evaluate the dealer using the CSI standard just as though you were buying a new car. Check with your local department of Consumer Affairs. Stay away from dealers that have a poor complaint record.

When it comes to price, you should use the same strategy as described previously for buying from a private owner. The exception is that the dealer will have to get more than wholesale for the car. He deserves it. But you should be able to negotiate a price below the retail figure suggested by the NADA.

Rental Company Cars, Are They Right for You?

Thousands of cars from rental company fleets hit the lots every year as low mileage used cars. I don't like most of them. Many rental cars accumulate hard mileage. Renters abuse them. Maintenance is kept to a minimum. If you want a used car that has been well cared for and babied by its owner, stay away from rental cars. Does that mean that all rental cars are a bad bet? Not at all. Just make sure your mechanic thoroughly checks the one you are considering.

When you buy a used car from a dealer, there is a chance that you are getting a former rental car. These are called "program cars." They are bought back from rental companies by the carmakers and sold at auction to dealers. Ask your dealer who owned the car you are considering. You can verify previous ownership by looking at the odometer statement. Otherwise ask for the previous owner's name and address and inquire directly about the car. If the dealer is reluctant to provide that information (more often than not they will not give it to you), consider another car.

Part II

Avoiding Ripoffs When You Get Your Car Fixed

What You Will Find in Part II

GETTING A car repaired has become so expensive that you cannot afford to let your guard down when dealing with auto repair shops. Although there are many honest shops employing mechanics of high integrity, finding such a facility is not easy. Any time you have your car repaired you stand a good chance of being ripped off by the many crooks and fast buck artists who use a large bag of tricks to fleece their customers. Part II will tell you what some of these tricks are and how to defend against them. You'll also learn how to find a competent mechanic you can trust.

Problems associated with getting your car fixed are not limited to situations involving paid repairs. Many pitfalls await you when you have your car repaired free under warranty. Part II will cover some of the common warranty-related difficulties and how to solve them.

Here's what you'll find in Part II

Contents

Chapter 4: Warranty Repairs

Chapter 5: Paid Repairs

Chapter 4

Warranty Repairs

How to Find a Dealer that Does Good Warranty Work

ENSURING THAT you get high-quality repairs under warranty begins with buying your car from a reputable dealership. The dealer who sells you a car is more likely to provide good warranty service than any other dealer. Assuming your selling dealer has a good Customer Satisfaction Index (CSI) rating, you are likely to get courteous and competent warranty service. Part I discusses this rating and its implications in detail.

But what do you do when you have moved far away from your selling dealer and require warranty repairs? Or, as happens so frequently, you made the unfortunate mistake of buying a new car from a disreputable dealership with an incompetent service department and now have to locate a dealership willing and able to fix your car under warranty?

If you are dissatisfied with the performance of your selling dealer and want the help of one of that dealer's competitors, you can expect resentment. Technically, under the terms of your warranty, any authorized dealer should agree to repair your car. In practice that doesn't happen. If you buy your car from dealer A and look for warranty help at dealer B, dealer B will resent that you did not buy the car from him. Although dealer B's service manager might not willfully refuse to fix your car, he could stall you by claiming that an appointment is not available in the shop for weeks. Even if your car finds its way into the shop, it could sit there for days before work commences. Despite lemon laws and miscellaneous state and local ordinances against consumer abuses, clever service managers have an uncanny ability to induce customers they don't want to go elsewhere voluntarily for repairs. In short, you'll be subjected to so much grief you'll *want* to find another dealership.

This does not mean your situation is hopeless. If you have bought your car from our hypothetical dealer A and need help from dealer B, there are ways to reduce the resentment you might encounter at dealer B. The best gambit involves telling the service manager at dealer B that you want his shop to do all the service on your car, including paid maintenance work such as oil changes, maintenance tune-ups, etc. When you request warranty repairs, also ask for an oil change or some other inexpensive maintenance for which you will pay. Your interest in using dealer B for paid maintenance as well as warranty work will soften the service department's prejudice against you for having purchased your car from a competing dealership.

There is, however, one step you must take before you begin doing business with dealer B. You must determine whether this dealership has a competent service department. If you were buying a new car from dealer B, your task would be simple. The fastest and easiest way to judge a service department is to review its CSI scores as explained in Part I. Since you are not negotiating the purchase of a car from dealer B, they will not agree to show you their CSI scores to satisfy your curiosity about their service department. It is very unlikely that a service manager would reveal CSI information to a prospective service customer. However, the sales department will reveal this information to a prospective new car buyer. If you're not averse to telling a white lie, you can *pretend* to be interested in buying a new car, in which case you can justify your demand to review dealer B's CSI scores. The sales manager will probably show them to you. If the CSI scores are poor, you might consider going elsewhere for warranty service because you are not likely to get any better results than you did at dealer A, where your problems began.

Beyond CSI scores, there are other ways to predict in advance the quality of the warranty work you might expect from a car dealership. Here are the things to look for. First, you need to find out if they employ competent mechanics specifically trained in the areas of service you require. For example, if you have trouble with your car's automatic transmission, does the dealership have at least one mechanic who has been factory trained and certified in automatic transmission repair? You can determine this easily. In the customer waiting area of most dealerships, mechanics' factory training certificates are displayed. Look for a certificate for the kind of service you need—in this example, automatic transmission repair. If you can't find the certificates, ask the service manager to show you where they are.

Suppose you find a certificate from General Motors indicating that Joe Dokes passed a factory training course in automatic transmission repair. Does Joe still work at the dealership? Find out! Will Joe himself work on your car or will they assign some less knowledgeable mechanic? You have the right to request that your car be worked on by a mechanic specifically trained in the area of service your car requires. You don't go to a podiatrist for dental work, do you? If you receive assurance that Joe himself will work on your car, you can corroborate this statement by examining the repair order, for Joe's signature. In most shops they record the name of the mechanic who did the job somewhere on the repair order or the mechanic signs the repair order. You are entitled to a copy of the repair order even if the work is free under warranty.

How to Get the Most Out of Your Car's Warranty

When you buy a new car you pay for the warranty that comes with it. The anticipated costs to the manufacturer of repairing the cars they build are factored into the retail selling price. Since you pay for your warranty, you have a right to use it as much as possible to minimize your future cost of ownership. Your objective is to uncover failing parts and various malfunctions before the warranty expires, at which time you'll have to pay for repairs.

The best way to do this entails having a comprehensive examination of your car performed by an independent mechanic. It is a mistake to have a dealer perform this inspection because most dealers do not want to do warranty work and are not likely to judge honestly the condition of your car. The fee for an independent mechanic's services should not exceed $50 to thoroughly evaluate all items of the car that are covered by the warranty. Any parts that are deficient should be documented and brought to a dealer's attention and repaired for free before the warranty expires. Make sure your documentation is thorough. Ask your dealer for a copy of all your warranty records. Insist that all of your complaints be recorded on a repair order, and request a copy of every repair order you sign.

Never lose sight of the fact that many parts on a car do not fail spontaneously. They can gradually deteriorate and function on a substandard level for quite some time before they finally break down completely. Just because your car is running fine today, while the warranty is in force, does not mean it will run fine tomorrow after the warranty expires.

Here are some of the items your mechanic should check:

Computer Fault Codes The computer in your car constantly monitors the performance of various sensors and relays that affect the operation of the engine and the automatic transmission. If a sensor or relay fails completely, the CHECK ENGINE or SERVICE ENGINE SOON light on the instrument panel will come on and stay on. Many times, however, the warning light can flash momentarily without your noticing it, and the car will run fine. This phenomenon indicates an intermittent problem, that is, one that comes and goes very quickly. Even though the problem is sporadic, the computer notices it and stores a fault code in its memory. This fault code will be in the car's computer memory even if the warning light on the instrument panel is not on continually.

Intermittent problems should be brought to a dealer's attention. A fault code in the computer's memory could mean that a sensor or relay is gradually failing, or that a problem in the vehicle's wiring harnesses is emerging. Retrieving fault codes from a vehicle's computer is generally very easy and takes no more than five minutes. All a mechanic has to do is to attach a device called a scanner to an electrical connector. On many cars the connector is referred to as the ALDL (assembly line data link) connector. This connector taps directly into the vehicle's computer. If your mechanic discovers any fault codes, ask him to write them on your inspection report. You must document intermittent problems with a letter to the dealer before the warranty expires. Also, obtain a repair order that clearly shows you complained about the condition before the warranty ran out. Don't underestimate how serious intermittent fault codes can be. If a fault code is associated with deteriorating wiring or electrical connectors, the cost of diagnosis and repair can easily reach $300 or more.

Engine Oil Leaks Your mechanic should check for leaking valve cover gaskets and leaking oil seals. The crankshaft front and rear seals should be checked for evidence of leakage. Oil stains are not the same as leakage. If oil actually drips from a seal or gasket it must be replaced.

Power Steering Fluid Leaks There should not be any fluid leaks from the power steering reservoir or the steering rack-and-pinion assembly seals.

Automatic Transmission Fluid Leaks Your mechanic should check for leaks at the transmission front and rear seals. He should also look for leaks at the transmission-to-radiator coolant tubes. The vehicle should be road tested to confirm that shift quality is normal with no slippage.

Shock Absorber and Strut Fluid Leaks Shock absorbers and MacPherson struts should be inspected for evidence of fluid leakage. Leaking struts or shocks must be replaced.

Steering Linkage and Suspension Steering linkage should be inspected for loose tie-rod ends, worn ball joints, sagging springs, and worn control-arm bushings.

Warped Brake Rotors or Drums The vehicle should be road tested to ascertain the ability of the brakes to stop the car. The cause of any brake pulsation should be identified. Brake pulsation should be corrected under warranty by machining the rotors and/or drums.

Engine Performance The vehicle should be road tested to evaluate engine performance. Your mechanic is probably more sensitive to abnormal engine operation than you are. If the engine hesitates or surges, corrective action must be taken under warranty. Ask your mechanic to listen for ping-ing, or detonation as it is more correctly called by auto technicians. If the engine pings on the correct octane fuel, there could be a problem requiring a revised computer Programmable Read-Only Memory (PROM). Other causes of pinging are incorrect igni-tion timing, a defective knock sensor, a mal-functioning turbocharger wastegate, an ob-structed turbocharger intercooler, excessive combustion chamber carbon, and a partially clogged exhaust system.

Charging System Performance Your me-chanic should check the alternator output and the condition of the battery.

Engine Belts and Hoses All drive belts and coolant hoses should be inspected. Cracked or otherwise damaged belts or hoses should be replaced under warranty.

Warranty Ripoffs—You're Paying for Work that Should Be Free!

Automotive tune-ups are very lucrative sources of service revenue for car dealers and independent repair shops. Often when a car's engine does not run properly, the owner is sold a tune-up as a solution. Peri-odic maintenance tune-ups are still needed on computerized cars, but these tune-ups virtually never correct engine performance problems (See *Tune-up* in Part III).

The majority of engine performance prob-lems that occur on computerized cars are attributable to malfunctions in computer sensors, relays, and wiring connectors, all of which should be covered by a 5-year, 50,000-mile emissions warranty. This war-ranty supplements the basic new car war-ranty and accompanies every new car sold in America. For details on the parts covered by this warranty, see *Tune-up* in Part III. What you have to keep uppermost in mind is that you should not be too anxious to pay for re-pairs connected with solving engine perfor-mance problems. Think emissions warranty, not tune-ups!

It is not unusual for a consumer to be-come so frustrated with his or her dealer's inability to solve an engine performance problem that the car is taken to dealer after dealer for a solution. In a final act of despera-tion the consumer decides to pay for correc-tion of the problem at an independent repair shop, sometimes with good results, some-times with no resolution of the problem. Keep in mind that you have a five-year emis-sions warranty and it must be honored by the car's manufacturer. Contact the manu-facturer's district service manager to remind him of his company's obligation, and you should get results.

Often, engine performance problems are connected with a vehicle's design defi-ciencies. In these cases, problems will persist despite routine corrective actions. The carmaker advises its dealers how to imple-ment special modifications to the vehicle through regularly released *Technical Service Bulletins*. The repair instructions contained in these bulletins are not found in the factory service manuals. In some cases dealers do not adequately catalog these bulletins. The bulletins can be misplaced, leaving the dealer's mechanics unaware of how to fix a particularly difficult problem.

If your car has a troublesome condition that a dealer cannot solve, contact the manufacturers before you rush out to another shop with your wallet opened. Describe the problem you are having and ask the district service manager whether a technical service bulletin covers that problem.

Secret Warranties

The term *secret warranty* refers to warranty coverage offered by a car manufacturer for repairs not ordinarily covered under warranty and not publicly announced. In other words, you'll get your problem fixed under warranty even if your car's warranty has expired, but only if you protest and complain. If you are timid, your dealer may charge you for a repair other customers are receiving free.

So how do you find out if the problem you are experiencing is covered by a so-called secret warranty? First, ask your dealer. Then try the manufacturer's zone office. Contact the customer relations department. The phone number is in your owner's manual. Simply state your problem and ask them if there is a policy adjustment provision covering the malfunction on your car. Avoid using the term "secret warranty" when talking to your dealer or the manufacturer. Dealers and manufacturers do not acknowledge the existence of secret warranties. They do acknowledge *policy adjustments,* which amount to case-by-case extensions of warranty coverage. In your case, if you complain enough, you may get the coverage!

If the customer relations department does not acknowledge a special policy in connection with your problem, there is another way to determine whether the difficulty with your car is related to some intrinsic design problem the manufacturer actually knows about. There are many problems with cars that can only be fixed using information disseminated in technical service bulletins. Here's a strategy for finding out whether there is a bulletin related to your car. First, contact a dealer about your problem and ask the service department whether there is a correction for the condition described in a technical service bulletin. If there is, ask how much the repair will cost. Also, get the number and date of the bulletin. You can then write to the manufacturer asserting that you are aware of the bulletin and that you feel your car should be fixed for free because an inherent design problem was there when you bought the car.

If the dealer does not acknowledge the existence of a bulletin, you can try an independent repair shop. Many shops have bound volumes of factory technical bulletins for all makes of cars. You can pretend to be interested in paying for a repair. Request that the shop's proprietor check the bulletin index for any bulletins pertaining to your car and the problem it has. Some shops have these bulletins on a computer database and can search and retrieve them very quickly.

As a last resort, you can contact the U.S. Department of Transportation. To obtain copies of technical service bulletins, write to:

National Highway Traffic Safety Administration
Technical Reference Library, Room 5108
400 Seventh Street, S.W.
Washington, DC 20590

You can also call (202) 366-2768 and ask for the technical reference library.

The library can provide a printout that lists all the bulletins the library has on file. From this printout you can select the bulletins that are of interest to you and order them from the library.

Are so-called secret warranties unfair? Probably not, although some consumer groups argue otherwise. Suppose a car manufacturer becomes aware that a certain percentage of cars it built in a particular model year may exhibit engine cam belt failure after 60,000 miles. The company knows only a small percentage will experience the problem, but it does not know exactly which cars will have the failure.

It has three choices: replace the belt on every car it made before the belts fail (this step costs a fortune), replace free of charge the belts on those cars whose owners vehemently complain about early failure, or replace none of the belts free of charge.

This scenario was actually faced by one Japanese carmaker. The manufacturer chose to replace the belt free of charge only for those owners whose cars experienced the problem and complained about the early failure of the part. Some consumer advocates branded this an unfair secret warranty. They insisted the company should have replaced the belts for free for everybody who owned the model in question.

That request, however, is not very realistic according to the Federal Trade Commission's Bureau of Consumer Protection. William MacLeod, director of the bureau, pointed out that if carmakers were forced to treat every customer identically, they might eliminate policy adjustments completely. In other words, when your warranty expires, you get absolutely nothing, period. At least with so-called secret warranties, if you are informed, you have a chance of getting something. Since you're reading this book, consider yourself one of the informed. Go for it!

What You Should Do If Your Engine Burns Too Much Oil

Modern automobile engines can run thousands of miles without burning a quart of oil, even small high-revving engines. Many four-cylinder, American-made engines commonly get 7500 miles to a quart of oil. Gone are the days when engines routinely burned a quart of oil every 500 miles.

Nevertheless, a consumer occasionally gets stuck with a new car that burns a lot of oil. High oil consumption in a new car can be considered oil usage in excess of one quart in 2000 miles of driving. Many car manufacturers and their dealers disagree. Car companies typically consider 750 miles or more per quart an acceptable figure for oil consumption in an engine covered by warranty. This is pure poppycock, and no consumer should ever accept so much oil usage in an engine that has been properly maintained and covered under warranty.

The question that really counts is, How many miles per quart of oil does the same engine as yours routinely get? If most owners get 5000 miles per quart of oil and you only get 750, obviously there is something wrong with your car! If your new car only gets 750 miles per quart of oil, there has to be something wrong with it.

I once worked for a carmaker that had some trouble with high oil consumption on many of its engines. Officially our policy was that 500 miles or more per quart was okay. Customers considered this nonsense. The problem was really created at the factory. The piston rings used in our engines were quite simply junk! They wore out in as few as 5000 miles of driving. An engine getting as few as 200 miles per quart of oil can be adjusted to get 3000 miles per quart very easily—we installed better quality piston rings and the problem was fixed.

Not all cases of high oil consumption are the result of bad piston rings. Sometimes a problem occurs in the valve stem seals. In other cases there is a defect in one or more cylinder walls. Whatever the cause, there is always some mechanical explanation for excessive oil consumption; it is usually the car manufacturer's fault, assuming you have maintained your car properly. One exception involves the use of synthetic motor oil. A new engine should be broken in using ordinary motor oil. After that, synthetic oil can be used. If synthetic oil is used in a brand new engine, the piston rings may never seat.

If your car is using too much oil and you can't get the problem resolved under warranty, there is a strategy you can use that often works. Dealers and carmakers are not always concerned about oil consumption per se, but they do get concerned when a new car violates exhaust emissions guidelines. Your first appeal has to be to your dealer. If that fails, contact the carmaker's district service manager. If you get no satisfaction there, you can draft a letter to the carmaker's zone office. Here's the essence of what the letter should say.

High oil consumption causes contamination of an emission control device called the oxygen sensor. When this part malfunctions due to contamination, the car's computer cannot correctly control fuel mixture. Consequently, exhaust emissions increase. Remind the manufacturer that you are aware of the connection between oil consumption and potentially high emissions. Also suggest that you are considering contacting the Environmental Protection Agency, but will not do so until you receive a reply to your letter. Give the car company two weeks to respond. If they do not react to your veiled threat, contact the Environmental Protection Agency's Field Operations and Support Division in Washington. Write to:

Warranty Complaint
Field Operations and Support Division (EN-397F)
U.S. Environmental Protection Agency
Washington, DC 20460
Telephone (202) 382-2640

This government agency does not get involved with general warranty complaints. Their only interest is in complaints pertaining to vehicle emissions and failure of dealers and carmakers to honor the 5-year, 50,000-mile emissions warranty. If a legitimate complaint reaches this agency, it is usually resolved quickly and to the consumer's satisfaction.

If you live in California, there is another agency you can contact. It is the California Air Resources Board, Warranty Section. Call them at (800) 242-4450.

Chapter 5

Paid Repairs

How to Find a Good Mechanic

INCOMPETENT AUTO mechanics far outnumber competent ones. Because they are so scarce, it is worth expending some effort to look for a good mechanic—in the long run it will save you a lot of money and grief. It is bad enough that you can generally expect mediocre service while your car is under warranty and repairs are performed for free. When you have to pay for repairs, however, there is greater incentive to be selective about who works on your car.

There are many objective ways to evaluate the quality of repairs you can expect from a mechanic before he starts working on your car. First, find out if he is certified by the ASE (Automotive Service Excellence, an organization previously called the National Institute for Automotive Service Excellence). ASE tests and certifies mechanics in several distinct areas of automotive repair. There are separate tests and certification for:

Brakes
Automatic Transmissions
Tune-up and Emission Control Systems
Electrical Systems

Air Conditioning and Heating
Front End
Manual Transmissions and Rear Axles
Engine Repair

Make sure the mechanic you are considering is certified to perform the kind of repair work your car needs. If he is, he will have a certificate which specifies the tests he took and passed and the date his certification expires.

However, merely possessing ASE certification is not enough. There are additional considerations you should factor into your decision to do business with a particular mechanic. Good mechanics regularly attend training seminars sponsored by auto industry associations and equipment manufacturers. Ask the mechanic you are considering if he attends these training programs. Request that he show you his certificates of completion. Do the certificates indicate his training is recent? The date of training is important. If he hasn't been to school in many years, there could be cause to be concerned about his current skill level.

Not only can you prejudge a mechanic, you can also evaluate the repair shop he works in. Check with your local Better Business Bureau and Department of Consumer Affairs. Find out if there have been an unusually high number of complaints about the repair shop you are considering. Stay away from shops that generate a disproportionate number of consumer complaints. Look at the physical condition of the shop. If it appears shabby with old parts littering the floors and work benches, this sloppiness could carry over in the shop's repair work.

Ask to see the shop's technical library. It should be neat and comprehensive. There should be manuals in the library covering your make and model of car. Of great importance is whether the shop maintains a library of technical service bulletins. No mechanic can effectively service modern cars without these bulletins, which contain special repair instructions provided by the car manufacturer. This information is not found in any service manual. Independent repair shops can obtain these bulletins in bound volumes or on CD-ROM computer databases. Either way, they are essential, and you must ask the shop manager to show you that his shop has bulletins that apply to your car. If a prospective repair shop is not conscientious enough to obtain these bulletins, you should find another shop. Without technical bulletins to assist in quickly finding and repairing problems, a shop could easily charge two to five times more for repairs than what they are worth and still not correctly fix your car!

Still more criteria establish whether a shop is the kind you would want to do business with. Ask the manager about their policy regarding written warranties. How long do they warranty their work, and is the warranty in writing? Never accept an oral commitment as to the length and terms of a repair warranty. If the shop does not issue written warranties, you should be suspicious about the way they treat their customers.

Some repair shops are approved by the American Automobile Association (AAA). These shops have to meet certain guidelines established by AAA. You should take AAA approval seriously as one of the considerations for deciding on the shop you do business with. The Automotive Service Association (ASA) is another organization that maintains certain guidelines for member shops. A shop's ASA affiliation should generally be considered a plus by a consumer seeking a reputable repair facility.

Can You Trust the Mechanic With Whom You Have Been Doing Business? (Beware the Dogs Who Bite the Hands that Feed Them!)

Many consumers think that doing business with a particular repair shop for many years provides insurance against being cheated. Maybe you remember hearing the line from an old song that summed up human nature pretty well: "we only hurt the ones we love." Believe it or not, some repair shops out there only hurt the customers they know best!

Why would a repair shop proprietor cheat his best and most loyal customers? The reason is simple: it's easy and it's safe! Here's the strategy that's often used. For every four times a particular customer visits a shop for repairs, he or she is fleeced three times. The fourth time there is little or no charge for work done, unless of course expensive parts have been replaced. The customer is led to believe that some magnanimous largesse has been extended by the proprietor. "What a nice guy my mechanic is," muses the happy customer. Little does the customer know that the three previous visits to the shop generated so much profit in overcharges that the apparent freebie was actually paid for many times over.

You are undoubtedly wondering why a mechanic might consider it "safe" to cheat his most loyal customers. Here's the reason. In many states, representatives of the Department of Motor Vehicles or the Consumer Affairs Department make visits to repair shops posing as customers in need of repairs. The cars they take to the shop are "bugged" to produce a malfunction symptom. Since they know what area of the car was bugged, they can accurately judge the fairness of the mechanic's bill to repair it. Aware that the authorities police repair shops in this way, many mechanics are afraid to flimflam anybody they don't know. One such indiscretion with a representative of the Department of Motor Vehicles could lead to a suspension of a repair shop's license, a fine, or in some cases a jail sentence.

There are many ways a dishonest mechanic can cheat his well known customers. Typically, bills are made out parts that are not replaced. The customer may be charged for a set of rebuilt brake calipers that have in fact been merely washed off with solvent to make them appear rebuilt. An engine may burn a lot of oil. The mechanic might fix it with the relatively simple replacement of valve stem seals and charge for a ring job (a motor overhaul). He could wash off the oil pan with solvent, mark the bolts to make it seem as though they had been removed, and apply a bead of silicone sealant along the oil pan-to-engine seam to create the illusion that the pan had been removed. The customer is then charged $1500 for a repair that should have cost $400. A representative of the Department of Motor Vehicles would uncover this chicanery. The average unsuspecting loyal customer will not.

How can you defend against this kind of fraud? You might consider occasionally policing your mechanic yourself to assess his honesty. One way to do this entails placing a miniscule punch mark on parts that may require replacement. Use a small hammer and a center punch to place a tiny depression in metal parts that are going to be evaluated for replacement by your mechanic. Cover the depression with some grease or grime from an adjacent area of the part. Later, you can look for the mark you made to confirm the mechanic's claim that he replaced it. In nonmetallic parts you can place a very small scratch mark to identify the part. Place such a mark on any part you suspect might be replaced, such as on the brake calipers if you are having brake trouble, or on the alternator if you are having electrical system trouble, and so forth.

If you are charged for replacement parts, ask for the old parts back. If your mechanic tells you he had to return them for "core" credit against his purchase of a rebuilt part, he could be telling the truth. For that reason, you should stipulate in advance that you want to see old parts before you pay the bill. Also, always ask that new or factory-rebuilt parts be installed in your car. Mechanics find it easiest to cheat a customer when a part is repaired in the shop. A rebuilt part comes with a manufacturer's warranty, it looks brand-new and works as good as new. Ask your mechanic to tell you the brand name of the rebuilt part he installed. This will discourage him from billing you for parts that were not replaced.

Which Repair Shops Do the Best Work—Dealers, Independents, or Chains?

So many consumers are dissatisfied with the quality of warranty service they get from dealers that they don't even consider dealers for paid maintenance and repair work. If a dealership does not do warranty work conscientiously, it does not deserve to be rewarded with customer-paid business. Car dealerships that do incompetent warranty work usually create just as many problems for their customers in making with paid repairs.

Nevertheless, simply because you have had bad experiences with one dealership does not mean that all are equally incompetent. Many car dealerships do excellent repairs under warranty and perform courteously and efficiently when it comes to customer-paid work. Furthermore, contrary to what many people assume, car dealerships are sometimes no more expensive than independent repair shops and franchised chains. Independent shops are privately owned, nonfranchised operations. Your local garage is such a shop. The chains are nationwide franchised operations such as Midas, Goodyear, and others. Some of the shops operated by the large chains are company owned, whereas others are privately owned.

Regarding cost of repairs, you are most likely to get the best prices from your local neighborhood independent repair shop. Such shops generally have low overhead and minimal advertising budgets. The national repair chains do a great deal of costly adver tising about how low their prices are, and in fact they are, if you purchase one of their repair packages. For example, if you have an advertised brake job done at one of the large chains, you may only pay the advertised $89. But don't count on it! Chances are this is just a lowball price designed to get you into the shop. The low prices advertised by the chains are excellent bargains if your car only needs the work included in the package deal. In many cases additional work is required, so you'll end up spending far more money than the advertised price. Ultimately, you could pay as much as or more than what a dealer or independent shop would charge you for the same work. In fairness to the chains, they will generally give you an accurate estimate when your car requires more work than what is covered by the special package price.

Independent repair shops sometimes use the same merchandising strategies, advertising low prices on repair packages that almost never suffice to accomplish a thorough repair. This gimmick "gets people in the door," as they say, so it can be considered an effective advertising tool. Before you become too jaded about how the auto repair industry attracts customers, remind yourself about how almost every other industry advertises. Lawyers announce worry-free $175 divorces that almost always turn into $10,000 donnybrooks. Airlines advertise $89 supersaver fares on many flights that might have all of two seats available at that price. So what makes the car repair business any worse?

Assuming the prices offered by dealers, chains, and independents were equal, where can you expect the best quality work? The best work is usually done by shops that have a low employee turnover. Independent repair shops have a definite advantage in this area. The proprietor is generally a working mechanic who takes a personal interest in retaining every customer. He also realizes how much it costs to recruit and train a new mechanic, so he will do everything he can to retain a competent employee.

Car dealers have the advantage of greater familiarity with particular makes and models because of continuous exposure to the same cars. This helps in resolving certain engine performance problems quickly. However, the chains and independents now have access to so much factory repair information that dealers no longer have a significant advantage when it comes to availability of technical support.

If your neighborhood's independently owned garage employs well-trained mechanics experienced in working on your make of car, chances are you will get the most courteous treatment there and the most conscientious repairs. Occasionally, your car may have a problem that is too difficult for an independent mechanic to solve. If your mechanic is honest, he will send you to a dealership for certain kinds of specialized repairs that dealers do best because of their greater familiarity with your make.

Besides their greater experience with the cars they service, dealers also offer another significant advantage that must be weighed when you decide about who services your car. Many dealers can offer superior warranties on repair parts and labor. General Mo-

tors dealers, for example, offer a 12-month/ 12,000-mile warranty on repair parts *and* labor. This warranty is backed up by the manufacturer.

Supposing though that you are completely loyal to your neighborhood garage in preference to a new car dealership, you should not be discouraged from getting the best bargains on auto maintenance and repairs by selecting a variety of specialty shops to do certain kinds of work. Here is a list of common repair and maintenance services and the kinds of shops that can best perform them at the lowest cost:

Maintenance tune-ups	General repair garages
	Tune-up specialty shops
	Tire dealers (Goodyear, etc.)
Engine performance diagnosis	New car dealers
	Tune-up specialty shops
	General repair garages
	Tire dealers
Automatic transmission repairs	Transmission shops
Exhaust systems	Muffler shops
Engine repairs	General repair garages
	New car dealers
Wheel alignment	Tire dealers
Brakes	General repair garages
	New car dealers
	Tire dealers
Antilock brake work	New car dealers
Air conditioner repairs	General repair garages
	New car dealers
Lubrication and oil changes	General repair garages
	Tire dealers
Electrical system work	New car dealers
	General repair garages

You might wonder why "fast lube" shops were not mentioned as good choices for lubrication and oil changes. Actually they are a good bet if no-appointment service and speed is your main interest. They are also pretty thorough. If you want rock bottom prices, however, they should generally be be avoided. Many fast lubrication shops find diverse creative ways to pick your pocket for more money than a lubrication and oil change are really worth. An oil and filter change that might cost you $19 at a general repair garage or discount tire store could easily run you $28 at a fast lube shop. Sure they vacuum your car and clean your windows, but it's a lubrication and oil change you are after, not a cleanup. Also, many fast lube shops attempt to pad the bill by selling air filters and windshield wiper blades that your car may not need. Furthermore, many new cars require 5W30 motor oil, and some fast lube shops try to tack on an extra charge for this oil.

If your car's automatic transmission is burned out, your local garage will probably subcontract the job to a nearby transmission shop. Very few small general repair garages are equipped to perform automatic transmission repairs competently and efficiently.

That's why transmission work is subcontracted. You'll be charged a markup for the transmission overhaul. The markup represents your mechanic's profit for subcontracting the repair to a transmission shop. It could be cheaper for you to deal directly with a transmission shop such as AAMCO or a similar facility that specializes in automatic transmissions.

When it comes to wheel alignments and front end work, tire specialty stores such as Goodyear are hard to beat. They usually have both good wheel alignment equipment and mechanics who know how to use it properly.

Billing Ripoffs and How to Avoid Them

Before your car is worked on, you will be required in most cases to sign a document known in the auto industry as a repair order. The repair order provides the repair shop with written authorization to work on your car. Depending on how the repair order is filled out, it can provide the shop with a license to steal!

Repair Estimates

In some states laws require repair shops to give their customers written estimates on request. Even if you live in a state that doesn't have such a law, you can still take action to reduce the risk of getting cheated. In many cases it is impossible for a mechanic to know what a repair will cost until he thoroughly examines your vehicle to determine

what, if any, parts will be needed. That is why your request for an estimate will be greeted with the statement, "I can't give you one until I begin working on the car." Under the circumstances, what you must do is to ask for a worst case scenario estimate. In other words, How much will the repair cost if the malfunction involves the most expensive parts and the most extensive labor? This is called a ballpark repair estimate. Any mechanic can provide an educated guess.

Once you know what your maximum financial exposure may be, you can ask for a written cost ceiling on the repair order. Suppose the mechanic tells you the most a job could cost under the worst circumstances is $400. You then insist that a note be written on the repair order indicating that no work shall be done exceeding $400 without your further authorization. You can write this yourself in the space above your signature when you sign the repair order. The statement could say: "Bill not to exceed $400 without my further authorization."

You must decide whether you will allow the shop to exceed the limit based on an oral approval from you over the telephone or an additional written approval. A written approval can be inconvenient for you and expensive. You must take the time to return to the shop. While the mechanic is waiting for your authorization he could begin another job, thereby delaying completion of your car's repairs. All this can be avoided by allowing the total cost to exceed the prearranged limit with an oral approval by telephone. Just make a note of the time you received the call for authorization, the person you spoke to, and the amount you approved. If a dispute arises, your written note can help resolve the disagreement in your favor.

Bill-Padding Gimmicks

There are many ways a repair shop can pad your bill. Preventing this begins with knowing something about how repair shops charge for their work. There are two basic methods used for computing your bill, the flat rate system and the clock hours system. You have to find out which billing system will be used before your car is worked on. First we'll look at the flat rate system.

The Flat Rate System

Flat rate billing entails multiplying the time allowed for the repair in a flat rate manual by the repair shop's posted hourly labor rate. In the flat rate system, most repair procedures have a corresponding repair code and repair time allowance assigned in the manual. Replacement of a carburetor for a particular car might have a code C1120, 1.2, for example. C1120 is the replacement code. The number "1.2" stands for 1.2 hours, the suggested time allowed to replace the part.

There are two kinds of flat rate manuals, aftermarket manuals and factory manuals. Every car manufacturer provides its dealers with a flat rate manual to bill the factory for warranty repairs. The dealership's warranty clerk finds the code applicable to a particular repair and the time allowance for that repair. The dealer's warranty labor rate is multiplied by the number of hours allowed in

the flat rate manual. This is the total reimbursed to the dealer for labor. The warranty cost allowance of the part is added to this.

There is a big difference between flat rate manuals supplied by car manufacturers and those printed by aftermarket publishers. The manuals provided by car manufacturers allow much less time for each repair! Car companies expect their dealers to do warranty work fast and efficiently. The modest times allocated in their flat rate manuals are difficult to achieve under the best of circumstances, and even more so on older cars on which parts have rusted and seized for one reason or another. Because warranty work is done on relatively new cars, they can be easier to fix because rust is not a factor and the parts are relatively clean.

Although the flat rate times allowed for repairs can be very low in car manufacturer's manuals, they can be unrealistically high in some aftermarket manuals. In almost every case, you will be billed according to time allowed in an aftermarket manual, not a manufacturer's manual, even if the work is done by a car dealership that has manufacturer's manuals. Aftermarket manuals try to take into account the possibility that older cars have rusted or corroded parts that can be hard to remove; a lot of built-up grime has to be cleaned before a part can be worked on, etc. Nevertheless, the times allocated in these manuals can be in many cases far in excess of what a reasonably competent mechanic would require to do a job.

Here's the rationale for allowing so much time. In some cases a mechanic would require much less time. In others, far more time would be needed because of corrosion, rust or some other problem associated with a car's age. Consequently, when all categories of repair situations are averaged out, the flat rate times allocated in aftermarket manuals are theoretically fair. Many consumers object to paying an *average* repair time if their cars are fixed in less than average time. This reasoning can be spurious. Suppose it requires a lot more than flat rate allocated time to fix your car? Would you want to pay the additional labor? Would you want to pay more labor if your mechanic is a slow worker and fails to achieve the recommended time? In these cases the flat rate manual protects you.

Problems arise, however, when repair shops get greedy and want more money than the flat rate manual allows. You might see additional charges on your bill for freeing up rusted parts. This is not acceptable. The generous repair times allowed in aftermarket flat rate manuals include time for extra labor associated with removing rusted parts. Carefully read your repair order when you receive the bill. Don't be too timid to question flat rate charges annotated on the bill. If you are not satisfied with the explanation, ask to see the flat rate manual and request that the shop manager explain how charges were computed.

The Clock Hours System

The clock hours system is much more simple than the flat rate system. You simply pay for the number of hours a mechanic works on your car multiplied by the posted hourly labor rate. Rarely do repair shops use this billing method. Generally, it is used only when diagnostic work is being done. In this case, the mechanic must search for the cause of a problem. How much time will be required is not possible to predict accurately because the mechanic does not know what the problem is.

Many consumers allow unscrupulous or incompetent mechanics to use this logic to bilk them mercilessly under the clock hours system. Although it is true that certain problems require diagnosis of unpredictable duration, nothing ever goes wrong with a car that can't be diagnosed within a certain maximum allocation of time. Let's look at an example.

Suppose your car's engine is not running well. You have a maintenance tune-up done, and there is no improvement. Your mechanic tells you it is going to be very difficult to locate your car's problem. He refuses to commit himself to any definite amount of time. Watch out, you're being set up! It is true that your mechanic does not know exactly how long it will take to locate the problem. Nevertheless, there are certain standard engine diagnostic procedures that can identify nearly any problem within a certain amount of time. Usually, no more than one hour should be required. If your mechanic refuses to commit himself to a time limit, there are several possible reasons:

1. He wants to fleece you.

2. He is incompetent and simply does not know what he is doing.

3. He is unfamiliar with your make of car and how to troubleshoot it efficiently.

4. He does not have proper test equipment to perform a speedy diagnosis.

5. He does not possess a library of technical service bulletins pertaining to your car and therefore lacks information about special procedures required to correct engine performance problems.

Item number four requires special comment. As will be pointed out in Part III, almost any good mechanic can diagnose and repair a computerized car with an inexpensive piece of test equipment called a scanner. However, using this device as the sole diagnostic tool can be time-consuming and inefficient. A computerized engine analyzer is an absolute must if engine performance problems are to be isolated quickly. If time is no object and you don't care what your bill is, then less sophisticated test equipment will suffice.

The "Leave the Car With Me" Con Game

Many mechanics use a proven strategy for bilking their customers, particularly in connection with the diagnosis and repair of engine performance problems. If your mechanic insists that your car's problem is so complex that you must leave your car with him for the day, there is a good chance you are going to be ripped off.

Most engine performance problems on computerized cars can be diagnosed and repaired within 30 minutes. Many mechanics would like to be paid two or three hours worth of labor in exchange for 30 minutes of work. If you are in the shop looking over your mechanic's shoulder, it is impossible for him to claim it took three hours to do a job that actually requires 30 minutes.

Furthermore, suppose you are in the shop watching him, and you see him fumbling through a service manual for an hour trying to find out how your car works! Do you want to finance your mechanic's education? Perhaps your mechanic wanted you to leave the car with him because he did not want to expose his lack of knowledge about your vehicle.

If your mechanic asks you to leave your car with him, insist on a written estimate of diagnostic time and set a limit as to the amount of time you will allow him to bill you. If he cannot assure you that he can do a thorough engine performance diagnosis in an hour, find another mechanic.

The "Hook It Up to the Analyzer" Scam

Computerized engine analyzers are essential to fast diagnosis of problems in late-model cars. Unfortunately, they are also very useful in bilking unwary consumers. Some mechanics are so creative in fleecing customers that they have devised a way to cheat those consumers shrewd enough to refuse to leave their cars for diagnostic work.

Here's how the scam works. Your car is hooked up to a computerized engine analyzer. The machine has a lot of flashing lights, scope traces, meters, and other gadgets that look very impressive. "Certainly, something important is being done to my car," you think silently. Meanwhile your mechanic has walked away from your car to work on another car in the shop. When questioned, he alleges that the machine is going through various automatic diagnostic tests. An hour can elapse as these alleged tests are performed by the analyzer. During this time, the mechanic occasionally returns to your car to make it seem as though he is working on it. Another hour can go by. More work is done on other customers' cars as the meter runs on *your* repair bill.

Is so much time really necessary for the supposed automatic diagnostic tests? Absolutely not! A computerized engine analyzer can run thorough a complete diagnostic sequence in less than ten minutes. Additional time is required for interpretation by the mechanic, but the machine can do its job in under ten minutes. Remember, the diagnosis of just about any engine performance problem should not require more than one hour of a good mechanic's time. After that, there will be some time required to replace the part or parts identified as the cause of the problem. If your mechanic is constantly walking away from the engine analyzer to other cars, you are being charged for work that isn't being done on your car!

What a Properly Written Repair Order Should Look Like

One of the best ways to avoid getting cheated on car repairs is to insist that the repair order you sign be filled out properly. Figure 2-1 on page 66 shows a well-written repair order. Let's analyze it.

The repair order shown was generated by a General Motors dealer, Steve West Motors, in Kendallville, Indiana. This dealer boasts one of the highest track records for customer satisfaction in the United States, and the repair order will reveal one of the reasons for this. Here are the important elements.

Customer Data Thoroughly Covered

The customer's name, in this case Greg Robinson, address and telephone number are clearly indicated, along with type of car, serial number, and mileage. Repair shops that care about their customers contact them from time to time to assess their satisfaction. Without a correct address and telephone number this cannot be done. It is important to you to have an accurate mileage reading at the time your car enters the shop. You can compare the odometer reading on the repair order with the reading when you pick up the car. This can tell you if the mechanic actually road tested your car to verify symptoms that might be evident only while driving. It also tells you if somebody in the repair shop used your car for personal transportation during the day—an unusual occurrence, but it does happen!

The time received and time promised are also important. Many repair shops are not conscientious enough to make any promises about when your car will be available to you. You should get this in writing when you sign the repair order.

Customer Complaint Clearly Stated

Do not sign a repair order unless it contains a clear definition of your complaint. The Instructions section of the repair order

COST	QUAN.	NUMBER	DESCRIPTION	PRICE
		PARTS		
	(1)	10463033	Alternator	178 37

☐ CASH
☑ CREDIT CARD – TYPE _MasterCard_
☐ DEALER CHARGE

67983

PONTIAC	BUICK	GM **STEVE WEST MOTORS** OLDSMOBILE **GMC TRUCKS**

U.S. 6 WEST   KENDALLVILLE, IN. 46755   347-1400

NAME _Greg Robinson_   DATE _4-10-91_
ADDRESS _612 Wakefield Blvd._   CITY _Kendallville_ 46755
YEAR _87_   MAKE _Buick_   TYPE OR MODEL _LeSabre_   RECEIVED _8:15_ A.M.
SERIAL NO. _1G4HP5432HH542595_   ENGINE NO. _3.8 Litre V-6_   PROMISED _4:30_ P.M.
SPEEDOMETER _63,725_   LICENSE NO. _570435_   PHONE WHEN READY YES ☑ NO ☐
CUST. ORDER NO.   ORDER WRITTEN BY _Kevin_   PHONE _347-2439_

DSS	ISJ		LABOR CHARGE
LUBRICATE	☐		
CHANGE OIL	☐		
CHANGE OIL FILTER CART.	☐		
TUNE UP	☐		
SERVICE EMISSION CONTROL	☐		
BALANCE WHEELS	☐		
FRONT END ALIGN.	☐		
X TIRES	☐		
SAFETY CHECK	☐		

OPER. NO.   INSTRUCTIONS:

Customer states battery goes dead overnight
Call customer if repair over $200.00 :

.6	Check charging system and check for current draw.	22 80
	Alternator output 20 amps max., Below specification	
.7	Replace Alternator	26 60

12 month/12,000 mile warranty on parts & labor

P.O. NO.   SUBLET REPAIRS

OUR LABOR RATE IS $ _38.00_ PER HR.

ACCOUNT	AMOUNT	INTERNAL		CLAIM			C	S

	C	S
LABOR-MECH.		49 40
LABOR-BODY SHOP		
SUBLET-MECH.		
SUBLET-BODY SHOP		
PTS. & ACC. MECH.		178 37
PTS. & ACC. BODY SHOP		
PAINT & MAT'L.		1 00
GAS, OIL & GREASE		
TAX		8 97
TOTAL		237 74

GAS, OIL & GREASE
GALS. GAS @
QTS. OIL @
LBS. GREASE @

PRELIMINARY ESTIMATED
PARTS   LABOR   TOTAL _200 00_

PHONE ESTIMATE FOR AUTHORIZED ADDITIONS
TALKED TO _Mr. Robinson_
TIME CALLED _10:00_ BY _Kevin_
ADDITIONAL REPAIRS
PARTS _178 37_   LABOR _50 40_   TOTAL _228 77_

NOT RESPONSIBLE FOR LOSS OR DAMAGE TO CARS OR ARTICLES LEFT IN CARS IN CASE OF FIRE, THEFT OR ANY OTHER CAUSE BEYOND OUR CONTROL.

Figure 2-1

shown in Figure 2-1 includes the statement, "Customer states battery goes dead overnight." Many instances of consumer dissatisfaction with auto repairs happen because the repair shop does not have a clear idea of what the customer is complaining about. Worse, the repair shop doesn't even bother to transpose accurately the complaint to the repair order. Don't sign a repair order until your complaint is correctly written on it.

Maximum Permitted Repair Expense Clearly Defined

Note the statement: "Call customer if repair over $200." This is a must for your protection. An honest repair shop will gladly agree to a written limit to the expense you will incur, beyond which your additional authorization is required. In the lower left corner of the repair order, the estimated total of parts and labor is noted as $200 in the TOTAL column.

Customer Authorization to Exceed Expense Ceiling Clearly Documented

In the case of the repair order shown in Figure 2-1, the total cost of parts and labor exceeded the $200 authorized by the customer. The dealer's service writer "Kevin" called the customer "Mr. Robinson" at ten in the morning and received authorization to perform repairs totaling $228.77 plus tax. This telephone transaction is noted in the lower left corner of the repair order in the box entitled PHONE ESTIMATE FOR AUTHORIZED ADDITIONS.

Work Done is Itemized and Method of Computing Labor Clearly Defined

The itemization of work is where many consumers get fleeced. A reputable repair shop such as Steve West Motors has no need to chisel its customers, so they itemize repairs very carefully.

The repair order in Figure 2-1 shows that the charging system was checked to determine why the battery had been losing its charge. The charging system test determined that alternator output was only 20 amperes, well below the specified rating for the car. In the OPER. NO. (operation number) column of the repair order "0.6" is annotated. This means the shop is using the flat rate system for billing. The flat rate labor allowance for a charging system test is six-tenths of an hour. This figure is multiplied by the dealer's labor rate of $38 per hour to arrive at a total labor charge or $22.80 for testing the alternator. Replacing the alternator carries a flat rate allowance of 0.7 hours, resulting in a labor charge of $26.60. The total of both labor operations is $49.40.

When a repair order is prepared this way, you know exactly what you are paying for. Shops that merely give you a lump sum bill without itemization of charges could be hiding overcharges. Many shops that do not itemize repair bills charge a different amount for the same work performed on different days. If profits are down, the charges could go up. If you are unlucky enough to show up on a day when the shop's proprietor needs to make up for poor earnings, you could pay more for a repair than it is worth. You should insist that repair charges be itemized.

Replacement Parts Clearly Defined and Itemized

A repair order should show the parts that were installed in your car and the amount charged for those parts. Figure 2-1 indicates that one alternator was installed in Mr. Robinson's car at a charge of $178.37 for the part.

Warranty Clearly Stated

You should get a written warranty when you have your car repaired. The repair order in Figure 2-1 indicates a 12-month, 12,000-mile warranty on parts and labor. Never accept an oral assurance for the terms of a repair warranty. Honest repair shops have no objection to putting their repair warranty in writing.

Gasoline and Oil Additives (Miracle Potions for Your Engine)

Some repair shops add extra money to their coffers by selling useless gasoline and oil additives. In nearly every case these additives either do not work as advertised or can actually do harm to your car.

Gasoline Additives

A favorite snake oil cure is fuel injector cleaner. Fuel injector cleaner is already in every brand of gasoline sold in the United States, so why should you pay for something that is already in your tank?

In the early 1980s clogged fuel injectors attributable to inadequate fuel detergency was a common problem. The oil companies have solved this problem. As of this writing, it is virtually impossible to find any gasoline in the United States that can cause fuel injector clogging. Furthermore, there are so many detergents and deposit control additives in all gasolines that fuel injectors simply do not become obstructed in the way they used to.

The only useful gasoline additive that may be helpful is so-called dry gas. Dry gas is actually methyl alcohol (methanol). If there is a lot of moisture in your car's fuel tank, methyl alcohol will make it easier for the engine to burn the water when it reaches the cylinders. Also, in cold weather alcohol can prevent freezing of the water in the fuel tank

and obstruction of the fuel lines. However, caution must be observed in using dry gas; too much can damage the coating inside the fuel tank. Other fuel system parts can also be ruined by excessive amounts of methyl alcohol. If you use this additive in cold weather, use it sparingly, carefully following the instructions on the can regarding the recommended quantity per tank of fuel. More is not necessarily better when it comes to dry gas! In no case should the percentage of methyl alcohol in your fuel tank exceed 5 percent of the available fuel.

Oil Additives

The only liquid that should ever be placed in your car engine's crankcase is motor oil. If you use a name-brand oil carrying an API (American Petroleum Institute) specification corresponding to the carmaker's requirement, your engine will get all the lubrication and wear protection it needs. As of this writing, the highest API specification for oil used in passenger car gasoline engines is "SG." This specification not only implies that the oil provides maximum protection against wear, but also denotes that the oil offers the best available protection against sludge. This means that the oil has the ability to keep potentially damaging particles in suspension so that they don't settle in the valve train and build up thick, gooey sludge.

PTFE Solid Lubricants

Some people advocate the use of "solid lubricants" in automobile engines. One of the most widely publicized solid lubricants is

PTFE, short for polytetrafluroethylene. This is the chemical name for what consumers better know as Teflon, Du Pont's brand name for PTFE. Minute particles of PTFE can be suspended in a liquid and mixed with an engine's motor oil. According to proponents of PTFE, the particles adhere to the metal in the engine and form a super slippery barrier to wear. It should be noted that Du Pont does not endorse the use of Teflon in motor oils.

Some very clever and persuasive television "infomercials" tout these miraculous lubricants in half-hour presentations that include the spectacle of an engine running throughout the program with no oil in the crankcase. Supposedly, the coating created by the addition of the $29-per-quart PTFE lubricant preserves the engine from destruction even after the oil is drained from the crankcase.

There is no great trick to making an engine run without oil in the crankcase. If operated under no-load conditions and adequately prepared before actually starting, an engine can run for quite a long time with an empty crankcase. This is especially true if the engine has been fitted with special oil-impregnated bearings. The bottom line—it's a circus stunt, not a miracle. PTFE is not required to accomplish the trick.

PTFE advocates point to its greater "slipperiness," in comparison with the lubricating ability of ordinary oil, as evidence that it is superior to motor oil. But lower friction in a motor oil and superior anti-wear properties do not necessarily go hand in hand. API SG oil is as friction free as it has to be. It is true that PTFE possesses lower friction, but claiming that this makes an engine last

longer is like asserting that because one vitamin pill a day is good for you, five vitamin pills are five times as good. Simply reducing friction in a lubricant does not necessarily improve wear.

In fact, the people who market PTFE additives have no evidence whatsoever that their products make an engine last longer in a controlled accelerated wear test. They strongly *imply* that your engine will last longer, but they have no proof. One of their implied proofs is that PTFE additives improve gas mileage. Improved gas mileage is obtainable in a quart of ordinary motor oil. Just buy "EC" or "EC II" oil. The rating "EC" stands for energy conserving. Oil rated EC means that a standard test engine run in a laboratory gets 1.5 percent better gas mileage than the mileage obtained with a laboratory reference oil. Oil given the rating EC II boosts gas mileage by 2.7 percent. You can buy oil with an EC rating for about $1.50 a quart. The people who peddle PTFE additives charge up to $35 per quart.

One of the largest marketers of PTFE motor oil additives enlisted the help of an automotive journalist and mechanic named Brad Sears to evaluate their PTFE product. Mr. Sears' testimonial is used by the company which offers his appraisal in the form of a draft copy of a one-page flier shipped with other product literature. In the flier, Mr. Sears talks about how he found that a car using this PTFE additive required less fuel than cars using ordinary oils, as evidenced by a change in the car computer's "block learn" after PTFE was added.

Without going into a lot of technical talk

about what block learn is, it can be said that the phenomenon Mr. Sears observed is fairly common. This event is due to contamination of the vehicle's oxygen sensor; what Mr. Sears interpreted as a wonderful benefit resulting from PTFE is more correctly interpreted as damage to the car's emission control system! Could the failure of the oxygen sensor have been an unfortunate coincidence not related to the use of the PTFE additive? Maybe. Just keep in mind the kind of evidence offered by Mr. Sears is no more credible than the circus stunt of getting an engine to run for half an hour without oil in the crankcase.

Counterfeit Mechanical Parts and Second-rate Crash Parts

You must be concerned about the quality of the parts installed in your car when mechanical repairs are done or body work is performed after an accident. Many of the parts supplied by makers other than the car manufacturers are pure junk. Parts made by the car companies are called "factory" parts or "original equipment" parts. Parts made by other companies are called "aftermarket" parts. Some aftermarket parts are as good as or even better than factory originals. All too frequently, however, they are substantially inferior.

Counterfeit Mechanical Parts

Some independent repair shops sell parts that are contained in packages that look nearly identical to those housing GM, Ford, or Chrysler parts. Sometimes these parts are counterfeit—cheap knockoffs that are far inferior to the genuine article. Cleverly, the bandits who distribute these parts pirate the car company's logo and trademark and make the package look authentic to the undiscerning eye. Even the repair shop owner can be duped into buying parts he believes are authentic, so he isn't necessarily cheating you.

If an independent repair shop claims to use factory-original parts, ask for the package the part came in. Later, show it to the parts manager of an authorized dealership. He can compare it with the packaging for a part in stock and determine whether you were sold a counterfeit.

Why should you be so concerned about the kind of parts installed in your car? Counterfeit parts are usually vastly inferior in quality and performance. In some cases they can be unsafe. Even some legitimately distributed aftermarket brands are pure garbage.

For example, a bargain-priced aftermarket distributor cap might cost $5 less than a factory original or a good quality aftermarket product. After six months, the distributor cap burns out. You get a bill for $95 for diagnostic time, labor, and a new distributor cap, not to mention the expense of towing, lost time from work, etc. All that to save $5. A good distributor cap would have lasted five years!

Ask your mechanic what brand of parts he uses. If the brand is not familiar to you, inquire at an auto parts store. The person attending the counter will generally be honest with you about what the good brands are.

Second-rate Crash Parts

Insurance companies talk a lot about how they want to save you money. One way they claim to do this entails forcing body shops to use sheet metal parts made by companies other than the car manufacturers. These parts are called "imitation crash parts." They are often made in foreign countries and always cost less than factory originals. But are they as good or better?

If you believe the Certified Automotive Parts Association (CAPA), then they are as good. But if you believe CAPA, you should also believe in the tooth fairy! CAPA is sponsored by the insurance industry, so its positions may be expected to further that industry's desire to increase profits by lowering the cost of claims.

The auto body repair industry is not as convinced as CAPA that imitation crash parts are as good as factory originals. In one survey, 85 percent of the body shops that use imitation crash parts considered them inferior to factory originals. Ford Motor Company tested CAPA-certified hoods and found them to be lacking sufficient welds and adhesives, a problem that could have serious safety implications. Tests run by car manufacturers have shown that CAPA-certified imitation crash parts do not have adequate corrosion protection.

In view of the carmakers' generally negative evaluations, you should ask your body shop what kind of parts they intend to use to repair your car if it has been in an accident. If CAPA-certified imitation crash parts have been designated, you have reason to protest to your insurance company and insist that factory original equipment parts be installed.

Maintenance Packages

Maintenance packages are favorites among car dealerships. And they are so lucrative they should be. A maintenance package is a long list of services packaged as a 15,000-mile service, a 30,000-mile service, and so on. You simply choose from a menu of packages, and for one price, a very high price, your car gets served the soup to nuts banquet of checks and services it supposedly needs. Generally, you should avoid menu maintenance packages and buy maintenance services à la carte.

A typical 30,000-mile maintenance package can cost about $300. For that sum your car gets a tune-up, oil change and lubrication, transmission filter and fluid change, and a host of other services. Most of the "other services" are just perfunctory visual checks that take all of two minutes to do. Many of these services are simply not needed. Check the maintenance schedule in your owner's manual to be sure.

For example, most American-made cars do not require a change of transmission fluid before 100,000 miles except under severe operating conditions. Changing the fluid sooner is a waste of money despite what some so-called experts claim. There is one exception: if your engine has ever overheated, the transmission fluid has overheated too, and the fluid should be changed promptly.

Tires need not be rotated unless they are wearing unevenly, so save your money on

this unnecessary maintenance item. Tune-ups simply do not exist anymore in the conventional sense. Your owner's manual mentions the term "tune-up" for want of simpler terminology. As pointed out in Section Three, all that is done is a maintenance tune-up, which includes replacing the spark plugs, positive crankcase ventilation (PCV) valve, PCV filter, air filter, fuel filter, and possibly the exhaust gas recirculation (EGR) filter. Timing can no longer be adjusted on most cars, nor can fuel mixture or idle speed. These parts may be worth $50 on most American-made cars, and the labor to install them could be worth about $50. Add to that about $25 for the oil change and lubrication and you have about $125 worth of work, for which you'll pay $300 if you buy the package.

The alternative? Just tell the repair shop manager you want an oil change, and replacement of the parts required by the maintenance schedule in your owner's manual. If your car dealer will not do the work at a reasonable price, have it done by an independent repair shop. Ask the shop to write a note on your bill that indicating that the required maintenance service was done to protect your warranty. For example, if the schedule calls for service at 30,000 miles, buy the needed maintenance à la carte and have your mechanic write "30,000 mile maintenance" on the bill. You'll save a lot of money, and protect your warranty, too.

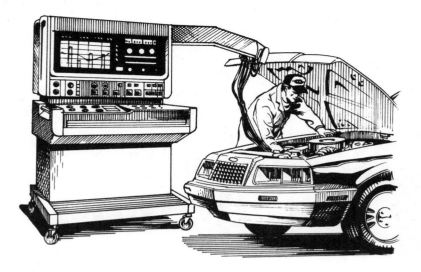

Part III

What To Do When Your Mechanic Says "Your Car Needs..."

What You Will Find in Part III

PART III CONTAINS valuable information about many of the problems that are likely to occur in your car, and what you should do when your mechanic tells you that certain repair work is needed. These problems will manifest themselves in the form of something abnormal that you can generally see, hear, or feel. You don't have to be a professional mechanic to know that your car is not working as it should.

Part III will give you the knowledge you need to identify what is probably wrong with your car based on your own observations, and the knowledge you need to properly explain these observations to your mechanic.

Additionally, you will be given information that you need to help control the cost of the repairs that are done to your car and the quality of those repairs. Sometimes mechanics make expensive and dangerous mistakes when they perform automotive service. In other cases they may deliberately attempt to deceive you to inflate your repair bill. To protect yourself as a consumer, you must be aware of the tricks some mechanics play and the mistakes they sometimes make. This much needed information is presented for you in a simplified way that any layman can understand.

Here's what you'll find in Part III

There Are 27 Major Topics In Alphabetical Order

If you don't find the subject that interests you in the list of major topics, see the index in the back of this book. The index contains references to many automotive related subjects that are discussed in connection with the major topics given in the list above.

How to Use Part III

The 5 Categories of Information

TO GET THE most out of the information contained in Part III, you must understand how this information is presented. Part III is structured alphabetically to present the automotive problems you are most likely to encounter. Each alphabetical entry contains five categories of information:

Symptoms
Typical Causes and Corrections
Parts and Terms
Mistakes and Ripoffs
Maintenance Tips

It is not necessary for you to read all the information in each category, or even each category for that matter. You may simply wish to find out more about a part for which you were charged on your repair bill. In this case, you would just read the definition found in Parts and Terms, which is a mini glossary. So that you can fully appreciate the value of each of the five categories of information and understand how to use them, read the following explanations of the categories.

Symptoms

Most malfunctions in an automobile produce symptoms that the driver will notice. Many of the more prominent symptoms are listed under each alphabetical entry. For example, if a problem is developing in the brake system, you may hear grinding noises, the car may pull to one side when the brakes are applied, or several other symptoms may be present. The major symptoms are listed in numerical order.

After you have found the symptom that most closely matches the problem you have observed, you will want to know the possible causes of the problem and what your mechanic should do to correct the condition. By knowing what *should* be done to your car, you can minimize the number of situations in which you are charged for unnecessary work. This information is contained in the section entitled Typical Causes and Corrections.

Typical Causes and Corrections

This section of every alphabetical entry includes a description of some of the possible causes of the symptoms listed in the Symptoms section. The proper actions your mechanic should take to correct the problem are also defined.

As in the Symptoms section, there is a numerical order to the presentation of causes and corrections for each corresponding symptom. First you must note the number assigned to the symptom listed in the Symptoms section. You must then locate the same

number adjacent to the symptom description in Typical Causes and Corrections. This number identifies the correct information pertaining to the symptom in question. It is not necessary for you to read any other information in the Typical Causes and Corrections section.

If you see a triangle (▲) symbol next to the number of the symptom causes and corrections you are reading, it means that additional information is contained in the section entitled Mistakes and Ripoffs. Reading this extra information is optional, but you may want to do so to get a good idea of the common errors mechanics make when attempting to correct the symptom in question and some of the tricks they sometimes use to overcharge unwary consumers.

If you see a term printed in *italics* in the Typical Causes and Corrections section, it means that a definition of that term (and possibly an illustration) is found in the section entitled Parts and Terms.

Parts and Terms

This section of every alphabetical entry is a glossary of mechanical terms and automobile parts. The entries in this section are the *italicized* words found in Typical Causes and Corrections. When you talk to your mechanic about your car, he will often use terms that you don't understand. To take the mystery out of your mechanic's jargon and to enable you to better understand your repair bill, many of these potentially confusing terms are explained for you. In some cases, your mechanic will offer to give you the old

parts that were removed from your car as evidence that they were really replaced. But how do you know what the parts should really look like? The illustrations referenced in Parts and Terms will help you considerably in this regard.

Mistakes and Ripoffs

Every alphabetical entry in this section contains a description of common errors mechanics make when attempting to correct the symptoms included in the Symptoms section, and some of the tricks they occasionally use to overcharge unwary consum-

ers. Mistakes and Ripoffs is designed to make you a more informed consumer. It will give you information you need to intelligently monitor and evaluate the repairs that are performed on your car.

Maintenance Tips

This section provides you with information about periodic maintenance that can help reduce the incidence of the symptoms listed in the Symptoms section. This information will also help you reduce the frequency of major repairs and the overall cost of owning your car.

Air Conditioner Tune-up

EVERY SPRING, repair shops advertise air conditioner service specials. For a flat fee, your car's air conditioning system will be checked out and R12 refrigerant will be added as needed, with the refrigerant costing extra. The cost of this substance will climb greatly in the near future because its manufacture will have been banned by the U.S. Environmental Protection Agency on the grounds that R12 refrigerant is a chlorofluorocarbon that is harmful to the ozone. Alternative refrigerants do not work as well as R12. Consequently, unless your car's air conditioner is not cooling properly, you should avoid routine air conditioner tune-ups because the cost will be prohibitive and the benefits minimal. All that is routinely required is a check of the compressor drive belt.

Symptoms

When an air conditioner tune-up is required, the following symptoms may be evident:

1. Air coming out of air conditioner ducts is too warm.

2. Air coming out of air conditioner ducts blows hot and cold.

Typical Causes and Corrections

Here are some of the most common causes of the aforementioned symptoms listed in numerical order. If you see a term printed in *italics*, it means that a definition of that term (and possibly an illustration) is found in the section entitled Parts and Terms. If you see a triangle symbol (▲) next to the number of the symptom you are reading, it means that additional information is contained in Mistakes and Ripoffs.

Here are some of the topics covered in detail in Mistakes and Ripoffs:

- Using bubbles in the sight glass as evidence that the system needs additional R12 refrigerant.

- Failure to evacuate the air conditioner system.

- Failure to check compressor oil level.

- Failure to clean the condenser.

- Overcharging the air conditioner.

- Failure to check the thermostat.

Air Coming Out of Air Conditioner Ducts is Too Warm (1) ▲

If your car's air conditioner will not provide cool air, the most common cause is lack of *R12* refrigerant (also called *Freon*). The techniques used to restore normal operation of the air conditioner vary depending on whether all the refrigerant or only a portion of it has been lost.

Any automotive air conditioner will lose its supply of refrigerant after time. Industry standards define the loss of more than one half pound of refrigerant per season as a significant leak; however, a system in good condition should hold its *charge* of refrigerant for several years. Most auto air conditioners hold at least two pounds of refrigerant. Even if 50 percent leaks out, the system will still operate at 90 percent efficiency and will cool the car very well. Therefore, the loss of half a pound of refrigerant in one season should not adversely affect cooling. If your car requires charging more frequently than every third season, it has an unacceptably large leak. Because refrigerant can damage the atmosphere's ozone layer, any detectable leak at all may be considered unacceptable by the environmentally conscious. Figure 3-1 shows a typical air conditioner system. Leaks generally occur where the hoses are attached by fittings.

If only a portion of the refrigerant has leaked out, your mechanic can add more in a matter of minutes. After that, he must check all fittings with a device called a *leak detector* to make sure there are no major leaks. Another common source of leakage is the seal behind the compressor clutch; this part must be checked too. If there are no major leaks, the air conditioner will probably require no additional service for some years. A mechanic can determine whether an air conditioner has lost all its refrigerant in several ways. The easiest is to check the *sight glass* if the system has one. Figure 3-1

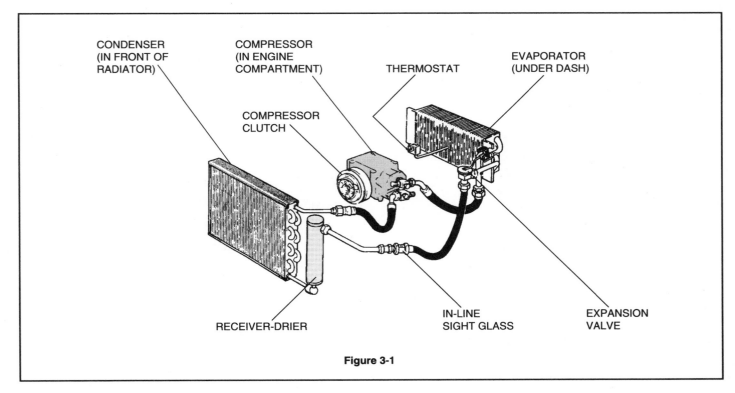

CONDENSER (IN FRONT OF RADIATOR)

COMPRESSOR (IN ENGINE COMPARTMENT)

THERMOSTAT

EVAPORATOR (UNDER DASH)

COMPRESSOR CLUTCH

RECEIVER-DRIER

IN-LINE SIGHT GLASS

EXPANSION VALVE

Figure 3-1

shows an in-line sight glass. Figure 3-2 shows a sight glass mounted on the *receiver-drier.* If there is a lot of foam or bubbles in the sight glass when the engine is running at a speed above idle, the supply of refrigerant is too low, but there is some refrigerant in the system. If there are no bubbles, and a film of oil is evident under the sight glass, there is no refrigerant at all in the system. The same determinations can be made by using pressure gauges.

If there is substantial leakage or if there is no refrigerant at all some refrigerant must be added to pressurize the system. It is then checked for leaks. Afterwards, the system is opened up to repair the leaks, the receiver-drier is replaced, and the hoses are reconnected and an *evacuation* is performed. After evacuation has been completed, the air con-

ditioner is charged with refrigerant. This process is much more complicated and more expensive than simply adding additional refrigerant. Therefore, you must ask your mechanic to distinguish between a situation where your air conditioner is low on refrigerant and completely out of refrigerant.

Many repair shops have refrigerant recovery systems that allow them to reuse any refrigerant that may be drained from your car's air conditioner. Ask your mechanic if he intends to reuse any refrigerant. If he does, the total quantity he charges you for should not exceed the capacity of the system by more than half a pound. The refrigerant capacity is written on a tag mounted somewhere on the compressor. Most cars do not require more than three pounds of R12 refrigerant to fully charge the system. You should be suspicious if you are charged for substantially more refrigerant than the rated capacity.

Air Coming Out of Air Conditioner Ducts Blows Hot and Cold (2) ▲

This symptom often indicates a problem in the electrical or electronic controls that regulate the air conditioner. *Charging* the system with additional refrigerant will not solve the problem. In fact, it could damage the air conditioning system.

One common area responsible for an air conditioner sometimes blowing hot air is the compressor clutch (Figure 3-3). This electrically operated device can slip or sometimes not engage at all due to a wiring defect or a problem in the clutch coil. A loose compressor drive belt can also cause intermittent operation of the air conditioner.

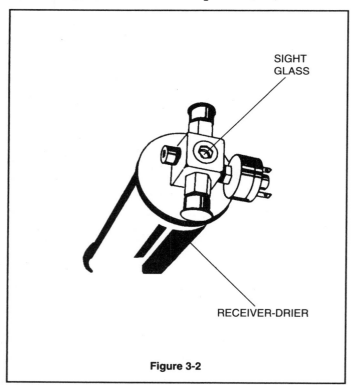

SIGHT GLASS

RECEIVER-DRIER

Figure 3-2

Some computerized cars are designed to turn off automatically the air conditioner during wide-open throttle acceleration. When normal speed is resumed the air conditioner comes back on. If your air conditioner behaves this way, check your owner's manual and fully read the section covering the air conditioner before you request service.

Another cause of this symptom is an icing *evaporator* (see Figure 3-1). The evaporator is located under the dash inside the car. Liquid refrigerant is metered into the evaporator by the *expansion valve* (see Figure 3-1). Because the pressure in the evaporator is low, the refrigerant vaporizes. When this happens, the refrigerant absorbs the heat from the evaporator fins and cools the air flowing through the fins. When the air flow-

ing through the fins is cooled, the moisture in it condenses. This moisture is directed into a drain pan, and from there it drains out a rubber hose under the car. This is the water you may see dripping under your car on a humid day when the air conditioner is running.

If the evaporator gets too cold, the moisture that condenses on its fins may turn to ice instead of draining into the drain pan. The ice blocks the flow of air through the evaporator, and the car gradually heats up. A defective *thermostat* (see Figure 3-1) is the usual cause of this problem, although the expansion valve and other parts can be responsible. In any case, mechanics often fail to properly diagnose this condition.

In response to a customer's complaint that the air conditioner sometimes blows hot, the mechanic might insert a thermometer into one of the ducts and note that the air is very cold. Thinking that colder is better, the mechanic might assume that an air temperature reading of 33°F or so, measured at a duct is excellent. Bad conclusion! If the air in the duct is 33°F, it's a lot colder at the evaporator, and ice will form on a humid day. If it's hot and dry, ice may not form. Most car air conditioners will not produce a temperature lower than 45° F measured at the ducts. This ensures that the evaporator will not freeze.

Parts and Terms

If your car needs air conditioner service, your mechanic could mention one or more of the following terms:

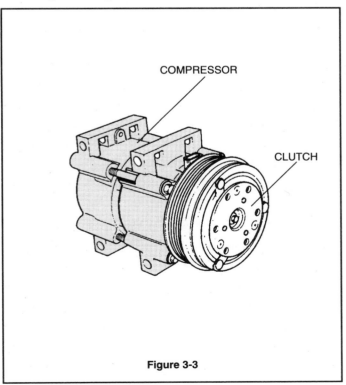

COMPRESSOR

CLUTCH

Figure 3-3

Charge This term refers to the quantity of refrigerant in the air conditioning system. It also refers to the act of adding additional refrigerant.

Compressor The compressor pumps refrigerant through the air conditioning system. Figure 3-3 shows a typical rotary compressor. Auto air conditioning compressors require a special oil. The oil level must be checked whenever the air conditioning system is opened for service. Failure to check the oil level is a common cause of compressor breakdown.

Evacuation Refers to the process of pumping air and moisture out of an air conditioning system. Air in the system increases pressure and reduces cooling efficiency. Moisture reacts with the refrigerant to form hydrochloric acid, which destroys system components. Moisture can also freeze internally, blocking the flow of refrigerant and causing a temporary loss of cooling. If an air conditioning system has lost all its refrigerant or if a line has been disconnected for any reason, a vacuum pump must be attached to the air conditioning system and operated for at least 30 minutes. The pump must run long enough to produce 29.5 inches of vacuum (at sea level) in the air conditioning system, as indicated on a vacuum gauge. In this vacuum, water boils at 72°F. All the moisture in the system will boil off and be pumped out by the evacuation pump.

Expansion Valve Some air conditioning systems use an expansion valve (see Figure 3-1) to meter the quantity of refrigerant that flows into the evaporator (see Figure 3-1). Other air conditioner designs do not use such a valve, incorporating a calibrated orifice instead.

Freon Freon is a brand name for Refrigerant 12 (R12). The chemical name is dichlorodifluoromethane. Through frequent use, Freon has become generic for R12.

Leak Detector A device used to locate refrigerant leaks. There are two kinds of leak detectors: the electronic type or the less sensitive halide detector, which uses a propane torch and a copper reactor plate. Some brands of refrigerant contain detection dye that can be seen when it leaks from a loose connection, a crack in a tube, etc. This dye is not suitable for use in certain cars and will void the manufacturer's air conditioner warranty.

Receiver-Drier Some air auto air conditioning systems contain a receiver-drier that stores refrigerant and a desiccant to remove moisture from the system. A typical receiver-drier is shown in Figure 3-1. The receiver-drier should be replaced whenever the system is opened for service.

Sight Glass Some auto air conditioners include a sight glass mounted on the receiver-drier (see Figure 3-2) or in-line in one of the hoses (see Figure 3-1). The sight glass may be used to evaluate the quantity of refrigerant in the system. Foam or bubbles seen in the sight glass with the engine running at a high rpm indicates a low level of refrigerant.

An oil slick seen on the sight glass indicates an empty system. If the sight glass is clear at a high rpm and the air conditioner is cooling, a full system is indicated.

Thermostat The thermostat is shown in Figure 3-1. It senses the temperature of the evaporator via a metal capillary tube inserted into the evaporator's fins. The thermostat is calibrated to ensure that the evaporator does not get cold enough to freeze the condensation that forms on it.

Mistakes and Ripoffs

The following information will help you control the cost of air conditioner service. The topics covered are those most likely to be associated with errors commonly made by mechanics or deliberate attempts to defraud the consumer.

Using Bubbles in the Sight Glass as Evidence that the System Needs Additional R12 Refrigerant

A favorite trick of some unscrupulous mechanics is to show a car owner bubbles in the sight glass of the air conditioner and use that as evidence that additional refrigerant is needed. Actually, even a fully charged air conditioner can have bubbles in the sight glass at a low engine rpm. If the engine is revved up and the bubbles remain, low refrigerant is indicated.

You should not be too quick to allow more refrigerant to be pumped into your car's air conditioner. Typically, an auto air conditioner that is 50 percent undercharged will operate at 90 percent efficiency. Its efficiency will drop to only 50 percent when the system is 10 percent overcharged. So remember, as little as 10 percent too much refrigerant in the system will reduce efficiency by 50 percent.

Failure to Evacuate the Air Conditioner System

If an auto air conditioner has lost all its refrigerant or if the system has been opened for an reason, it must be evacuated before adding more refrigerant. Failure to do so will result in loss of cooling capacity and possible deterioration of components. Many mechanics do not take the time to evacuate an air conditioner. You should ask your mechanic if he intends to do this procedure when servicing your car. Special evacuation equipment is required. If your mechanic does not have this equipment but claims he can use the car's compressor to evacuate the system, do not allow him to do so. Using the car's compressor to produce a vacuum in the system can seriously damage the compressor.

Failure to Check Compressor Oil Level

Auto air conditioning compressors are lubricated by a special oil that mixes with R12 refrigerant. If for any reason the system is opened up, the oil must be checked and topped off if necessary. Any time any air conditioner hose ruptures, it is very likely that a good deal of compressor oil will be sucked out of the system due to the rapid loss of refrigerant.

Mechanics often neglect to check the compressor oil level. This is one of the reasons why an air conditioning compressor that should last ten years could fail after two or three years. Make sure to remind your mechanic to check the oil level in the compressor if he is going to perform major system service.

Failure to Clean the Condenser

The condenser is mounted in front of the radiator. A typical condenser is shown in Figure 3-1. The condenser works in a way similar to the car's radiator in that it removes heat. Air passing through the condenser cools the hot gaseous refrigerant so that it returns to a liquid state. The refrigerant of course picks up heat from the evaporator inside the car, which absorbs heat from the air in the car.

If the condenser is clogged with leaves, bugs or other road debris, its ability to cool the refrigerant is greatly reduced. This results in lower cooling capacity, higher pressure inside the air conditioner, and greater wear on the compressor. Sometimes a mechanic will convince a customer that extensive service is required to restore normal air conditioner operation when only a quick cleaning of the condenser with compressed air or pressurized water is necessary.

Overcharging the Air Conditioner

Overcharging an air conditioner by as little as 10 percent will reduce its cooling efficiency by as much as 50 percent. The concept that more is better does not apply to refrigerant. You should not allow your mechanic arbitrarily to add more refrigerant every summer season, as overcharging may

both reduce cooling efficiency and damage the compressor.

Many repair shops have refrigerant recovery systems. These devices can extract all the refrigerant from an air conditioner, filter it, and reuse it. Sometimes it is difficult for the mechanic to tell exactly how much refrigerant is in an air conditioner by reading the gauge pressure. If a mechanic has any doubt, it is best to extract all the remaining refrigerant and pump in an exact known quantity equal to the refrigerant capacity written on the tag on the compressor.

Failure to Check the Thermostat

Some auto air conditioners use a thermostat that measures the temperature of the evaporator. The thermostat prevents the evaporator from getting too cold and icing up, thereby reducing air flow and causing the air conditioner to blow hot air. If your air conditioner initially works fine on a hot humid day and then blows warm air, it could be that the system is getting too cold!

Many mechanics fail to check the thermostat. There is a relationship between the so-called "suction side" pressure and the temperature of the evaporator. By hooking up gauges, your mechanic should be able to determine whether the evaporator is getting too cold. Ask him to do this simple check. If he doesn't know what you are talking about, you should seek the services of an air conditioner specialist.

Maintenance Tips

The following maintenance tips will help

ensure maximum air conditioner life and minimal cost of maintenance:

- Run the air conditioner for a few minutes from time to time, even in cool weather. This will help ensure maximum life of the seals.

- Have the compressor drive belt checked every year.

- Do not have the system charged with more refrigerant unless there is a problem with cooling capability.

Alternator
(See also Battery)

Symptoms

Failure of an alternator is accompanied by the following symptoms:

1. Charge warning light on instrument panel illuminated or ammeter shows discharge.

2. Whining noise from alternator as engine speeds up.

Typical Causes and Corrections

Here are some of the most common causes of the aforementioned symptoms listed in numerical order. If you see a term printed in *italics*, it means that a definition of that term (and possibly an illustration) is found in the section entitled Parts and Terms. If you see a triangle symbol (▲) next to the number of the symptom you are reading, it means that additional information is contained in Mistakes and Ripoffs.

Here are some of the topics covered in detail in Mistakes and Ripoffs:

- Failure to perform alternator maximum output test.

- Failure to check charging circuit resistance.

- Replacing the alternator when only a new voltage regulator would suffice.

Charge Warning Light on Instrument Panel Illuminated or Ammeter Shows Discharge (1) ▲

Illumination of the charge warning light or a discharge indication on the ammeter could signal the failure of the alternator (Figure 3-4). A loose alternator drive belt or a bad *voltage regulator* could also cause these conditions, so both these possibilities must be checked before the alternator is replaced.

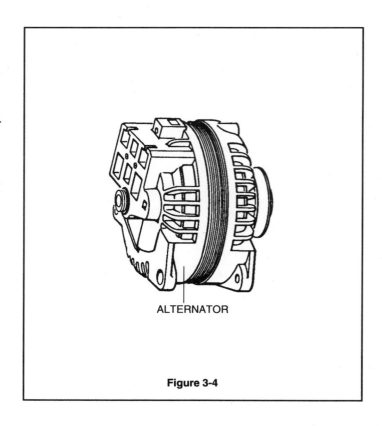

ALTERNATOR

Figure 3-4

Whining Noise from Alternator as Engine Speeds Up (2)

A shrill noise that increases in pitch as the engine speeds up can be caused by a bad alternator *diode*. If a diode has failed, the alternator's maximum output can be reduced. This problem may not reveal itself on cars equipped with an ammeter unless several accessories are turned on, in which case the ammeter will indicate a discharge.

Parts and Terms

If your car needs an alternator, your mechanic could mention one or more of the following terms:

Diode   A diode is a solid-state electronic device inside an alternator. The purpose of alternator diodes is to change or rectify alternating current into direct current for use by the car's electrical system.

Voltage Regulator   The voltage regulator is a device that controls the output voltage of the alternator. The regulator can work as a separate device or it can be built into the alternator. Voltage regulators are usually calibrated to regulate voltage to a range of 13.8 to 14.2 volts.

Mistakes and Ripoffs

The following information will help you control the cost of alternator service. The topics covered are those most likely to be associated with errors commonly made by mechanics or deliberate attempts to defraud the consumer.

Failure to Perform Alternator Maximum Output Test

Often mechanics do not properly check alternator maximum output to verify that it is capable of handling the maximum electrical load placed on it. The mistake they make entails checking the voltage at the battery with the engine running and no accessories turned on. This is not an accurate way to measure alternator performance. Every car manufacturer specifies the maximum current an alternator must provide at a certain engine rpm. To perform the test, the alternator field circuit is connected to battery current by the mechanic. The battery is loaded down by a special current draining device, or in lieu of that, all the car's accessories are turned on. An ammeter connected in the alternator output circuit will indicate how many amperes of current are being provided by the alternator at a certain engine rpm. If output current is below specifications, the alternator must be replaced.

Failure to Check Charging Circuit Resistance

Charging circuit resistance must be checked whenever work is performed on the alternator. Failure to check circuit resistance and correct any related problems can result in repeated incidences of a dead battery even with a perfectly good alternator.

Current from the alternator must flow to the battery. If there is a bad connection between the alternator's positive terminal and the battery's positive terminal, the battery can eventually go dead. A bad connection will manifest itself as a voltage reading on a voltmeter connected to the alternator and the battery's positive terminal. Any voltage reading represents a voltage drop, that is, the difference in voltage provided at the alternator and what's left of that voltage when it reaches the battery. The loss of voltage is due to charging circuit resistance. The voltage drop should not exceed 0.1 volt on most cars.

There is another very important part of this test that most mechanics forget to do. The test just described covers the positive side of the charging circuit. The negative side must be tested too. In this case, the voltmeter is connected to the alternator exterior frame and the battery's negative terminal. Any voltage drop indicated in this test means there is high resistance somewhere in the battery's negative circuit. A normal negative side voltage drop should not exceed 0.3 volt.

If high resistance is indicated in either phase of the above mentioned tests, the connections must be cleaned or repaired. Failure to do so can cause the battery to go dead, difficulty in starting, and many other electrical system problems. Make sure you remind your mechanic to perform a charging circuit resistance test if your car has any alternator trouble.

Replacing the Alternator When Only a New Voltage Regulator Would Suffice

In many cases the inability of the alternator to supply sufficient current results from a defective voltage regulator, not a malfunc-

tioning alternator. To distinguish between the two, your mechanic must perform an alternator maximum output test and check charging circuit resistance. Some alternators have a built-in voltage regulator. In many cases the regulator can be removed and replaced inexpensively. In some cases it is cheaper to replace the entire alternator (including the built-in regulator) with a rebuilt unit.

Maintenance Tips

The following maintenance tips will help ensure maximum alternator life and minimal cost of repair:

- Have alternator drive belt tension checked and adjusted every year.

- Make sure battery connections are clean and tight.

- If you jump start another car, make sure you avoid reverse polarity. Connect the positive terminal to the positive terminal, and the negative terminal to the negative terminal. Reverse polarity (connecting the positive of one car to the negative of another) can destroy the alternator.

- If the alternator in your car is suspected of being defective, ask your mechanic to perform a maximum output test and to check charging circuit resistance.

Ball Joints

(See also Shock Absorbers,
Struts, Wheel Alignment,
and Wheel Balancing)

Symptoms

Worn ball joints can produce the following symptoms:

1. Shimmy in front end and vibration in steering wheel.

2. Audible clunk when brakes are applied.

Typical Causes and Corrections

Here are some of the most common causes of the aforementioned symptoms listed in numerical order. If you see a term printed in *italics*, it means that a definition of that term (and possibly an illustration) is found in the section entitled Parts and Terms. If you see a triangle symbol (▲) next to the number of the symptom you are reading, it means that additional information is contained in Mistakes and Ripoffs.

Here are some of the topics covered in detail in Mistakes and Ripoffs:

• Failure to tighten wheel bearings before checking ball joints.

• Charging for new ball joints when only wheel balancing is required.

Shimmy in Front End and Vibration in Steering Wheel (1) ▲

Front end shimmy can be caused by worn *ball joints*. A ball joint is a part that connects the *lower control arm* of the front suspension to the *steering knuckle*. The location of the ball joint in a MacPherson strut front suspension is shown in Figure 3-5. Some older suspension designs have an upper and a lower ball joint.

Before you allow a mechanic to replace the ball joints in your car to correct a vibration, have the front wheels balanced. Most cases of steering wheel vibration and front end shimmy are caused by improperly balanced wheels.

If your car requires a new ball joint on one side of the car, it is not always necessary to replace the ball joint on the other side. For

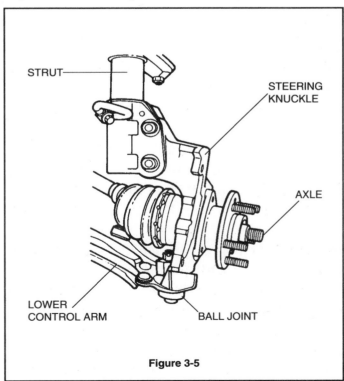

STRUT

STEERING KNUCKLE

AXLE

LOWER CONTROL ARM

BALL JOINT

Figure 3-5

example, if the right front lower ball joint is bad, the left front lower joint can be left in the car if it passes a ball joint *axial* and *radial* free play test.

Audible Clunking Sound Heard When Brakes are Applied (2) ▲

A loud clunk from the front end heard when the brakes are applied could be due to a badly worn *ball joint* (see Figure 3-5). Usually, a ball joint worn sufficiently to produce a loud noise will also cause severe steering wheel vibration and front end shimmy. Refer to symptom number one for additional details.

Parts and Terms

If your car needs a ball joint, your mechanic could mention one or more of the following terms:

Axial Play   Refers to up and down play in a ball joint (as opposed to side-to-side play). Refer to radial play.

Ball Joint   A ball joint is used to attach the lower control arm (see Figure 3-5) to the steering knuckle. A view of the inside of a ball joint is shown in Figure 3-6.

Grease Fitting   A grease fitting is shown in Figure 3-6. Ball joints that have grease fittings installed should be greased at every lubrication. If grease fittings are not installed at the factory, you can have your mechanic install them very inexpensively. Some ball joints are "permalubed" and can-

not be fitted with a grease fitting. This means the inside of the ball joint is made of an oil-impregnated porous metal or a metal with a Teflon coating.

Lower Control Arm   The lower control arm (see Figure 3-5) attaches the steering knuckle to the frame of the car.

Radial Play   Looseness (side-to-side play) in a ball joint is measured by jacking up the car, grabbing the top and bottom of the tire, and forcing the bottom of the tire toward and then away from the car. The total movement of the bottom of the tire corresponds to radial play in the ball joint.

Steering Knuckle   A steering knuckle is shown in Figure 3-5. The steering knuckle

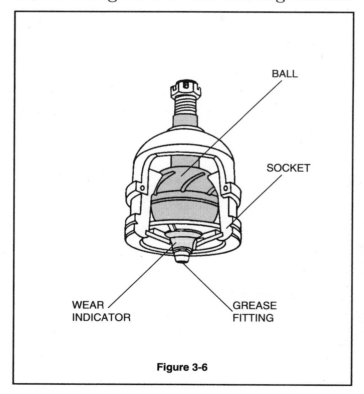

Figure 3-6

supports the axle assembly and the entire wheel.

Wear Indicator Some ball joints have a built-in wear indicator. Figure 3-6 shows such a ball joint. As the ball and socket wear, the wear indicator recedes into the ball joint housing. A quick way to check a ball joint with such an indicator entails simply grabbing the grease fitting and wiggling it. If it moves up and down or side to side easily, the ball joint is worn out.

Mistakes and Ripoffs

The following information will help you control the cost of ball joint service. The topics covered are those most likely to be associated with errors commonly made by mechanics or deliberate attempts to defraud the consumer.

Failure to Tighten Wheel Bearings Before Checking Ball Joints

The type of lower ball joint shown in Figure 3-5 is checked by placing a jack under the lower control arm. The control arm is jacked up, thereby removing the vehicle's weight from the ball joint and permitting measurement of *axial* and *radial play*. If the wheel bearing is loose, radial play can result from movement of the wheel bearing, not movement of the ball joint. Make sure you ask your mechanic if he checked for loose wheel bearings before he measured ball joint play.

If your car has ball joints equipped with a *wear indicator*, the lower control arm need

not be jacked up. The wear indicator can be measured, or the grease fitting can be grabbed and wiggled. If it moves, the ball joint is worn out.

Charging for New Ball Joints When Only Wheel Balancing Is Required

Ball joints on cars equipped with Mac-Pherson strut front suspension last a lot longer than they do on other suspension designs. In fact, if you have the ball joints lubricated periodically, they often last the entire life of the car. Therefore, you should be suspicious if your mechanic recommends new ball joints on your car if it has a strut suspension.

If your problem is steering wheel vibration and front end shimmy, have the front wheels balanced first. Usually that will correct the problem. If your mechanic insists a ball joint is bad, you might ask him to check the play while you are watching. Make sure he checks the tightness of the wheel bearing first. Loose wheel bearings can mimic worn ball joints.

Maintenance Tips

The following maintenance tips will help ensure maximum ball joint life:

- Have the ball joints lubricated regularly. If grease fittings are not installed, have your mechanic put them in.

- Do not drive your car for a long period with incorrectly balanced wheels.

Battery
(See also Alternator and Starter)

ANY GOOD quality battery should last at least four years. When a battery goes completely dead, it does not mean that it cannot be recharged and used for many additional years. Mechanics sometimes make mistakes servicing a dead battery that can totally ruin it. In other cases they misdiagnose the cause of the run-down battery. It is not uncommon for consumers to be sold batteries they don't need. Even worse, when a vehicle experiences a starting problem, there is the chance that an alternator, voltage regulator, or starter will be replaced unnecessarily.

There is much confusion on the part of consumers as to what a so-called maintenance-free battery is. There are three types of batteries:

1. Vent cap.

2. Semisealed low maintenance.

3. Sealed maintenance-free recombinant.

Twelve-volt vent cap batteries have an individual cap for each of the six battery cells. Each vent cap can be removed to add distilled water to replenish each cell. Vent cap batteries are designed with materials that cause substantial cell gassing and evaporation of water; therefore, water must be added frequently. Cell gassing causes battery terminal corrosion; consequently, vent cap batteries require frequent cleaning of the terminals.

By contrast, semisealed low maintenance batteries rarely require additional water. These batteries usually have two vent panel covers, each of which expose three cells when removed. If necessary, water can be added. Low maintenance batteries contain less antimony than do vent cap types, or antimony is replaced with calcium or strontium lead alloy. These materials cause less cell gassing than that which occurs in vent cap batteries, so the terminals do not corrode nearly as much. Also, low maintenance batteries that use calcium or strontium lead alloy have less internal electrical resistance than vent cap batteries. This produces approximately 20 percent more cold cranking amperage than a vent cap battery of the same size.

Sealed maintenance-free recombinant batteries do not have vents. No water can be added to this kind of battery. In vent cap and low maintenance batteries, hydrogen is released at the negative plates and oxygen is released at the positive plates. In maintenance-free batteries, however, virtually no hydrogen is released during charging. Oxygen that is released from the electrolyte at the negative plates chemically recombines (thus the term recombinant) with the negative plates, so there is no cell gassing, no need to vent the battery, and no corrosion of the terminals.

When you purchase a new battery for your car, the extra cost of a sealed maintenance-free battery is usually worth the money. Many cases of failure of an engine to start are due to corroded battery terminals. With a maintenance-free battery, corrosion does not occur.

Symptoms

Battery failure does not ordinarily occur spontaneously. Usually there are telltale symptoms that warn you of impending battery failure. Here are some of the symptoms you may see that indicate the need for a new battery:

1. Engine cranks too slowly.

2. Battery requires frequent recharging.

Typical Causes and Corrections

Here are some of the most common causes of the aforementioned symptoms listed in numerical order. If you see a term printed in *italics*, it means that a definition of that term (and possibly an illustration) is found in the section entitled Parts and Terms. If you see a triangle symbol (▲) next to the number of the symptom you are reading, it means that additional information is contained in Mistakes and Ripoffs.

Here are some of the topics covered in detail in Mistakes and Ripoffs:

- Misrepresenting the "eye" on a maintenance-free battery.

- Failure to install a new battery having adequate cold cranking rating.

- Failure to thaw a frozen battery before servicing it.

- Failure to perform a capacity test at the proper battery temperature.

- Failure to check starter current draw.

- Failure to check alternator maximum output.

- Failure to check electrical resistance in the charging circuit.

- Unnecessary replacement of the alternator or voltage regulator.

Engine Cranks Too Slow (1) ▲

If your engine seems to crank more slowly than it normally does, it could indicate a gradually failing battery. However, there are some other problems that can cause slow cranking even with a brand-new battery. Among these are a defective starter, bad electrical connections at the battery, starter, or chassis ground, wrong grade of motor oil, and incorrect ignition timing.

If your mechanic tells you a new battery is required, you must be suspicious if the battery is less than four years old. On some batteries, you can get an idea of their condition by looking at the built-in *hydrometer*. Certain maintenance-free batteries have a built-in hydrometer "eye" that tells you the state of charge. A green, red or blue dot in the eye means the battery is at or above 65 percent of charge. A black dot indicates a charge below 65 percent. A clear or light yellow dot means the battery has lost its electrolyte and must be discarded.

Of the three possibilities, only the last (clear or light yellow dot) automatically necessitates replacement of the battery. If the charge indicator eye indicates a charge that is greater than 65 percent, that in itself does not mean the battery is good. Furthermore, if the eye indicates less than 65 percent charge, it doesn't mean the battery is bad. There are two important parameters that define a battery's condition: its state of charge and its capacity. A battery can appear well charged but lack sufficient current capacity to crank the engine properly and provide other electrical system current needs. If your indicator eye shows a charge of less than 65 percent, a recharge could restore the battery to normal operation. But the cause of the low battery charge must be located. Some causes of low battery charge are a loose alternator belt, a defective alternator, a defective voltage regulator, and defective electrical wiring.

Some mechanics make the mistake of placing too much faith in the charge indicator eye. Other mechanics use the condition of the eye to deceive the customer into buying a new battery that is not needed. Ask your mechanic to perform an *open circuit voltage test* and a *capacity (load) test* on your battery even if the charge indicator eye indicates a high level of charge. The open-circuit voltage test is much more accurate for checking maintenance-free batteries than the indicator eye. If the state of charge is low, charging the battery may be all that is needed to restore its operation. Thereafter, the mechanic must find out what caused the battery charge to deplete. If the state of charge appears adequate, the capacity test could reveal deficiencies that necessitate installation of a new battery.

In very cold weather it is possible for the *electrolyte* in the battery to freeze. A fully charged battery will freeze somewhere between -60°F and -90°F. If the battery is partially discharged, it can freeze at 5°F or higher. If your car fails to start in very cold weather due to a run-down battery, do not allow your mechanic to charge it immediately. The battery must be fully thawed out at room temperature before charging, or it can be damaged or even explode.

Battery Requires Frequent Recharging (2) ▲

A battery may not hold a charge for more than a day or so if it is defective. Other problems, however, can cause a battery to require frequent recharging. Among these are low *alternator* output, bad *voltage regulator*, loose alternator belt, and high *parasitic draw* from the battery. Many mechanics forget to check *parasitic draw*. The result is that the recharged or new battery will rapidly go dead if parasitic draw is excessive.

Parts and Terms

If your car needs a battery your mechanic could mention one or more of the following terms:

Alternator The alternator provides electricity for the car as soon as the engine starts. Until the engine is actually running, all electrical energy is provided by the battery. At engine speeds slightly above idle, all electricity is provided by the alternator. At idle speed the alternator may not turn fast enough to meet the car's electrical demands. In this case, the extra electricity is drawn from the battery. As the engine speeds up, the alternator supplies enough electricity to power all accessories and a little extra to recharge the battery. An alternator does essentially the same thing as a generator, but it performs more efficiently.

Capacity Test Also called load test. A battery can be adequately charged but not have sufficient capacity. Capacity is the ability of the battery to provide a certain number of amperes of electrical current while maintaining an adequate voltage level. To perform a capacity test, the battery must be fully charged and at room temperature. If the battery is cold, it will show a capacity lower than what it actually has. During the capacity test a device called a load tester (also sometimes called a carbon pile) is attached to the battery, which drains half its rated cold cranking amperage for 15 seconds. For example, if the battery has a cold cranking rating of 400 amps, 200 amps are drawn from it. If the cold cranking rating is not known, about 250 amps are drawn for V8 engines, 200 amps for six-cylinder engines, and 175 amps for four-cylinder engines. While the current is being drawn from the battery the mechanic observes a voltmeter. At the end of 15 seconds, the voltmeter should not indicate less than 9.6 volts. If it does, the battery is bad.

Cold Cranking Rating Also called cranking performance rating. This measurement tells you how much current can be drawn from the battery by the starter for 30 seconds at 0°F while maintaining a battery voltage of at least 7.2 volts. The cold cranking rating is an important measure of how well a battery will stand up when the weather is very cold and you have to crank the engine for a prolonged period before it starts.

Electrolyte The sulfuric acid in the battery is referred to as electrolyte. When water is added to a non-maintenance-free battery, it quickly becomes sulfuric acid as the battery charges. Only distilled water should be added to a battery.

Fast Charge A battery is being fast charged when the current going into the battery exceeds 15 amps. Fast charging can destroy a battery if it is not done carefully. If a battery that is not maintenance-free is fast charged, the electrolyte temperature must not exceed 125°F and electrolyte should not spew out of the cell caps. Voltage must not exceed 15.5 volts; if it does, the charge rate must be reduced. Extreme care must be used when fast charging a maintenance-free battery. The voltage measured across the battery terminals must not go over 15.5 volts, or battery damage or an explosion may occur.

Hydrometer An hydrometer is a device

that measures the charge of a battery by measuring the specific gravity of the electrolyte in each cell. Maintenance-free batteries sometimes have a built-in hydrometer called a charge indicator eye. An hydrometer can measure the state of charge of a battery but not its capacity. The hydrometer can indicate a fully charged battery even though the battery will not do its job properly in the car.

Load Test   See Capacity Test.

Open-circuit Voltage Test   This test is used as an alternative to an hydrometer check on sealed maintenance-free batteries. The test must be performed with the battery temperature somewhere between 60°F and 100°F. If current has been drained from the battery, it must be allowed to stabilize for ten minutes, with no current at all being drawn from the battery. When the test is done with the battery in the car, the negative cable must be disconnected. If the battery has just been charged, some current should be drained from it for 15 seconds. Then a digital voltmeter is connected to the battery to measure voltage to the nearest tenth of a volt. A fully charged battery will indicate 12.6 volts or higher. A reading of 12.2 volts indicates a 50 percent charge. Less than 11.7 volts means the battery is dead.

Parasitic Draw   Also called parasitic drain. Parasitic draw refers to a certain amount of current that drains from the battery even with the engine turned off and all accessories turned off. If parasitic draw is too high, a battery can go dead in a day or less. Exces-

sive parasitic draw can be caused by a defective alternator diode or a very dirty battery. Many mechanics forget to check parasitic draw when servicing the battery or charging system.

Reserve Capacity Rating   This rating tells you how many minutes a battery can supply current if the alternator fails. To determine a battery's rating, it is fully charged and maintained at a temperature of 80°F. Then it is discharged at a constant rate of 25 amps until the battery voltage drops to 10.5 volts. The number of minutes it takes for the voltage to reach that level is the reserve capacity rating. Typical reserve capacities range from one to three hours. Reserve capacity gives you an idea of how long the battery will last if you turn off the engine and leave the lights on, or how long the engine will run if your alternator fails. Make sure your mechanic installs a new battery having at least the same reserve capacity rating as the original.

Slow Charge   Refers to a charging rate of 5 to 15 amperes or less. Slow charging a battery takes a long time, but it is the safest method. A battery run down to 75 percent of full charge will require 90 minutes of charging at a slow charge rate of 10 amps to restore the battery to 100 percent charge.

Specific Gravity   Refers to the density compared to water of the electrolyte (acid) in the battery. Specific gravity is measured with an hydrometer in vent cap batteries (nonsealed batteries). When a battery is fully charged, the specific gravity of the electrolyte will be 1.265 at 80°F. In a 12-volt battery having six cells, no cells should have a specific gravity variation greater than 0.050 (50 points). For example, if all cells read 1.265 except one which reads 1.205, the variation is 60 points, and the battery is considered bad.

Sulfation   This term refers to the deposition of lead sulfate on the plates of a battery as it discharges. If sulfation is severe, the battery cannot be recharged. There is a test that can be done on non-maintenance-free batteries to determine if sulfation is too severe to permit recharging. It is called the three-minute charge test. The battery is subjected to a high rate of charge (approximately 40 amps) for three minutes. If the battery voltage exceeds 15.5 volts, the sulfation is too heavy to be broken up and the battery cannot be recharged.

Starter Current Draw   This refers to the amperage drawn from the battery by the starter when the engine is cranked.

Three-minute Charge Test   See Sulfation.

Voltage Regulator   The voltage regulator is an electronic device that maintains voltage between 13.8 and 14.2 volts when the engine is running. When a voltage regulator fails, it usually causes voltage to drop too low and the battery eventually goes dead. Sometimes, however, a voltage regulator can cause voltage to climb too high, resulting in alternator damage and/or several burned-out light bulbs in the instrument panel and elsewhere on the car.

Mistakes and Ripoffs

The following information will help you control the cost of battery service. The topics covered are those most likely to be associated with errors commonly made by mechanics or deliberate attempts to defraud the consumer.

Misrepresenting the "Eye" on a Maintenance-Free Battery

Certain maintenance-free batteries have a so-called built-in hydrometer "eye" that tells you the state of charge. A green, red, or blue dot in the eye means the battery is at or above 65 percent of charge. A black dot indicates a charge below 65 percent. A clear or light yellow dot means the battery has lost its electrolyte and must be discarded. Sometimes mechanics tell consumers that a black dot automatically necessitates a new battery. This is not true. All the black dot means is that the state of charge is low and that a recharge might restore normal battery operation.

Failure to Install a New Battery Having Adequate Cold Cranking Rating

If your car absolutely requires a new battery, make sure your mechanic installs one having at least as great a cold cranking rating (cranking performance) as the original. The cold cranking rating tells you how much current can be drawn from the battery by the starter for 30 seconds at 0°F while maintaining a battery voltage of at least 7.2 volts. If the cold cranking rating of the battery installed in your car is lower than that of the original, it could go dead prematurely when you start the car in cold weather.

Failure to Thaw a Frozen Battery Before Servicing It

If a battery goes dead in cold weather, the electrolyte in the battery can freeze. Any attempt to recharge the battery before it thaws out can ruin it or cause it to explode. Remind your mechanic to make sure the battery has had sufficient time to thaw out at room temperature before recharging it.

Failure to Perform a Capacity Test at the Proper Battery Temperature

If a battery is tested when it is cold, it will show a lower capacity than it really has. This falsely low heading can sometimes mislead a mechanic into believing a new battery is necessary.

Failure to Check Starter Current Draw

A starter with a shorted armature can draw far more current from a battery than it is supposed to. The excess draw will cause the engine to crank very slowly and run the battery down quickly. Typically, a starter draws about 250 amps for a V8 engine, 200 amps for a six-cylinder engine, and 175 amps for a four-cylinder engine. The amount of current consumed by the starter can be determined by doing a starter current draw test.

An inductive ammeter is placed over the battery cable (either positive or negative). If an inductive ammeter is used, none of the cables has to be disconnected, and the test can be done in less than a minute. The engine is cranked, and the current drawn by the starter is indicated by the ammeter. If the current level exceeds specifications, it usually means the starter is defective. Often mechanics fail to perform this simple test, resulting in rapid failure of a new battery.

Failure to Check Alternator Maximum Output

Sometimes a perfectly good battery will go dead over and over again because the alternator cannot supply adequate current when several power-consuming accessories are turned on. For example, suppose that you are driving on a rainy summer night with the air conditioner and radio turned on. The head lights, air conditioner, windshield wipers, radio, and ignition system might draw 35 amperes of current. If the alternator can only produce 30 amperes, 5 amperes must flow out of the battery. In time that loss will kill the battery.

Often mechanics do not properly check alternator maximum output to verify that it is capable of handling the maximum electrical load placed on it. The mistake they make entails merely checking voltage at the battery with the engine running and no accessories turned on. This is not an accurate way to measure alternator performance. Every car manufacturer specifies the maximum current an alternator must provide at a certain engine rpm. To perform the test, the alternator field circuit is connected to battery current by the mechanic. The battery is loaded down by a special current-draining device, or in lieu of that, all the car's accessories are turned on. An ammeter connected in the alternator output circuit will tell how many amperes of current are being provided by the alternator at a certain engine rpm. If current output is below specifications, the alternator must be replaced.

Failure to Check Electrical Resistance in the Charging Circuit

Consumers sometimes experience one battery failure after another because their mechanic did not perform a simple test of the car's electrical wiring. Current from the alternator must flow to the battery. If there is a bad connection between the alternator's positive terminal and the battery's positive terminal, the battery can eventually go dead. A bad connection will manifest itself as a voltage reading on a voltmeter connected to the alternator and the battery's positive terminal. Any voltage reading represents a voltage drop, that is, the difference in voltage provided at the alternator and what's left of that voltage when it reaches the battery. The loss of voltage is due to charging circuit resistance. The voltage drop should not exceed 0.1 volt on most cars.

There is another very important part of this test that most mechanics forget to do. The test just described covers the positive side of the charging circuit. The negative side must be tested too. In this case, the voltmeter is connected to the alternator exterior frame and the battery's negative terminal. Any voltage drop indicated in this test means there is high resistance somewhere in the battery's negative circuit. A normal drop in negative side voltage should not exceed 0.3 volt.

If high resistance is indicated in either phase of the above-mentioned tests, the connections must be cleaned or repaired. Failure to do so can cause the battery to go dead, hard starting, and many other electrical system problems. Make sure you remind your mechanic to perform a charging circuit resistance test if your car has any battery trouble.

Unnecessary Replacement of the Alternator or Voltage Regulator

If the battery in your car fails, it does not necessarily mean a new alternator and voltage regulator are required. Unfortunately for many consumers, they are charged for these parts whether they need them or not.

Old-fashioned electromechanical voltage regulators used to wear out. Routine replacement of these devices was a necessity. Modern solid-state electronic voltage regulators have no moving parts to wear out. These components normally last the life of the car. Occasionally, a voltage regulator can work properly when the weather is cool and malfunction when the outside temperature gets very warm. This condition is rare. If the voltage regulator in your car regulates the charging system's voltage between 13.8 and 14.2 volts, that is probably good.

An alternator should be tested using the technique described previously in the section Failure to Check Alternator Maximum Output. The alternator should be replaced only if it fails the test. Some alternators have the voltage regulator built in. In this case, the alternator and regulator may be replaced as an assembly. In many cases, however, it is possible just to replace the regulator section of the alternator. You should ask your mechanic about this possibility. He will generally want to replace the entire assembly with a rebuilt combination alternator-regulator unit, even though you could save money by just having the regulator replaced.

Maintenance Tips

The following maintenance tips will help ensure maximum battery life:

- Have battery cables and connections checked every year and have them cleaned if necessary.

- Have the alternator's drive belt checked and adjusted periodically.

- Use only distilled water in a battery.

- If your car requires a new battery, make sure you buy one having the correct cold cranking capacity.

Brake Job

Symptoms

Brake problems rarely occur suddenly. Usually there are telltale signs that something is going wrong long before a possibly disastrous brake failure occurs. Here are the common tip-offs:

1. Grinding noises when you step on the brake pedal.

2. Squeaking, squealing, or rattling noises when you step on the brake pedal.

3. Vibration in the steering wheel or throughout the car when the brakes are applied, or pulsation when brakes are applied; or vibration or pulsation recurs shortly after a brake job that included machining the discs.

4. Brake pedal feels soft or spongy.

5. Brake fluid leaks (fluid must be added frequently).

6. Car pulls to one side when brakes are applied.

7. One wheel locks up and skids when brakes are used.

8. Unusually large force must be applied on brake pedal to make car stop.

9. Brake pedal sinks slowly to floor when brakes are applied very lightly; brake warning light comes on.

Typical Causes and Corrections

Here are some of the most common causes of the aforementioned symptoms listed in numerical order. If you see a term printed in *italics*, it means that a definition of that term (and possibly an illustration) is found in the section entitled Parts and Terms. If you see a triangle symbol (▲) next to the number of the symptom you are reading, it means that additional information is contained in Mistakes and Ripoffs.

Here are some of the topics covered in detail in Mistakes and Ripoffs:

- Failure to replace damaged brake hoses.

- Failure to replace crazed or blue-spotted discs.

- Unnecessary or dangerous machining (cutting) of discs.

- Failure to replace brake fluid.

- Improper caliper maintenance that causes dragging brakes.

- Unnecessary wheel cylinder replacement.

- Failure to replace crazed or blue-spotted drums.

- Unnecessary or dangerous machining (cutting) of drums.

- Failure to replace drum brake return springs and other hardware.

Grinding Noises (1) ▲

You will hear grinding noises when the brake linings are worn down to their metal backing plates in the case of *bonded linings*, or worn down to the rivets in the case of *riveted linings*. The problem may be in the front or rear brakes. The location can be determined by carefully listening to where the grinding noises originate. The front brakes can be worn out while the rear brakes are fine, or vice versa. However, the front brakes usually wear out the fastest because they do most of the work to stop the car.

You must have grinding noises corrected promptly to avoid major damage to the brake *discs* or *drums*. These parts are very costly, whereas the brake linings (*pads* or *shoes*) are relatively inexpensive. Grinding noises that have been audible for even a short time will likely result in some damage to brake discs or drums. If the damage is minor, it can be corrected by *cutting* or *machining* these parts (the terms "cutting" and "machining" mean the same thing). If the damage is

severe, the affected part must be replaced.

Keep in mind that it is not always necessary to do a front and rear brake job at the same time. Over the life of your car, new front brake linings could be required two to four times as frequently as rear brake linings. However, pads or shoes must be replaced in matched sets. For example, if the pads on the right front disc brakes are badly worn, they and the pads on the left front brakes must be replaced. If the shoes on the right rear drum brakes are worn out, they and the shoes on the left rear brakes must be replaced. Refer to the section entitled Maintenance Tips for more information about when to replace pads or linings.

Squeaking Noises (2) ▲

Brake squeaks or squeals are high-pitched sounds that are often likened to the chirping of certain kinds of birds. These noises can be caused by *scoring* of the brake *drums* or *discs*. Excessive dirt or dust on the drums or discs can also cause squeaking, as can the failure or absence of the disc brake *antisqueal shims*. Many disc brake designs included *wear sensors*. These devices can produce squeaking sounds, which warn you that the brake pads are sufficiently worn to merit attention.

Rattling noises are not the same as squeaks or squeals. On cars equipped with disc brakes, rattling is usually heard when slowly rolling over small bumps without the brakes applied. The noise is caused by missing or broken *antirattle springs*, allowing the brake pads to vibrate in the *calipers*. In drum brakes, rattling can be caused by broken *return springs*, weak or broken *retaining springs* and pins, or other damaged hardware.

Rarely is squeaking or squealing noise indicative of major brake problems. Often the problem can be corrected by cleaning the brake drums or discs or by replacing defective antisqueal shims. Sometimes the brake discs or drums must be *cut* or *machined* (the terms "cutting" and "machining" mean the same thing) to correct a problem known as *scoring*. If brake pads are worn down to the wear sensors, you should have your mechanic replace them promptly to avoid future damage to the discs.

Squealing is a natural tendency in some disc brake designs and can be extremely difficult to eliminate, even when all the correct (and undamaged) parts are in place. Occasionally your mechanic will solve the problem by using a brake lining of different hardness, or by trying a *bonded lining* in lieu of a *riveted lining* or vice versa. On some cars a special high-temperature antisqueal lubricant can be used on the brake pad backing plates to eliminate squeal. Sometimes, using a special brake disc grinder to create a nondirectional finish on the disc will eliminate squealing.

Rattling noises are not acceptable in either drum or disc brakes. Frequently, these noises occur after a mechanic has performed brake repairs improperly, forgetting to install the antirattle springs or reusing worn or damaged springs.

Vibration (3) ▲

Vibration or pulsation which occurs when you step on the brake pedal is usually caused by "warped" *discs* or *drums*. Most cars have disc brakes in the front and drum brakes in the rear. You can tell whether the problem is due to the front discs, the rear drums, or rear discs (if so equipped) fairly easily.

If you feel a severe vibration throughout the car when the brakes are applied forcefully, but the steering wheel itself does not vibrate or shimmy in any way, the problem is most likely due to one or more warped rear drums or rear discs. A warped drum is out-of-round. The only way to correct the problem is by *machining* both rear drums or discs, or replacing them if their condition does not permit machining. It is never acceptable to machine or replace a drum or disc on one side of the car without machining or replacing the opposite drum or disc. If one drum or disc is replaced, the other should also be replaced to ensure that the set is matched, with equal friction.

If you feel a slight pulsation in the brake pedal when the brakes are applied gently, the problem is most likely caused by one or both rear drums being slightly out-of-round, or by one or both rear discs being warped. Machining both rear drums or discs and installing new brake shoes will usually correct the condition. On cars equipped with antilock brake systems (ABS), a slight pulsation in the brake pedal during very hard braking is normal. This pulsation is not caused by out-of-round brake drums or warped discs. Instead, it results from the action of the ABS system, whereby the ABS computer causes rapid automatic application and release of the brakes to prevent wheel lock.

Regarding the aforementioned condition, in which there is a slight pulsation when the brakes are applied gently, it is entirely possible that the problem is due to warped front discs and not out-of-round rear drums or warped rear discs. Some front wheel drive cars have a suspension design that can greatly dampen disc brake-related vibrations and isolate these vibrations from the steering wheel. The pulsation could feel like out-of-round rear drums or warped rear discs even though it actually originates at the front discs. There is a simple way to differentiate front disc-related pulsation from rear drum- or rear disc-related pulsation, but great caution must be exercised while the test is performed. Here's how it's done.

While driving at about 10 mph on a road without traffic or in a vacant parking lot, take your foot off the gas pedal and gradually apply the parking brake (do not apply the regular brakes). Don't apply the parking brake too forcefully or the rear wheels will lock. If you feel pulsation as the car slows down, the rear drums are out-of-round (or the rear discs are warped if the car is equipped with four-wheel disc brakes). If there is no pulsation, the problem is in the front discs. After completing the test, make sure you release the parking brake.

If the steering wheel vibrates when you apply the brakes, it is usually due to one or more warped front discs. In the case of discs, warping can mean a side-to-side wobbling of the disc or waviness in the disc's surface. These conditions are corrected by machining both front discs or replacing them. It is never acceptable to machine or replace a disc on one side of the car without machining or replacing the opposite disc. If one disc is replaced, the other should also be replaced to maintain a matched set having equal friction characteristics.

Sometimes (but rarely) vibration can be felt in the steering wheel when the brakes are applied because there is a problem in the vehicle's front suspension. Badly worn tie-rod ends or other parts can cause such vibrations. If normal brake repairs fail to correct a vibration when the brakes are used, you should have the suspension checked.

Occasionally, a brake vibration is corrected by machining the discs, shortly after which the vibration comes back. In some cases the problem is caused by a condition referred to as excessive runout (side-to-side wobbling) of the wheel *hub*. The wheel hub is the part the disc is attached to. The only way to correct this problem is to replace the hub.

Pedal Soft or Spongy (4)

If the brake pedal feels soft or spongy, there is probably air in the hydraulic system. If the brake pedal gets substantially higher by repeatedly pumping the pedal, air in the system is confirmed. The air can be removed by *bleeding* the system. This process can generally be done in less than half an hour.

If the pedal feels soft or spongy immediately after a brake job, there are two frequent causes. One is that the mechanic failed to bleed the brakes properly after replacing the *master cylinder*, or after rebuilding or replacing *wheel cylinders* or *calipers*. The other common cause is that the mechanic excessively *machined* the rear brake *drums*. If the inside diameter of the drum is made too large by excessive machining, the brakes can feel spongy because of poor contact between the linings and the drum. New drums are usually the only solution to this problem.

On very rare occasions, a spongy brake pedal can be caused by brake fluid vapor lock. This is a condition in which localized boiling of the fluid occurs. The tremendous heat generated by continued forceful braking, combined with very thin (badly worn) brake pads and some moisture in the brake fluid, can lead to fluid vapor lock. Moisture eventually gets into any brake system because the brake fluid is hygroscopic, that is, it attracts and absorbs water, primarily past the lip seals in the wheel cylinders and the calipers. However, moisture can get into the system because of careless maintenance.

When the master cylinder reservoir is opened to add brake fluid, care must be taken to put the cover back on the reservoir quickly, especially under conditions of high humidity. If the reservoir is left exposed for long periods, the brake fluid will absorb a considerable amount of moisture from the air. Moisture lowers the boiling point of brake fluid.

If you suspect fluid vapor lock, have a mechanic completely flush the hydraulic system. He must add new disc brake fluid that meets the manufacturer's specifications. Brake fluid graded DOT 3 or DOT 4 is commonly specified.

Brake Fluid Must Be Added Frequently (5)

This symptom indicates a leak from the hydraulic system. Leakage usually occurs at the rear *wheel cylinders* of drum-type brakes. Disc brake *calipers* are also common sources of leakage, as is the *master cylinder*.

Brake fluid leakage is dangerous. To avoid a possible accident due to loss of brakes, you must immediately have a mechanic determine the source of the leakage and repair it. Merely adding fluid is not acceptable. You must not use a vehicle with leaking brakes.

Car Pulls to One Side When Brakes Are Used (6) ▲

This condition can be caused by excessively worn brake *pads*. Replacement of the pads will often correct the problem.

Sometimes a brake pull is caused by front *discs* that are unequal in thickness because they were carelessly *machined*. Also, if only one disc was replaced, a brake pull can result because there is a mismatched set on the front of the vehicle. Because of the unequal friction characteristics of the two discs, the vehicle veers to one side when the brakes are applied.

Another cause of a brake pull is a sticking *caliper* piston. This situation requires rebuilding or replacement of the affected caliper and replacement of the brake pads. Although a caliper can be rebuilt by a competent mechanic, it is better to use a remanufactured or new unit than one that has been repaired. A caliper piston can also leak brake fluid, and this problem will often cause a brake pull. Again, the solution is rebuilding or replacing the affected caliper. After a brake job has been performed, a brake pull can exist because the mechanic failed to clean the floating caliper support brackets.

Occasionally a brake pull will result from badly worn front suspension components or unequally inflated tires. Make sure the tire pressure is correct. Have a mechanic inspect the suspension and replace worn parts.

Wheel Locks Up and Skids (7)

This problem is usually caused by contamination of the brake *linings* by brake fluid from a leaking caliper or wheel cylinder. Contamination by grease from a leaking axle seal is also a possible cause. Contaminated linings should be replaced instead of cleaned. They must be replaced in matched sets, that is, left front and right front, or left rear and right rear. The source of the fluid leak must be repaired.

It is not necessary to machine or replace a brake disc or drum that has been contaminated by brake fluid or grease. Cleaning with special solvents is all that is required to restore it to useful service.

Larger than Normal Force Required to Stop Car (8)

If this condition occurs only after you have used the brakes repeatedly and very forcefully, it may be due to brake overheating and *fading*. Some brake *linings* have a greater tendency to produce fading than others. Have the *pads* or *shoes* checked and replaced as necessary. Overheated *discs* or *drums* could develop *blue-spotting*, a condition requiring their replacement.

If unusually high brake pedal effort is always required, there may be a failure of the power brake *booster*. A vacuum hose to the booster may be broken, or the booster itself may have failed. If a vacuum hose is bad, the engine will probably always run roughly. If the booster has failed, you will probably notice that the engine runs very rough when you step on the brake while the car is standing still.

Some cars equipped with antilock brake systems use an hydraulic power brake booster instead of a vacuum-operated booster. If the hydraulic power booster is inoperative, a much greater brake pedal force is required to stop the car. If the hydraulic booster fails, some kind of visual warning will be indicated on the instrument panel. Typical warning messages are ANTILOCK DISABLED, CHECK ANTILOCK BRAKES, and ANTILOCK.

Brake Pedal Sinks to Floor with Light Pressure on Pedal (9)

Typically, this condition is noted by the driver after having stopped at a traffic light. With light foot pressure the pedal gradually sinks to the floor, and the warning light on the instrument panel comes on. Under very firm pressure, the pedal does not sink to the floor.

This is characteristic of a defective *master cylinder* in which there is an internal leak. Therefore, no loss of brake fluid will be noticed. You must have the master cylinder replaced immediately to avoid the risk of an accident.

The brake warning light can also illuminate situations in which there is an external leak and loss of brake fluid from the system. This condition must be corrected immediately.

Parts and Terms

When your mechanic repairs your car's brakes, he will probably mention one or more of the following brake system components and terms. Listed in alphabetical order are those items you should know about so that you can make an informed decision about the extent of the repairs you will permit. Remember to refer to the section entitled Mistakes and Ripoffs for the detailed information to help control the cost and safety of brake repairs on your car.

Antirattle Springs Antirattle springs prevent the brake pads from vibrating and rattling in the calipers. Typical antirattle springs are shown in Figure 3-7. Normally, these springs can be reused when performing a brake job.

Antisqueal Shims These shims help prevent high-pitched noises from being generated by disc brakes. Normally, these shims can be reused when performing a brake job. Figure 3-7 shows a typical kind of antisqueal shim. Many disc brake designs do not require antisqueal shims and utilize antisqueal lubricant instead.

Bleeding Bleeding the brakes is a procedure that removes the air from the hydraulic lines. If all the air is not removed, the brake pedal will feel spongy and will require pumping to bring it up to its normal height.

Blue Spotting Dark blue spots appear on a brake drum or disc due to excessive heat.

The blue spots are locations where the metal has hardened. In some cases it is possible to remove blue spots by machining, but this is not a desirable solution. Blue-spotted discs or drums should be replaced.

Bonded Linings A bonded lining is a section of brake friction material attached (with a special adhesive) to the metal backing plate of a disc brake pad or drum brake shoe. This kind of attachment of the friction material differentiates a bonded lining from a riveted lining, which uses rivets for attachment to the backing plate. Figure 3-8 shows a bonded disc brake pad. Either bonded or riv-

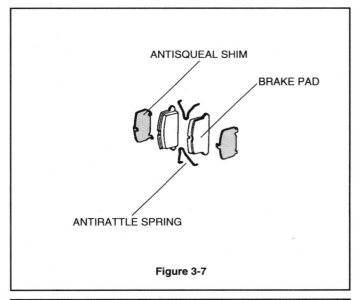

ANTISQUEAL SHIM

BRAKE PAD

ANTIRATTLE SPRING

Figure 3-7

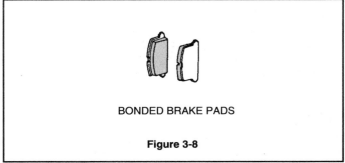

BONDED BRAKE PADS

Figure 3-8

eted linings can be used, but switching from one type to the other can lead to brake squeal on some cars.

Booster A brake booster is usually a vacuum-operated device (Figure 3-9) used in power brake systems to reduce the amount of pedal effort required to stop the vehicle. Virtually all disc brake systems use a booster. Failure of a booster is extremely rare. In most cases when there is a reduction in brake power boost, so that much greater effort is needed to stop the vehicle, it is due to a crack in the vacuum hose leading to the booster.

Some cars that are equipped with antilock brake systems use a hydraulic power brake booster (Figure 3-10) instead of a vacuum-operated booster. If the hydraulic power booster is inoperative, a much greater brake pedal force is required to stop the car. However, if the hydraulic booster fails, some kind of visual warning will be indicated on the instrument panel. Typical warning messages are ANTILOCK DISABLED, CHECK ANTI-LOCK BRAKES and ANTILOCK.

Caliper This device is used in disc brakes. It exerts a clamping force on the brake disc to stop the car. It is not routinely required to rebuild or replace calipers in a brake job. However, a caliper can leak brake fluid or seize, in which case repair or replacement is necessary. It is better to replace a defective caliper with a new or remanufactured unit than to repair it. A caliper is shown in Figure 3-11. The clamping action of the caliper against the disc is shown in Figure 3-12.

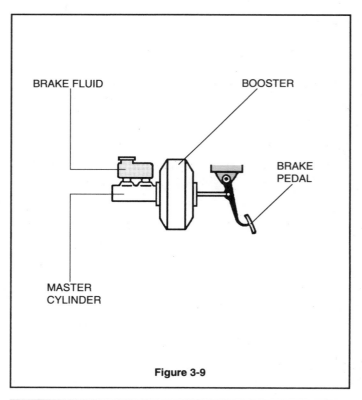

Figure 3-9

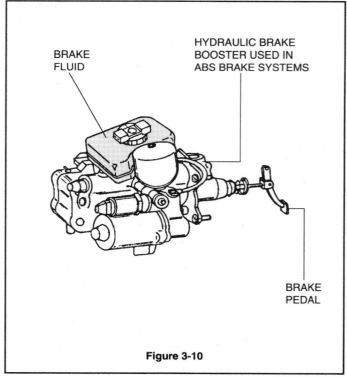

Figure 3-10

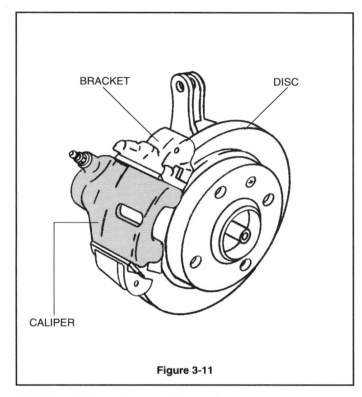

BRACKET

DISC

CALIPER

Figure 3-11

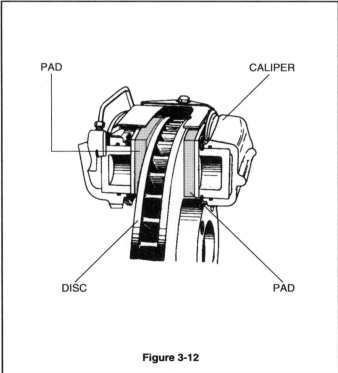

PAD

CALIPER

DISC

PAD

Figure 3-12

Cutting See Machining.

Discs A brake disc is shown in Figure 3-11. The disc rotates with the wheel or axle. The clamping action of the caliper and brake pads against the disc slows its rotation and stops the vehicle. The clamping action of the caliper against the disc is shown in Figure 3-12. A brake disc can warp, causing pulsation or vibration when the brakes are applied. Warping refers to waviness and certain other irregularities in the disc's surface. Disc brakes do not require any periodic adjustment.

Drums Brake drums are usually used on the rear wheels. A drum is shown in Figure 3-13. Brake drums can become out-of-round, causing pulsation or vibration when

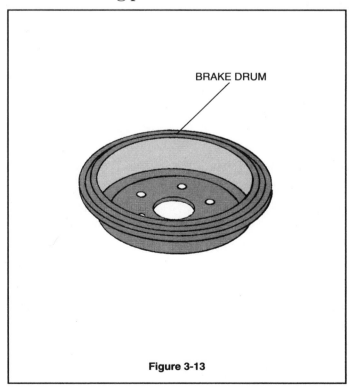

BRAKE DRUM

Figure 3-13

the brakes are applied. Brake drums are typically made from cast iron, but steel and aluminum have also been used. Drums designed to be used with asbestos linings should not be used with metallic linings.

Fading Fading refers to a loss of braking efficiency due to excessive heat. Fading usually occurs after repeated forceful use of the brakes or continuous use of the brakes during downhill driving. When the brakes have "faded," greater pedal effort is required.

Hub The hub is the part of the car to which the brake disc or drum is normally attached. Brake vibrations that cannot be corrected by machining the discs or drums can be due to defective hubs. A typical hub is shown in Figure 3-14.

Linings The lining is the relatively soft friction material attached to disc brake pads or drum brake shoes. The shaded portion of each disc brake pad shown in Figure 3-8 is the lining. Linings are either asbestos or metallic. Metallic linings generally cost more to replace than asbestos linings. Because of legislation banning the use of asbestos for health reasons, asbestos linings will soon be discontinued. Linings can be either riveted or bonded. See Bonded Linings for details.

Machining Also called cutting, machining refers to using a lathe to restore a smooth surface to a disc or drum. In some cases a brake job can be done satisfactorily without machining either the drums or the discs.

However, if one disc or drum requires machining, the corresponding disc or drum on the opposite side of the vehicle must also be machined. Excessive machining of a brake disc or drum is very dangerous because it weakens the part. Every car manufacturer publishes safety specifications that require a minimum thickness for a disc and a maximum inside diameter for a drum. Machining a brake disc on a lathe may not be sufficient to eliminate squealing noises. Sometimes these noises only can be corrected by creating a nondirectional finish on the discs with a special grinding device.

Master Cylinder The master cylinder (see Figure 3-9) is basically a hydraulic pump that sends brake fluid under pressure to the vehicle's brakes when the brake pedal is pressed. Even if the master cylinder does not develop external leaks (which is possible), it can leak internally. In the interest of maximum safety, it is wise to replace the master cylinder after 80,000 miles of use even if it shows no apparent signs of failure.

Pads Brake pads are shown in Figure 3-8. They are used with disc brakes. Pads with riveted linings must be replaced if the linings are worn to 0.030 inch (1/32 of an inch) or less above the rivets. Pads with bonded linings must be replaced if the lining thickness is approximately 0.100 inch (3/32 of an inch) or less.

Power Booster See Booster.

Retaining Spring Retaining springs and

pins of one type or another are used in drum brakes. These parts keep the brake shoes properly positioned and prevent rattling. They should be replaced with new parts after 50,000 miles if brake work is performed. Typical retaining springs and pins are shown in Figure 3-15.

Return Spring Return springs are used in drum brakes. Typical return springs are shown in Figure 3-16. These springs return the brake shoes to their proper position after the brake pedal is released. If the springs are weak or broken, brake drag can result, a condition in which the lining remains in contact with the drum and wears out prematurely. The return springs should be replaced after 50,000 miles if brake work is performed.

Riveted Linings A riveted lining is a section of brake friction material attached to the metal backing plate of a disc brake pad or drum brake shoe with rivets. This kind of attachment of the friction material differentiates a riveted lining from a bonded lining, which uses special adhesive for attachment to the backing plate. Either bonded or riveted linings can be used, but switching from one type to the other can lead to brake squeal on some cars. See Bonded Linings.

Scoring This term refers to deep circular grooves worn into the friction surface of a brake disc or drum. Scored discs are repaired by machining them. It is not good practice to use a scored disc or drum with new linings.

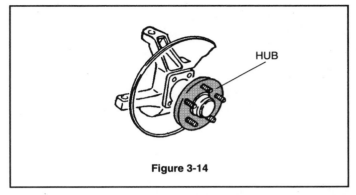

Figure 3-14

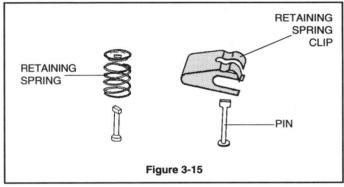

Figure 3-15

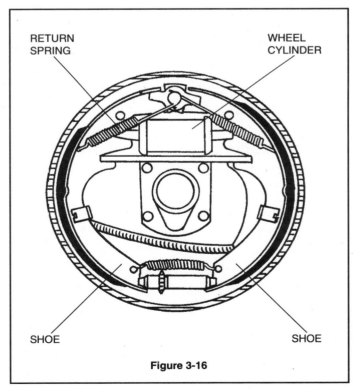

Figure 3-16

Shoes Drum brake lining assemblies (the lining and the metal backing plate) are usually referred to as shoes, as opposed to disc brake lining assemblies, which are called pads. Brake shoes are shown in Figure 3-16. Sometimes, just the metal backing plate of a brake pad assembly or drum brake lining assembly is called the shoe; however, the term is more commonly used in conjunction with rear brake linings. Shoes with riveted linings must be replaced if the linings are worn to 0.030 inch (1/32 of an inch) or less above the rivets. Shoes with bonded linings must be replaced if the lining thickness is 0.060 inch (1/16 of an inch) or less.

Wear Sensor This device is made of spring steel attached to a disc brake pad. When the lining material wears sufficiently, the wear sensor contacts the brake disc and produces a squealing noise. The wear sensor itself does not damage the disc; however, severe damage will occur if the noise is ignored and additional wear is permitted. A wear sensor is shown in Figure 3-17.

Wheel Cylinder This is a hydraulic device used with drum brakes. It forces the rear

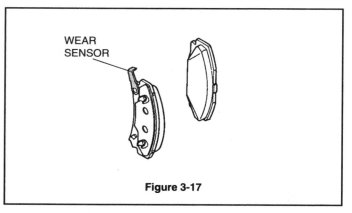

WEAR SENSOR

Figure 3-17

brake shoes outward so that the linings contact the drum. Wheel cylinders can leak or seize. It is best to replace a defective wheel cylinder with a new part instead of repairing it. A wheel cylinder is shown in Figure 3-16.

Mistakes and Ripoffs

The following information will help you control the cost of brake work done on your car. The topics covered are limited to those that are most likely to be associated with errors commonly made by mechanics or deliberate attempts to defraud the consumer. Disc brakes are covered first, then drum brakes.

Disc Brakes (Drum Brakes—Page 118)

Many bargain-priced disc brake jobs amount to no more than a replacement of the disc brake pads. Their replacement alone may not be enough to ensure your safety. In some cases, consumers are baited into a shop by the promise of an inexpensive brake job, only to be sold additional unnecessary work, sometimes in the form of disc machining. More common, however, are situations where too little work is done, not too much. In this sense, you are ripped off because you leave the shop with a small bill and a false sense of security about the condition of your car's brakes. Slipshod work at any price is no bargain.

Here are a few things a second-rate disc brake job might omit, leading to the possibility of subsequent brake failure and an accident:

- Replacement of cracked flexible brake hoses.

- Replacement of crazed or blue-spotted discs.

- Replacement of discs machined below manufacturer's tolerances.

- Draining the brake fluid and flushing the hydraulic brake lines.

- Cleaning of sliding caliper support brackets.

Failure to Replace Damaged Brake Hoses

The flexible hoses (Figure 3-18) installed on the front brakes must be inspected for damage such as cracks, abrasion, etc. Me-chanics frequently forget to do this. These hoses must handle brake fluid under ex-tremely high pressure, so they have to be in good shape. Make sure they are inspected, and get the results of the inspection in writ-ing on the repair order.

If your car has more than 80,000 miles on it, it's a good idea to have both front brake hoses replaced even though they show no apparent signs of deterioration. It's cheaper to have this done concurrently with other brake work.

Failure to Replace Crazed or Blue-Spotted Discs

Disc Crazing A brake disc is said to be crazed when it has small hairline cracks (Fig-ure 3-19) in the friction surface on which the pads make contact. These cracks are caused

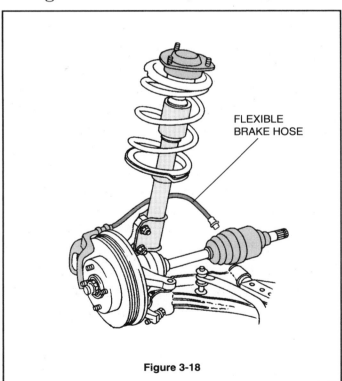

FLEXIBLE
BRAKE HOSE

Figure 3-18

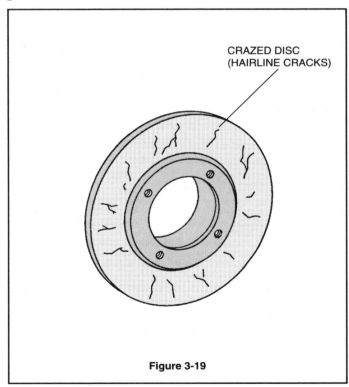

CRAZED DISC
(HAIRLINE CRACKS)

Figure 3-19

by expansion and contraction due to heat. The cycle of expansion and contraction leads to stresses in the disc, metal fatigue, and cracking.

If the cracks are very slight, machining the disc will get rid of them; however, they will probably reappear. Given enough time, what begins as minor crazing will end in severe cracks, disc fracturing, and perhaps an accident.

Many mechanics fail to recognize crazing in its early stages, or if they do, they often machine the discs only to clean up the friction surfaces. This kind of work is not satisfactory; crazed discs must be replaced.

Blue Spotting   Dark blue spots on the surface of a brake disc are areas where the metal has overheated and hardened due to severe brake use. In some cases it is possible to machine away the hardened metal and continue to use the disc. However, the safest policy is to replace a disc that has shown signs of failure as evidenced by blue spots. If one disc is replaced, the other should also be replaced to ensure that a matched set is on the car.

Unnecessary or Dangerous Machining (Cutting) of Discs

Disc machining, that is, cutting the discs on a lathe, is an area of automotive service where the consumer is very likely to fall victim to deceit or incompetence because:

• Your car's brake discs really don't require machining, or

• The discs actually do need to be machined but the job isn't done, or

• The discs are cut dangerously too thin, or

• The wheel hub is defective, causing vibration.

Several things can go wrong with brake discs that can require machining to restore the friction surfaces. If you feel a pulsation or vibration in the brake pedal or steering wheel when the brakes are applied, it is possible that one or both discs are warped. Technically, warping involves problems in a disc's lateral runout or surface parallelism, conditions that can be verified by taking measurements with a dial indicator and a micrometer. Lateral runout refers to a side-to-side wobbling of the disc as it rotates. Lack of parallelism refers to unequal thickness of the disc around its circumference. Both defects are corrected by machining the disc on a lathe. Another problem that is correctable by machining the discs on a lathe is surface scoring. Scoring (Figure 3-20) involves the presence of deep circular grooves in the friction surfaces.

Sometimes discs may be machined to correct vibration attributed to warping when the problem is really a "warped" wheel hub (see Figure 3-14). The disc is attached to the wheel hub. If the hub has excessive runout (usually more than 0.003 inch is considered excessive), its rotation will result in side-to-side wobbling of the disc and vibration in the brake pedal. If a brake job that has included disc machining has been done on your car and the vibration was not corrected, excessive runout of one or more wheel hubs must be suspected. This should be brought to the attention of the mechanic, who can verify the condition using a tool called a dial indicator. If a wheel hub is warped, it must be replaced. Replacement of wheel hubs in matched sets is not necessary.

Sometimes, a mechanic will tell you that your car's discs need to be machined to correct rattling or squealing. Rattling is never caused by surface irregularities on the disc. Usually, the cause is a missing, worn, or broken antirattle spring. A simple and inexpensive replacement of the affected spring(s) is all that is required to solve the problem. Disc machining and new pads are not necessary in this case.

Squealing can be a more difficult problem to solve. In this case, machining the discs and replacing the pads can work, but these efforts are not always required. Often after a major brake job including disc machining and new pads, the same problem comes

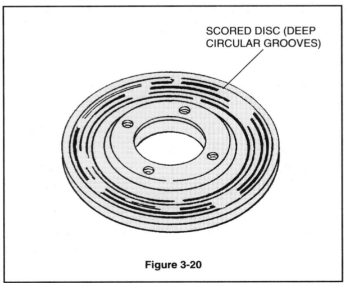

SCORED DISC (DEEP CIRCULAR GROOVES)

Figure 3-20

back once the car has been driven a few hundred miles. Sometimes the squealing is caused by the mechanic's failure to install the antisqueal shims. Or he may have used the wrong type of brake pads. On some cars a special high-temperature antisqueal lubricant can be used on the brake pad backing plates to eliminate squeal. Make sure your mechanic exhausts these simple, low-cost options before selling you another expensive brake job!

How You Can Tell that Your Car's Discs Need to be Machined

Consumers are sometimes charged for disc machining that is not necessary. If you feel a pulsing or vibration during braking, the problem could be in the rear drums (or rear discs), not the front discs. To distinguish between the two, observe whether you feel any vibration in the steering wheel or the front suspension when the brakes are applied. If not, then the condition is probably in the rear drums, not the result of warped front discs. A simple test outlined in the section entitled *vibration* can positively determine whether vibration is caused by front or rear brakes. If a vehicle is equipped with an antilock braking system (ABS), a slight pulsation in the brake pedal during very hard braking is normal. The pulsation is caused by the action of the ABS computer, which automatically initiates rapid application and release of the brake linings to prevent wheel lockup. Machining the brake discs or drums will not eliminate this kind of pulsation.

If a disc is scored, machining is necessary to restore a smooth surface. To confirm that your car's discs are scored, you'll have to be present in the repair shop when the wheels are removed. Make sure the disc isn't hot when you perform the following check. Run your finger nail across the friction surface of the disc, starting at the disc's inside diameter and proceeding in a straight line toward the outside diameter. If you feel grooves with your nail, the disc is scored. If the disc is smooth and doesn't have blue spots on it indicating overheating, very little will be gained by machining it.

A mechanic might try to convince you that machining is needed to restore correct "porosity" of the cast iron, the disc's coefficient of friction and full braking efficiency. There's a kernel of truth to this assertion. However, the minimal improvement in braking efficiency produced by machining a smooth, undamaged disc is short-lived and not worth the cost when a new set of replacement pads alone would work just fine, assuming other brake system components are okay. Besides, the less a disc is machined, the longer it is likely to last. Unfortunately, in most instances, discs are sufficiently scored to require machining.

If a disc is scored, it is best to restore a smooth friction surface by machining it. If one front disc is machined, the other must be machined regardless of whether it is scored or not. Failure to machine both discs can result in uneven braking. Uneven braking can also result if both discs are not machined to approximately the same final thickness.

If only minor disc scoring is present, machining is not absolutely mandatory. How-

ever, it will take some time for new brake pads to bed into the grooved discs, and much squeaking and other annoying noise can be expected in the process, along with accelerated initial pad wear. Because of these factors, many repair shops refuse to replace disc pads without machining the discs. In the interest of avoiding customer complaints about squeaking noises, this policy makes good sense.

How Much Disc Machining is Too Much?

Excessive machining of brake discs is very dangerous. When a disc is machined too much, it is too thin to dissipate heat properly. This problem could lead to fracturing and an accident. If your mechanic tells you that your car's brake discs need machining, insist that he measure the final thickness of the discs. He should record the measurements on the repair order.

If only one of the front discs is too thin after machining to safely use it, it's a good idea to replace both discs with new ones. The properties of replacement discs can differ somewhat from those of the originals, and you shouldn't have a mismatched set on your car.

Failure to Replace Brake Fluid

Brake fluid is one of the most neglected and improperly serviced components of any car's hydraulic brake system. If you plan to get 100,000 miles of driving out of your car, you should ask your mechanic to drain the brake fluid and flush the hydraulic brake lines after the first five years or 50,000 miles, whichever comes first, or on the first occasion when routine brake work is done.

Most auto service manuals simply suggest draining and flushing the brake system if evidence of fluid contamination or deterioration is observed. The fact is, however, that contamination and fluid deterioration are inevitable and usually unnoticeable. And certainly by the time it is noticeable, damage has already occurred.

It is well known that brake fluid is exceptionally hygroscopic, that is, it absorbs moisture from the atmosphere. What is not so commonly known is that the fluid can absorb moisture even when the master cylinder is kept closed. Some experts have stated that flexible brake hoses have microporous openings that do not cause external leaks but can admit some atmospheric moisture that slowly contaminates the brake fluid. The rubber seals in front brake calipers and rear wheel cylinders can also allow moisture to pass through to the fluid.

Once contaminated by moisture, the brake fluid begins to break down. Its ability to prevent corrosion is reduced along with its boiling point and lubricating properties. Consequently, wheel cylinders and brake calipers can slowly corrode, eventually leading to fluid leaks, or seizure of the parts and "dragging" brakes, that is, brakes that stay partially applied even though you take your foot off the brake pedal. A lowered boiling point can result in a serious loss of braking during repeated quick stops or prolonged use while you are descending steep grades.

These problems are severe enough for the automotive industry to have sought out nonhygroscopic alternatives to conventional brake fluid. One solution has been the sili-cone-based fluids, which do not absorb water. They do, however, have some drawbacks, so it's not likely that your car's manufacturer will recommend them.

Improper Caliper Maintenance that Causes Dragging Brakes

Sloppy mechanics frequently overlook the need to clean sliding caliper support brackets when they perform disc brake work. This oversight typically results in uneven braking and premature wearing out of the new brake pads.

A sliding caliper disc brake, found on many cars, is characterized by the use of a single piston caliper that moves freely (slides) from side to side on its fixed, or immovable support bracket (see Figure 3-11). A floating caliper operates on a similar principle but slides on guide pins affixed to the support bracket. When the brakes are applied, the expansion of the caliper piston toward the

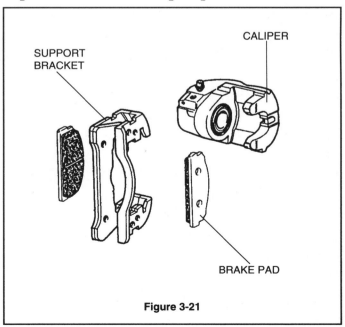

CALIPER

SUPPORT
BRACKET

BRAKE PAD

Figure 3-21

disc forces one pad against the disc while the caliper jaws pull the opposing pad into the disc. For this type of brake to work correctly, the caliper must float freely on the support bracket, and the brake pads must also move freely.

Figure 3-21 shows a disassembled view of a typical sliding caliper, including the fixed support bracket, the caliper, and the brake pads. You will note from the illustration that certain surfaces of the caliper and the support bracket must be clean. During prolonged use, after exposure to moisture and road salt, these surfaces rust and corrode. They should be thoroughly cleaned with a wire brush and coated with a suitable brake lubricant. If this work is not done, the caliper will not float freely on the bracket and the new brake pads may not apply and release evenly.

Failure to clean these surfaces adequately is a common mistake made by sloppy or poorly trained mechanics. Sometimes rusted or corroded calipers and support brackets are reassembled by beating them into place with a hammer. This results in very short brake life after the job has been completed. Also, the vehicle will probably pull to one side when the brakes are applied.

Drum Brakes

Here are some of the mistakes and rip-offs frequently associated with drum brake repairs:

- Unnecessary replacement of wheel cylinders.

- Failure to replace crazed or blue-spotted drums.

- Unnecessary machining of brake drums.

- Failure to machine drums that require it.

- Excessive machining of brake drums.

- Failure to replace return springs and other hardware.

Unnecessary Wheel Cylinder Replacement

When you step on the brake, fluid pressure causes the rubber cups (movable seals) and the pistons in the wheel cylinders (Figure 3-22) to move outward, forcing the brake linings against the drum and slowing it down.

The outside of a wheel cylinder is surrounded by a rubber boot that helps keep out dirt and water. Some minor brake fluid seepage can accumulate beneath the boot, leaving a damp stain (Figure 3-23) on the wheel cylinder. This seepage is normal and does not represent a problem.

Some unscrupulous mechanics will point to this stain as evidence of wheel cylinder leakage and convince an unwary customer that a new wheel cylinder is required when in fact it is not. If the boot is pulled away from the wheel cylinder and fluid drips out, that constitutes an unacceptable leak requiring rebuilding or replacement of the wheel cylinder.

If your car does have one or more leaking wheel cylinders, you are generally better off asking for new ones than having the old cyl-

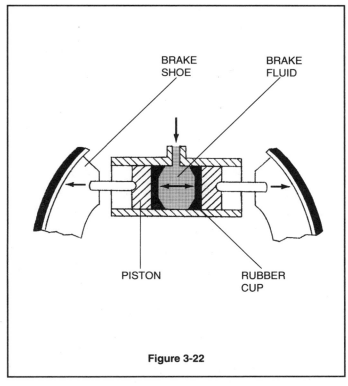

BRAKE SHOE

BRAKE FLUID

PISTON

RUBBER CUP

Figure 3-22

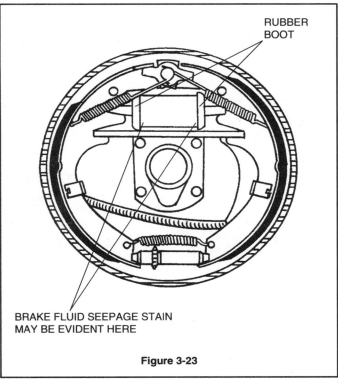

RUBBER BOOT

BRAKE FLUID SEEPAGE STAIN MAY BE EVIDENT HERE

Figure 3-23

inders rebuilt. Whether a wheel cylinder can be successfully reconditioned is a judgment call that many mechanics are incapable of making. Go with new parts to be on the safe side.

Failure to Replace Crazed or Blue-Spotted Drums

Drum Crazing   A brake drum is said to be crazed when it has small hairline cracks in the friction surface on which the linings make contact. These cracks are caused by expansion and contraction due to heat. This cycle of expansion and contraction leads to stresses in the drum, metal fatigue, and cracking.

If the cracks are very slight, machining the drum will get rid of them; however, they will probably reappear. Given enough time, what begins as minor crazing will end in severe cracks, fracturing of the drum, and, possibly, an accident.

Many mechanics fail to recognize crazing in its early stages, or if they do, they often just machine the drums to clean up the friction surfaces. This should not be done. Crazed drums must be replaced in matched sets.

Blue Spotting   Blue spots on the friction surface of a brake drum are caused by excessive heating and result in alterations in the drum's hardness and friction characteristics. In some cases machining can cut away the hardened areas, but replacement is the safest option. If one drum is replaced, the other should also be replaced to ensure that there is a matched set on the car.

Unnecessary or Dangerous Machining (Cutting) of Drums

As is the case with discs, brake drums are sometimes unnecessarily machined. If a drum's friction surface is smooth, machining generally is not necessary. Scoring, as previously described for discs, justifies machining a drum. However, if the scoring is minor, it will not adversely affect the performance of new brake linings. But, if a drum is out-of-round (warped), it must be machined. You can tell if a rear brake drum is out-of-round if you feel pulsation or chatter when you apply the brakes, but no simultaneous vibration occurs in the steering wheel or the front suspension of the vehicle. A more accurate test for out-of-round brake drums is described in the section entitled Vibration.

It is desirable to avoid machining rear brake drums whenever possible. Drums have a greater tendency to warp than discs do. Cutting away metal from the inside of the drum weakens it and increases this tendency, along with it the likelihood that additional cutting will be necessary later on.

Another reason to avoid cutting a brake drum is that new linings will not properly fit the machined drum. When a drum is cut, its inside radius is increased. However, the radius of the linings does not. Consequently, the new linings will initially achieve only partial contact with the drum (Figure 3-24), sometimes causing overheating and damage to the lining and drum.

In the past, this was prevented by a procedure called *radius grinding,* also commonly referred to as arc grinding. Radius grinding entailed using a special machine to grind off some of the new brake lining to a radius matching that of the machined drum (see Figure 3-24). Because of recent discoveries about the adverse health effects of asbestos, radius grinding is rarely done anymore. The procedure throws off a lot of dangerous asbestos dust from the linings as they are ground.

If it is absolutely necessary for your mechanic to machine your car's brake drums, ask him to record on your repair order the final drum diameter after machining and the manufacturer's maximum recommended diameter. It is not uncommon for mechanics to cut drums dangerously thin. Insisting that the machining specifications be made available to you will go a long way in motivating your mechanic to do the best and safest possible brake job on your car.

As a rule of thumb, no brake drum should be cut more than 0.060 inch greater than its original diameter. Also, the diameters of the two rear drums should be within 0.010 inch of each other to ensure equal rear braking action.

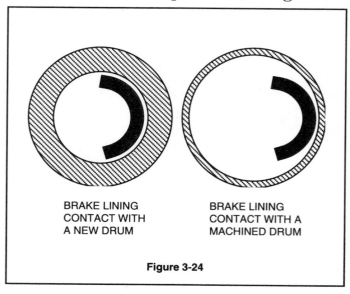

BRAKE LINING CONTACT WITH A NEW DRUM

BRAKE LINING CONTACT WITH A MACHINED DRUM

Figure 3-24

Failure to Replace Drum Brake Return Springs and Other Hardware

There are several important pieces of hardware associated with rear drum brakes, some of which mechanics sometimes fail to replace.

Figure 3-16 shows the brake shoe return springs. These springs fatigue after time because of exposure to heat and other factors. Often they are reused, but in many cases they should be discarded and replaced with new parts. As a general rule, if your car has more than 50,000 miles of use, it's a good idea to request new return springs when brake work is required. The added cost is minimal, but the benefits are reduced squeaking noises and a lesser tendency of the brake linings to drag and wear out prematurely.

Figure 3-15 shows two very common types of brake shoe retainer springs. These parts wear out and become fatigued, with the result being annoying rattles from the rear brakes. In some cases the pins can break, causing severe damage to the brake linings and drums. It is a good idea to replace the retainers when brake work is done if the car's mileage exceeds 50,000 miles.

Maintenance Tips

The following maintenance tips will help you avoid costly premature brake failures.

• Have brake shoes and pads checked every 6000 miles or annually, whichever comes first. Bonded linings on drum brake shoes worn to a thickness of 0.060 inch (1/16 of an inch) or less must be replaced. Riveted linings worn to 0.030 inch (1/32 of an inch) or less above the rivets must be replaced. Pads with riveted linings must be replaced if the linings are worn to 0.030 inch (1/32 of an inch) or less above the rivets. Pads with bonded linings must be replaced if the lining thickness is approximately 0.100 inch (3/32 of an inch) or less.

• Check brake fluid level at least monthly regardless of mileage.

• Have the master cylinder replaced at 80,000 miles regardless of its condition.

• Have flexible brake hoses checked every 6000 miles or annually for leakage, cracks or other physical damage. Have flexible brake hoses replaced at approximately 80,000 miles regardless of their condition.

• Have steel brake tubing inspected for rust or corrosion annually. Any rusted or corroded tubing should be replaced.

• Have brake system flushed and new fluid put in after 5 years or 50,000 miles of driving, whichever comes first.

• When adding brake fluid to the master cylinder, put the cover back on the reservoir quickly to minimize the amount of atmospheric moisture absorbed by the brake fluid. This step will reduce internal corrosion of brake parts and will keep the boiling point of the fluid stable.

Cam Belt

Symptoms

Many car manufacturers do not mention periodic replacement of the engine's cam (camshaft) belt in their maintenance schedules. Nevertheless, you should have your car's cam belt replaced every 50,000 miles. A broken cam belt causes massive internal engine damage. A belt that has "jumped" due to worn or broken teeth causes loss of engine power and can cause engine damage. Don't wait for symptoms to manifest themselves before you have the cam belt replaced! Here are some of the symptoms of a damaged or broken cam belt:

1. Loss of engine power.

2. Engine will not start.

Typical Causes and Corrections

Here are some of the most common causes of the aforementioned symptoms listed in numerical order. If you see a term printed in *italics*, it means that a definition of that term (and possibly an illustration) is found in the section entitled Parts and Terms. If you see a triangle symbol (▲) next to the number of the symptom you are reading, it means that additional information is contained in Mistakes and Ripoffs.

Here are some of the topics covered in detail in Mistakes and Ripoffs:

• Failure to properly adjust belt tensioner.

• Failure to properly set valve timing.

Loss of Engine Power (1) ▲

A loss of engine power not traceable to routine causes can be due to a shift in *valve timing* caused by a partially failed *cam belt*. A typical cam belt is shown in Figure 3-25. The cam belt's job is that of maintaining a fixed relationship between the position of the crankshaft and the camshaft at all times. If some teeth are worn off the belt, the position of the crankshaft relative to the camshaft can change. This alteration reduces engine compression and power. If the cam belt has

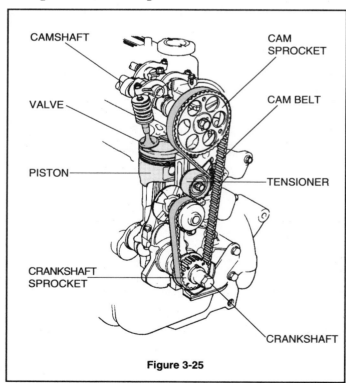

Figure 3-25

stretched, or the tensioner (see Figure 3-25) is improperly adjusted, the cam belt can "jump" on the cam sprocket, altering the relationship between the crankshaft and the camshaft.

If your mechanic tells you your engine requires a new cam belt as a maintenance item, his advice is sound if your car has been driven 50,000 miles or more. If he suggests a new cam belt as a solution to an engine performance problem, you should ask him how he made the determination that a cam belt would cure the difficulty.

You should ask your mechanic if he checked valve timing directly. Some mechanics perform a compression test on an engine, find low compression in all cylinders, and assume the valve timing is incorrect. Usually the assumption is correct, but it should be corroborated by a direct inspection of the valve timing. If the valve timing is off because of a stretched cam belt, it should be replaced.

Engine Will Not Start (2) ▲

If your car's engine will not start and the problem is related to the *cam belt,* chances are the belt is broken. A cam belt is shown in Figure 3-25. It is not uncommon for these belts to snap, particularly on engines with high mileage.

Frequently, a mechanic will replace the belt and the engine will start, but the car does not run as well as it did before the original belt fractured. Often the reason for this trouble is that one or more engine valves bent when the belt snapped. As shown in Figure 3-25, the pistons come very close to

the engine valves at the top of the piston stroke. When the cam belt breaks, the crankshaft keeps turning (and the pistons keep moving up and down) but the camshaft stops. Some valves are left open when they should be closed. As a result, a piston can strike an open valve on its way up, causing the valve to bend. Depending on how much the valve bends, the affected cylinder can lose some or all of its compression and power because the bent valve will no longer fully close.

If your mechanic replaces your car's cam belt because it snapped, remind him to perform a compression test after the new belt has been installed. If one or more cylinders has low compression, bent valves can be assumed, in which case you are in for an expensive valve job.

Parts and Terms

If your car needs a cam belt, your mechanic could mention one or more of the following terms:

Cam Belt The cam belt (see Figure 3-25) connects the engine camshaft to the crankshaft. As the crankshaft rotates, the camshaft rotates in the same direction. For every two revolutions of the crankshaft, the camshaft revolves once.

Camshaft An engine camshaft is shown in Figure 3-25. The design shown is an overhead cam configuration. The camshaft, as it revolves, opens the engine's intake and exhaust valves.

Valve Timing See Figure 3-25. Notice that the cam belt has cogs or teeth that mesh with the grooves in the crankshaft sprocket and the camshaft sprocket. The cogs ensure that the position of the crankshaft relative to the camshaft will remain constant for every revolution. This in turn ensures that the engine valves open and close at precisely the correct time for each stroke of each piston. The opening and closing of the valves relative to the position of the pistons is referred to as valve timing.

Mistakes and Ripoffs

The following information will help you control the cost of cam belt service. The topics covered are those most likely to be associated with errors commonly made by mechanics or deliberate attempts to defraud the consumer.

Failure to Properly Adjust Belt Tensioner

If your mechanic doesn't correctly adjust the cam belt tensioner (see Figure 3-25) when he replaces the cam belt, the belt can "jump," causing a change in valve timing, or it could break completely after a few thousand miles. If another cam belt is required shortly after installation of a replacement belt, you can generally assume your mechanic failed to adjust the tensioner properly.

Failure to Properly Set Valve Timing

If you have your engine's cam belt re-placed during routine maintenance and the engine runs poorly thereafter, your mechanic probably failed to properly set valve timing. The position of the cam sprocket (Figure 3-25) relative to the crankshaft sprocket must be perfectly aligned when the belt is installed. On some engines, if one sprocket is misaligned by only one tooth, the engine will not run well.

If a sprocket is misaligned by a few teeth, the pistons can strike the valves, causing permanent damage. If your car goes into the shop running well and receives a new cam belt and leaves the shop needing a valve job, your mechanic botched the valve timing. Encourage him to replace the bent valves free of charge!

Maintenance Tips

The following maintenance tips will help ensure maximum cam belt life and minimal engine repair related to cam belt problems:

- Avoid frequent jackrabbit acceleration. This adds extra load to the cam belt and increases stretching and wear.

- Have your car's cam belt replaced every 50,000 miles even if the maintenance schedule doesn't call for it. Some manufacturers have had great difficulty with failing cam belts that were not mentioned as a routine maintenance item in the maintenance schedule.

Carbon Removal

(See also Diagnostic Checkup
and Tune-up)

Symptoms

Carbon buildup has become a significant problem in late-model automobiles, particularly those equipped with multiport fuel injection. Carbon can accumulate in the intake manifold, on the idle air control motor and on the underside (the "tulips") of engine intake valves. Engines with severe carbon buildup are the victims of two major problems: the chemical properties of many of the gasolines that were on the market in recent years and crankcase oil vapors.

Regarding gasoline as a cause of carbon buildup, consumers must understand that not all gasolines are alike. What makes individual brands of gasoline unique is something called the additive package. While the basic fuel may come from a common source, each gasoline company injects its own special additives at the terminal. One additive, the detergent concentrate, is very important because it keeps your car's fuel injectors or carburetor clean and free of deposits and may keep the engine relatively free of carbon deposits. Not all detergents are equally effective, and some can actually contribute to heavy carbon buildup in the combustion chamber, in the intake manifold and in idle air motors of cars with fuel injection.

All gasolines in the past have contained carburetor detergents that did what their name implied—they kept carburetors free of excess deposits. Recently, most cars have been manufactured with fuel injection systems instead of carburetors. The type of fuel injection system known as multiport fuel injection was, in the past, prone to injector clogging due to the chemical nature of gasoline. To keep this type of injector from clogging, gasoline companies (at the request of certain auto manufacturers) increased the concentration of carburetor detergent. This also alleviated the injector clogging problem, but in many cars it created an entirely new problem.

At high temperatures, carburetor detergents can be unstable and can cause heavy carbon deposits to build up on the intake valves and in the intake manifolds of many engines. The carbon deposits can interfere with fuel-air flow and the combustion process in the engine, causing a variety of performance problems.

Certain types of engines are more susceptible to these deposit-induced performance difficulties; among them are some engines found in BMWs, Audis, and Volkswagens. These manufacturers design for exceptionally high performance from a small displacement combustion chamber using the so-called fast burn technique. Nevertheless, all engines made by every manufacturer can be adversely affected by these carbon deposits. The carbon buildup on the intake valves interferes with a process referred to as combustion chamber swirl, thereby slowing combustion and effectively retarding ignition.

To combat intake valve carbon, many gasoline companies have changed their additive packages, substituting deposit control additives for carburetor detergents. These chemicals not only keep injectors clean, but they also keep intake valves relatively free of carbon. Gasolines that do the best job of keeping an engine clean meet or exceed the so-called *BMW detergency standard.* Unfortunately, if your car manifests symptoms of heavy intake valve or intake manifold carbon buildup, gasolines that meet the BMW detergency standard will not correct the problem. These chemicals can *prevent* the problem but cannot correct it entirely once it is present.

Furthermore, regardless of what brand of fuel you use, intake manifold carbon buildup can still occur in multiport fuel injected engines. In these engines, detergent-carrying fuel does not travel through the manifold as it does in throttle body injected engines. Consequently, the manifold does not benefit from the cleansing action of the additives used to control deposits.

Here are some of the telltale signs that indicate the possibility of carbon buildup:

1. Engine hesitates or stalls when it is cold.

2. Loss of power and loss of fuel economy.

3. Erratic idle speed.

4. Engine pings even though fuel of the correct octane is being used.

Typical Causes and Corrections

Here are some of the most common causes of the aforementioned symptoms listed in numerical order. If you see a term printed in *italics*, it means that a definition of that term (and possibly an illustration) is found in the section entitled Parts and Terms. If you see a triangle symbol (▲) next to the number of the symptom you are reading, it means that additional information is contained in Mistakes and Ripoffs.

Here are some of the topics covered in detail in Mistakes and Ripoffs:

• The performance of unnecessary tune-ups to correct the symptoms of a carbon problem.

• The performance of carbon removal procedures without proper diagnosis.

• Unnecessary engine overhauls to correct a carbon problem.

Engine Hesitates or Stalls When it is Cold (1) ▲

If your car's engine sags, stumbles, hesitates, coughs or sputters for the first few minutes after it is started and then runs well when the engine is warm, it may have a problem involving excessive carbon buildup on the tulips of the *intake valves.* This condition causes the most pronounced problems in small, high performance engines that use what the auto industry refers to as the fast burn design.

To correct the problem of carbon buildup on intake valves, the carbon must be removed either mechanically or chemically.

Mechanical removal of carbon is time-consuming and costly. Parts and labor can easily exceed $400 for this repair. It involves removing the *intake manifold* and blasting the carbon off with, of all things, ground nut shells! In the auto repair business they refer to this treatment as the "walnut."

Chemical removal is less reliable and less thorough, but it can be done for less than $100. If your car has been driven 80,000 miles or more, there are serious risks associated with chemical removal of intake valve carbon. The same powerful solvents that remove the carbon from the intake valves can remove some carbon from certain areas of the pistons. The side effect can result in excessive consumption of oil after the procedure has been completed.

Loss of Power and Fuel Economy (2) ▲

Excessive carbon buildup in the *intake manifold* of a fuel-injected engine can seriously reduce power and gas mileage. In severe cases, power can be lowered so much that a car will have trouble reaching normal highway cruising speed.

As is the case with intake valve carbon removal described previously, manifold carbon can be removed mechanically or chemically.

Erratic Idle Speed (3) ▲

If your car's engine stalls unpredictably or the idle speed varies, the problem could be carbon buildup on the idle *air control motor assembly*. The idle air control pintle can stick because of carbon deposits, or the air passages can become obstructed. Replacement of the idle air control assembly, and mechanical or chemical decarbonization are the possible solutions.

Engine Pings Even Though Fuel of the Correct Octane is Being Used (4) ▲

Pinging is an abnormal form of combustion that results in metallic sounding noises inside the engine, usually audible while you are accelerating moderately or cruising at moderate speed. A gasoline's octane rating, which is posted at the pump, tells you about the fuel's ability to resist pinging. Typical octane ratings are 87 for regular unleaded and 93 for premium unleaded. The higher the octane, the greater the ability to resist pinging.

After a car has been driven for thousands of miles, the engine's "octane appetite" goes up. An engine that ran well when new on 87 octane fuel might later require 89 octane fuel to run without pinging. The increased octane requirement could be due to excessive carbon buildup in the combustion chambers. Sometimes the solution is simply to drive the car at high speed for a few hours to burn off some of the carbon. Unfortunately, this maneuver can be difficult to do in view of current speed limits and enforcement. Alternatively, chemical decarbonization may work. Barring that, mechanical carbon removal is called for. The last option is very expensive because it entails removing the engine's cylinder head or heads.

Parts and Terms

If your car requires carbon removal, your mechanic will probably mention one or more

of the following components. Remember to refer to the section entitled Mistakes and Ripoffs for detailed information you need to help control the cost of carbon removal.

BMW Detergency Standard The BMW fuel detergency standard defines a gasoline's ability to keep engine parts free of deposits. Fuels that meet the BMW standard are most likely to ensure a clean, efficiently running engine over many thousands of miles.

Idle Air Control Motor Assembly Figure 3-26 shows a typical idle air control motor assembly. Carbon buildup on this part can cause engine stalling or erratic idle speed.

Intake Manifold A portion of an intake manifold is shown in Figure 3-27. Carbon can accumulate in the passage in front of the fuel injector.

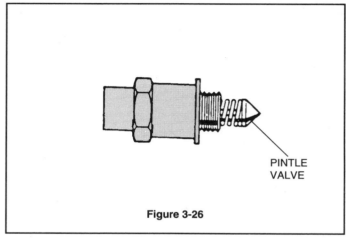

Figure 3-26

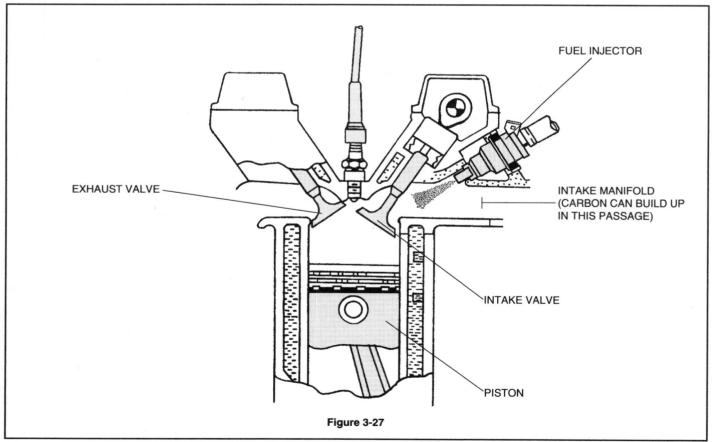

Figure 3-27

Intake Valve An intake valve is shown in Figures 3-27, 3-28(a) and (b). Figure 3-28(a) shows an intake valve with the underside of the valve (called the tulip) relatively free of carbon and other deposits. Figure 3-28(b) shows an intake valve with a heavy accumulation of deposits on the tulip. These deposits are caused by chemicals in gasoline and motor oil vapors.

Mistakes and Ripoffs

The following information will help you control the cost of engine carbon removal. The topics covered are limited to those that are most likely to be associated with errors commonly made by mechanics or deliberate attempts to defraud the consumer.

The Performance of Unnecessary Tune-ups to Correct the Symptoms of a Carbon Problem

Maintenance tune-ups rarely produce significant improvement in the performance of modern engines. You should not bow to the pressure to have a tune-up done as a cure-all for an ailing engine if your car's maintenance schedule does not call for one.

The Performance of Carbon Removal Procedures Without Proper Diagnosis

You should not be too quick to allow a mechanic to talk you into an engine decarbonization procedure. Often, mechanics suspect a carbon buildup in an engine's intake manifold or on the intake valves but do not take the time to confirm the diagnosis. The best equipped shops have a special tool called a borescope, which is a fiberoptic device that allows the mechanic to view the inside of the engine. A borescope viewing is a good idea before the mechanic performs an expensive mechanical removal of carbon deposits.

Chemical removal is far less expensive and might be a wise gamble; however, there are dangers with this procedure. The solvents used to remove engine deposits are

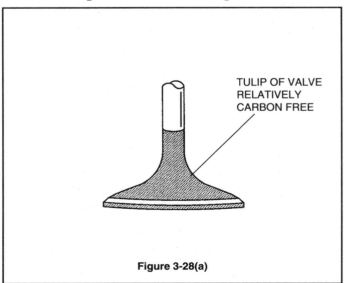

TULIP OF VALVE
RELATIVELY
CARBON FREE

Figure 3-28(a)

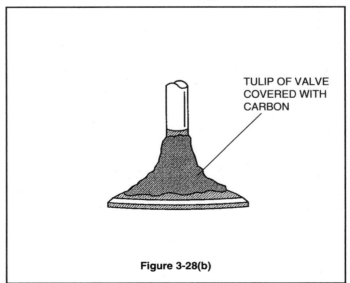

TULIP OF VALVE
COVERED WITH
CARBON

Figure 3-28(b)

extremely powerful. After the procedure has been finished, a neutralizer must be utilized. If the mechanic fails to perform this final step, engine damage can occur. Also, the motor oil must be changed after the procedure is completed. On engines with high mileage, chemical decarbonization can result in increased oil burning; therefore, the procedure may not always be appropriate on engines used more than 80,000 miles.

Some mechanics try to pass a can or two of gas tank additive as a chemical decarbonization procedure. This is a fraud. The effective removal of engine carbon using chemical solvents requires temporary installation of special devices in the fuel system. A can of solvent poured into the gas tank will not do the job.

Unnecessary Engine Overhauls to Correct a Carbon Problem

Many old time mechanics still think in terms of the old-fashioned "carbon and valve job." This procedure, however, is very expensive. Before a mechanic disassembles your car's engine to remove carbon, ask for confirmation of excessive carbon with a borescope. Alternatively, invest in a relatively inexpensive chemical carbon removal available at some tune-up specialty shop. Although chemical removal of carbon will not be as thorough as mechanical removal, it usually improves engine performance dramatically.

Even if mechanical removal of carbon is required, an engine overhaul or "valve job" usually is not needed. Carbon deposits can be blasted off of intake valves using special tools. Only the engine's intake manifold need be removed to perform this task. Removal of the cylinder head or heads is not necessary, and a complete valve job is certainly more than most engines require.

Maintenance Tips

The following maintenance tips will help ensure a relatively carbon-free engine.

- Use brands of gasoline that meet or exceed the BMW detergency standard.

- If your car's engine does not feel like it is running correctly, have it repaired immediately. Misfiring and over-rich mixtures encourage carbon buildup in an engine.

- Have your car's motor oil changed at least as often as is recommended by the manufacturer.

- Subject your car to rapid acceleration in low gear from time to time to help dispel carbon from the engine combustion chambers.

Carburetor

Symptoms

Failure of a carburetor can be accompanied by the following symptoms:

1. Hard starting, stalling, rough idle, engine misfiring, black smoke from tail pipe.

Typical Causes and Corrections

Here are some of the most common causes of the aforementioned symptoms listed in numerical order. If you see a term printed in *italics*, it means that a definition of that term (and possibly an illustration) is found in the section entitled Parts and Terms. If you see a triangle symbol (▲) next to the number of the symptom you are reading, it means that additional information is contained in Mistakes and Ripoffs.

Here are some of the topics covered in detail in Mistakes and Ripoffs:

• Unnecessary replacement of carburetor when charcoal cannister purge valve is defective.

• Misdiagnosis of bad choke when heat riser tubes in intake manifold are plugged.

• Misdiagnosis of bad carburetor when ignition system is faulty.

Hard Starting, Stalling, Rough Idle, Engine Misfiring, Black Smoke from Tail Pipe (1) ▲

These symptoms can be caused by a wide variety of carburetor malfunctions. Unfortunately, a defective carburetor is one of the more difficult items to diagnose accurately. An engine analyzer can, however, take much of the guesswork out of the diagnostic process. Using an *exhaust gas analyzer*, your mechanic can check for the presence of too much *carbon monoxide* at the tail pipe. Most bad carburetors increase carbon monoxide, so that the readings are too high. On cars equipped with a catalytic converter it can be difficult to measure carbon monoxide, but there are ways to do it that a competent mechanic should be aware of. Sometimes mechanics misinterpret a high *hydrocarbon* reading at the tail pipe. The presence of too high a concentration of hydrocarbons in the exhaust indicates engine misfiring, usually due to ignition system problems. It is not uncommon for some mechanics to conclude mistakenly that high hydrocarbons are caused by a bad carburetor.

Another frequent mistake made by mechanics entails condemning the carburetor when in fact the emission control system *purge valve* is bad. Refer to Mistakes and Ripoffs for details. If a mechanic tells you your car needs a new carburetor, ask him if he used an exhaust gas analyzer to help him make that determination. Not having this piece of test equipment can be a big disadvantage and may force the mechanic to guess what the problem is. With some carburetors costing over $500, you cannot afford guesswork.

Parts and Terms

If your car needs a carburetor, your mechanic could mention one or more of the following terms:

Carbon Dioxide   Also called CO_2. This gas is a component of an engine's exhaust and can be measured with an exhaust gas analyzer. Carbon dioxide and oxygen readings can be compared to evaluate the condition of the carburetor.

Carbon Monoxide   Also called CO, carbon monoxide is a by-product of the combustion process. This noxious gas is measured as a percentage of the engine's exhaust using an exhaust gas analyzer. Excessive carbon monoxide can result from a defective carburetor. Because a catalytic converter cleans up most carbon monoxide from the engine's exhaust, it can be difficult to get an accurate reading of the amount of CO in the exhaust. To overcome this difficulty, a device called a four-gas analyzer is used.

This device measures the oxygen and carbon dioxide content of the exhaust gas as well as carbon monoxide and hydrocarbons. Oxygen and carbon dioxide readings can be compared to evaluate the efficiency of the combustion process and the performance of the carburetor.

Choke   The choke is a device on a carburetor that provides a "richer" (more fuel; and less air) fuel mixture when the engine is cold. Figure 3-29 shows a typical two barrel carburetor. A spring in the choke housing contracts when it gets cold. The spring pulls the choke plate lever down and closes the choke plate. When the choke plate is closed, the engine gets more fuel and less air.

Exhaust Gas Analyzer   A device that measures the components of the engine's exhaust. To perform an accurate exhaust gas analysis on a car equipped with a catalytic converter, a four-gas analyzer should be used. This device measures the level of carbon monoxide, carbon dioxide, oxygen, and hydrocarbons.

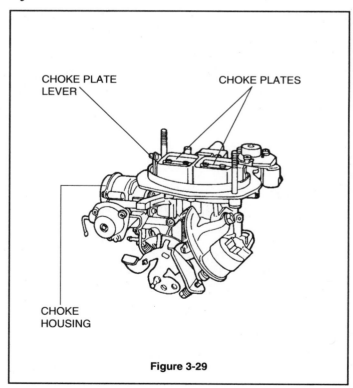

CHOKE PLATE LEVER

CHOKE PLATES

CHOKE HOUSING

Figure 3-29

Hydrocarbons   Also called HCs, hydrocarbons are chemical components of gasoline. Hydrocarbons in the exhaust gases are measured in parts per million by an exhaust gas analyzer. Excessive hydrocarbons indicate an ignition problem or leaking engine valves.

Oxygen   Also called O_2. The exhaust from an engine contains a certain percentage of oxygen by volume. This percentage can be measured using an exhaust gas analyzer. Oxygen and carbon dioxide readings can be compared to evaluate the efficiency of the combustion process and the performance of the carburetor.

Purge Valve   The purge valve opens a passage to the charcoal cannister, a device that stores evaporated gasoline vapors. When the engine is turned off, fuel vapors from the carburetor and the gas tank are stored in the charcoal cannister instead of being vented to the atmosphere. When the engine is running and warmed up, the purge valve opens to allow the carburetor to draw in the accumulated gasoline vapors from the charcoal cannister. The vapors are burned in the engine. If the purge valve gets stuck open or opens prematurely for some reason, the engine can idle rough and black smoke can spew from the tail pipe.

Mistakes and Ripoffs

The following information will help you control the cost of carburetor service. The topics covered are those most likely to be associated with errors commonly made by mechanics or deliberate attempts to defraud the consumer.

Unnecessary Replacement of Carburetor When Charcoal Cannister Purge Valve is Defective

Improper operation of the *purge valve* can cause symptoms that imitate a bad carburetor. If your mechanic tells you that your car requires a new carburetor, ask him whether he checked the purge valve.

Misdiagnosis of Bad Choke When Heat Riser Tubes in Intake Manifold are Plugged

Many carburetors are condemned because of an apparently sluggish operation of the choke, which manifests itself as poor engine performance when the engine is cold. In some cases, improper choke operation is not caused by the carburetor itself, but by a problem in the intake manifold. Figure 3-30 shows a typical intake manifold for an eight-cylinder engine. The coolant passages allow

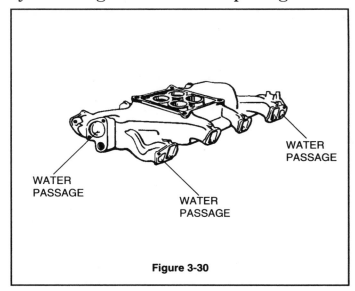

WATER PASSAGE

WATER PASSAGE

WATER PASSAGE

Figure 3-30

hot water to circulate in the manifold. This warms up the carburetor, provides more efficient fuel/air mixing, and ensures proper choke operation. If the coolant passages clog, carburetor performance will suffer.

Water-heated intake manifolds are not as likely to clog as exhaust gas-heated manifolds. In the latter design, hot engine exhaust gases are circulated through the manifold. After a period, the exhaust passages in the manifold can become completely plugged by carbon deposits. The results of a clogged manifold are inefficient carburetor operation and poor engine performance.

Misdiagnosis of Bad Carburetor When Ignition System Is Faulty

Sometimes mechanics misinterpret exhaust gas readings. They might assume that excessive hydrocarbons indicate a defective carburetor. In fact, this is not true. High hydrocarbons are caused by ignition system flaws or engine mechanical problems. Make sure your mechanic has thoroughly checked your car's ignition system before the carburetor is replaced.

Maintenance Tips

The following maintenance tips will help ensure maximum carburetor life and minimal repair costs:

- Do not use fuels containing more alcohol than that recommended by the car manufacturer. Alcohol can damage carburetor parts. It can also damage the coating inside the gas tank, thereby releasing debris into the fuel lines that can clog the carburetor.

- Have the fuel filter replaced at regular intervals.

- Do not waste money on carburetor cleaners sold in stores. Any major brand of gasoline contains an ample concentration of carburetor detergent.

- If the carburetor in your car is suspected of being defective, have it checked by a mechanic who has a four-gas exhaust gas analyzer and knows how to use it properly.

Clutch

Symptoms

Here are some of the symptoms you will notice that indicate the need for a new clutch:

1. Engine races when clutch pedal is released; clutch slips.

2. Chattering or vibration when clutch pedal is released.

Typical Causes and Corrections

Here are some of the most common causes of the aforementioned symptoms listed in numerical order. If you see a term printed in *italics*, it means that a definition of that term (and possibly an illustration) is found in the section entitled Parts and Terms. If you see a triangle symbol (▲) next to the number of the symptom you are reading, it means that additional information is contained in Mistakes and Ripoffs.

Here are some of the topics covered in detail in Mistakes and Ripoffs:

- Replacement of clutch when a clutch adjustment would suffice.

- Failure to machine the flywheel.

- Failure to replace pilot bearing.

- Failure to check for driveline misalignment as a possible cause of clutch chattering.

Engine Races when Clutch Pedal is Released; Clutch Slips (1) ▲

If the clutch in your car does not engage firmly when you release it, it is possible that the *disc* is worn out. Figure 3-31 shows the components of a typical clutch assembly. The disc contains friction material that functions much in the same way as a brake lining. When the friction material wears out the disc slips.

Before you allow a mechanic to replace the clutch in your car, you should remind him to check the clutch adjustment. On many cars the clutch release mechanism is designed in such a way that an incorrect adjustment can mimic a burned-out disc. Often a simple adjustment can restore normal clutch operation for many thousands of miles of driving.

There is a way that you can determine whether the clutch in your car requires an adjustment. Very gently and slowly depress the clutch pedal. For the first inch or two of pedal travel, movement should be very easy with almost no effort required. After the initial range of effortless travel you should begin to feel a sudden resistance to the force applied to the pedal. The first inch or two of easy movement of the clutch pedal is referred

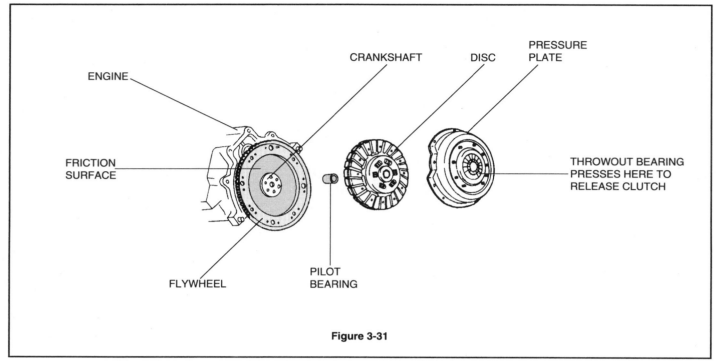

ENGINE

FRICTION
SURFACE

CRANKSHAFT   DISC   PRESSURE
PLATE

THROWOUT BEARING
PRESSES HERE TO
RELEASE CLUTCH

FLYWHEEL

PILOT
BEARING

Figure 3-31

to as free play. Most clutch designs require this free play. If there is no free play, the clutch can slip.

Chattering or Vibration when Clutch Pedal is Released (2) ▲

Vibration or chattering felt throughout your car when you release the clutch pedal has several possible causes (see Figure 3-31). The springs in the clutch *pressure plate* can be weak. The friction material on the *disc* can be defective. The surface of the *flywheel* can be uneven or damaged. Often overlooked by mechanics is the pilot bearing, which when worn causes clutch chattering. Occasionally, gear oil can leak from the transmission *front oil seal* (Figure 3-32). The oil gets on the clutch disc and can cause slipping, grabbing, chattering, and other clutch malfunctions.

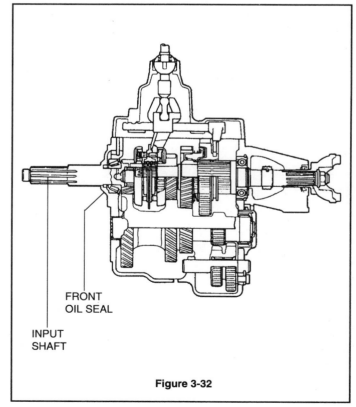

FRONT
OIL SEAL

INPUT
SHAFT

Figure 3-32

Another possible cause of perceived clutch vibration or chattering is a misaligned driveline on rear wheel drive vehicles. Refer to Mistakes and Ripoffs for details.

Parts and Terms

If your car needs a clutch, your mechanic could mention one or more of the following terms:

Disc See Figure 3-31. Also called friction disc. The disc is the friction element portion of a clutch assembly and works the same way as a brake lining does.

Flywheel See Figure 3-31. The flywheel is attached to the engine. The clutch friction disc comes into contact with the surface of the flywheel.

Free Play Free play is the small distance the clutch pedal must be depressed before the clutch begins to release. In actuality, free play originates at the clutch pressure plate (see Figure 3-31). There is a small clearance between the throwout bearing and the clutch pressure plate. This clearance at the pressure plate results in free play felt in the clutch pedal. On many cars, if there is no free play, the clutch will slip and burn out. The slippage is caused by the throwout bearing constantly pressing against the pressure plate. This condition forces the pressure plate into partially releasing the clutch; thus the slippage.

Front Oil Seal See Figure 3-32. The front seal on the transmission can leak gear oil, causing oil contamination of the clutch assembly.

Pilot Bearing Also called pilot bushing. A typical pilot bearing is shown in Figure 3-31. The pilot bearing is installed in the engine crankshaft. The input shaft of the transmission (see Figure 3-32) fits through the center opening in the clutch pressure plate and the disc. The tip of the input shaft fits into the pilot bearing. If the pilot bearing is worn, the input shaft can wobble, causing chattering of the clutch.

Pressure Plate See Figure 3-31. The pressure plate is the section of the clutch that squeezes the friction disc onto the flywheel.

Throwout Bearing Also called clutch release bearing. The throwout bearing is attached to a lever that forces the bearing against the pressure plate (see Figure 3-31) when you step on the clutch pedal. If the throwout bearing is bad, you will hear noise when you step on the clutch.

Mistakes and Ripoffs

The following information will help you control the cost of replacement of a head gasket. The topics covered are those most likely to be associated with errors commonly made by mechanics or with deliberate attempts to defraud the consumer.

Replacement of Clutch When a Clutch Adjustment Would Suffice

If the clutch in your car is slipping, a new clutch is not necessarily required. Sometimes an adjustment of the clutch *free play* can correct the problem. You can check for adequate clutch free play as described in symptom number one.

Failure to Machine Flywheel

A flywheel is shown in Figure 3-31. The surface the friction disc contacts must be flat and smooth, but not glazed. After a new clutch has been installed in your car, you may experience chattering or rough engagement of the clutch. Even worse, the new clutch might wear out very quickly. This problem could be the result of your mechanic having failed to check the flywheel friction surface. In many cases the flywheel should be removed and machined to ensure that the surface has good friction. Before your mechanic does a clutch job on your car, remind him to check the flywheel.

Failure to Replace Pilot Bearing

If you had the clutch in your car replaced because of chattering or vibration and the problem persisted, it could be due to your mechanic having failed to replace the pilot bearing (see Figure 3-31). In actuality, the part depicted in Figure 3-31 is technically a pilot bushing, which is even more prone to causing clutch chattering than a pilot bearing is (although functionally the two parts do the same thing). If a new clutch does not correct chattering and your mechanic did not bill you for a pilot bearing, there is a chance he overlooked this important component.

Failure to Check for Driveline Misalignment as a Possible Cause of Clutch Chattering

If your car has a case of clutch vibration that just won't go away, it is possible the problem has nothing to do with the clutch itself. On some rear-wheel drive cars, an incorrect drive shaft angle can cause severe vibration when you release the clutch to accelerate from a standstill. The solution is to shim the rear springs to establish the correct drive shaft angle. Mention this to your mechanic if normal corrective actions do not rectify a chattering clutch.

Maintenance Tips

The following maintenance tips will help ensure maximum life of your clutch and minimal cost of repair if your car does need a clutch:

- Have the clutch adjusted at least once a year.

- Do not drive with your foot resting on the clutch pedal.

- If your car's clutch is slipping, have it adjusted before you pay for a new clutch.

- If your car's clutch is chattering, ask your mechanic to check the drive shaft angle before he replaces the clutch.

- If the clutch requires replacement, ask your mechanic about the cost of a rebuilt clutch compared with that for a new unit. Rebuilt clutches work fine and when properly rebuilt can last just as long as a new assembly.

- Remind your mechanic to check the clutch pilot bearing when he replaces the clutch.

Cooling System Flush

Symptoms

A car's cooling system should be drained and flushed every three years. By the time you notice anything that indicates the need for a cooling system flush, damage to the cooling system has probably already occurred. Here are some of the symptoms you may see that indicate the need for a cooling system flush:

1. Water/antifreeze mixture in radiator contains suspended particulates.

2. Heater does not provide as much heat as it did when car was new.

Typical Causes and Corrections

Here are some of the most common causes of the aforementioned symptoms listed in numerical order. If you see a term printed in *italics*, it means that a definition of that term (and possibly an illustration) is found in the section entitled Parts and Terms. If you see a triangle symbol (▲) next to the number of the symptom you are reading, it means that additional information is contained in Mistakes and Ripoffs.

Here are some of the topics covered in detail in Mistakes and Ripoffs:

- Failure to back-flush cooling system.

- Failure to replace thermostat.

- Using boil-out tanks to clean aluminum radiators.

Water/Antifreeze Mixture in Radiator Contains Suspended Particulates (1) ▲

You can take a sample of the fluid from your car's coolant overflow tank. Check the owner's manual for the location of the tank. If it looks and feels filthy or contains rust, don't delay in having the cooling system *back-flushed*. Keep in mind that back-flushing is not the same as simply draining the radiator. When the cooling system is back-flushed, the thermostat must be removed. Ask your mechanic to install a new thermostat. The part only costs a few dollars and is well worth the investment.

Heater Does Not Provide As Much Heat as it Did When Car Was New (2) ▲

There are many possible causes of reduction of heater efficiency. One of them is the accumulation of rust and sediment in the heater core. If your car's cooling system has not been *back-flushed* for three years or more, ask your mechanic to perform this service before authorizing him to replace the heater core. When the back-flush is performed, the engine *thermostat* should be replaced.

Parts and Terms

If your car needs cooling system work,

your mechanic could mention one or more of the following terms:

Back-flush To back-flush a car's cooling system, the radiator is drained and the thermostat is removed. Special attachments are used to pump fresh water through the engine cooling system until the water runs clear. This indicates that rust and sediment have been removed.

Thermostat The thermostat (Figure 3-33) is a device that regulates engine coolant temperature. The thermostat should be replaced whenever the cooling system is back-flushed.

Mistakes and Ripoffs

The following information will help you control the cost of cooling system service. The topics covered are those most likely to be associated with errors commonly made by mechanics or deliberate attempts to defraud the consumer.

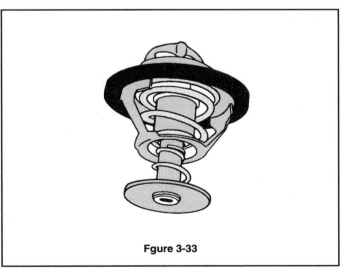

Fgure 3-33

Failure to Back-flush Cooling System

A car's cooling system should be drained and flushed every three years. Left in the engine too long, antifreeze loses its rust inhibiting properties and its ability to prevent corrosion. This leads to a clogged radiator and a greater likelihood of the car's overheating in hot weather. After several years, the engine can develop serious coolant leaks due to insufficient rust inhibition. Also, the heater core can clog, thereby reducing its efficiency and its ability to heat the car's interior.

Many repair shops advertise cooling system maintenance, which they claim includes draining and flushing the cooling system and adding fresh antifreeze. Almost invariably, they do not do what their advertisements claim. What they purport to be a cooling system flush usually amounts to no more than draining the radiator and adding some antifreeze. This procedure is completely unsatisfactory because only 40 or 50 percent of the total coolant is in the radiator; the rest is in the engine block, heater core, cooling system hoses, and coolant expansion reservoir.

In a cooling system with a ten-quart capacity, more than five quarts of deteriorated antifreeze/water mixture can be left behind if only the radiator is drained. This creates two problems. First, the corrosion protection offered by the fresh antifreeze is reduced by the presence of the worn-out residual mixture. Second, the addition of fresh antifreeze may increase the percentage of antifreeze to a level harmful to the engine.

Mechanics generally add new antifreeze in proportion to the total cooling system capacity to create a 50/50 mixture of water and antifreeze. In a ten-quart system, your mechanic would typically drain the radiator and then add five quarts of antifreeze expecting to produce a 50/50 mixture. Unfortunately, this doesn't take into account the residual water/antifreeze mixture left in the engine block, heater core, etc. Consequently, the percentage of antifreeze could wind up being a lot higher than 50 percent of the total coolant capacity. An excessively high concentration of antifreeze can cause problems. Studies have shown that when antifreeze makes up more than 50 percent of the total coolant capacity, deposits can form in certain areas of the engine, thereby reducing thermal conductivity. Put simply, this means some spots inside the engine can overheat.

Considering how important it is for your car's cooling system to be serviced properly, you should ask your mechanic to clarify how he normally performs a cooling system flush before you let him do the job. If he just intends to drain the radiator, you should advise him that you also want the engine block drained and the entire system *back-flushed.* Back-flushing is a procedure that entails using clean water to pump coolant out of the cooling system until the water runs clear. Back-flushing removes a great deal of rust and sediment from an engine's cooling system.

To back-flush a cooling system the *thermostat* must be removed. If your mechanic tells you a story about how tough it is to back-flush a cooling system, you might remind him that do-it-yourself back-flush kits are sold in department stores. If the job is easy enough for a novice to handle, it shouldn't be too difficult for a skilled mechanic.

Failure to Replace Thermostat

When a cooling system is *back-flushed* a new *thermostat* should be installed in the engine. Although this part only costs a few dollars, could cause total engine failure if it ceases to work properly. Ask your mechanic to replace the thermostat when he back-flushes the cooling system.

Using Boil-out Tanks to Clean Aluminum Radiators

If a cooling system has not been *back-flushed* for many years, sufficient rust and corrosion can build up in the engine and partially obstruct the radiator. One technique used to clean copper alloy radiators involves submersing the radiator in a boil-out tank, which contains caustic chemicals formulated to clean the deposits from the radiator. This process can work fine on copper-alloy radiators but will ruin radiators fabricated from aluminum. If your mechanic says he is going to send your radiator to a radiator speciality shop for cleaning, ask him to check whether it is made of aluminum. If it is, it can be flushed with clean water; if that doesn't work, a new radiator will be necessary.

Maintenance Tips

The following maintenance tips will help ensure maximum cooling system life:

- Have your car's cooling system drained and back-flushed every three years.

- Use major brands of antifreeze. Some discount brands do not provide adequate protection against rust and corrosion and do not even give the antifreeze protection claimed on the container.

- Have the engine thermostat replaced when the cooling system is flushed.

- Do not use chemical additives to stop minor leaks. These chemicals can cause damage to the cooling system. Have any minor leaks properly repaired by a competent mechanic.

CV Joint

Symptoms

CV joints are used in cars with front-wheel drive. Failure of a CV joint (constant velocity joint) is accompanied by the following symptoms:

1. Clicking noises from front of car in turns.

2. Clunk, vibration or shudder when the car is accelerating or at highway speeds.

Typical Causes and Corrections

Here are some of the most common causes of the aforementioned symptoms listed in numerical order. If you see a term printed in *italics*, it means that a definition of that term (and possibly an illustration) is found in the section entitled Parts and Terms. If you see a triangle symbol (▲) next to the number of the symptom you are reading, it means that additional information is contained in Mistakes and Ripoffs.

Here are some of the topics covered in detail in Mistakes and Ripoffs:

• Failure to properly adjust length of CV joint boot.

• Charging for new CV joint when only a new boot is needed.

Clicking Noises from Front of Car in Turns (1) ▲

If you hear clicking noises coming from the front of your car during turns, it could be due to a worn outboard *CV joint*. Figure 3-34 shows the inner and outer CV joints on one side of a car with front-wheel drive. Each side of the car has an inner and outer joint. Each joint is covered by a protective seal or *boot,* as it is sometimes called.

Some mechanics try to convince their customers that a torn boot necessitates replacement of the entire CV joint. This is not true. If you do not hear unusual noises from the front of the car or you do not feel shudder or vibration, the CV joints are probably fine. If

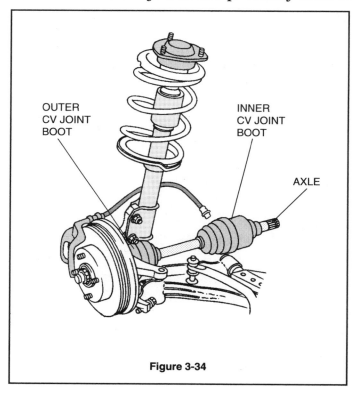

OUTER CV JOINT BOOT

INNER CV JOINT BOOT

AXLE

Figure 3-34

a CV joint boot is torn, the boot should be replaced promptly or the joint will ultimately fail. You should have the CV joint boots inspected every time your car is lubricated.

Clunk, Vibration or Shudder When the Car is Accelerating or at Highway Speeds (2) ▲

These symptoms can indicate a defective inner or outer *CV joint* (see Figure 3-34). If the noise or vibration is more pronounced when your car turns, the culprit is probably an outer CV joint.

Parts and Terms

If your car needs a CV joint, your mechanic could mention one or more of the following terms:

Boot A CV joint is covered by a protective seal called a boot (see Figure 3-34).

CV Joint CV stands for constant velocity. A constant velocity joint is a flexible joint that permits smooth application of power to the wheels of a car with front-wheel drive.

Mistakes and Ripoffs

The following information will help you control the cost of CV joint service. The topics covered are those most likely to be associated with errors commonly made by mechanics or deliberate attempts to defraud the consumer.

Failure to Properly Adjust Length of CV Joint Boot

A CV joint boot is secured at each end by a clamp (Figure 3-35). The boot has accordion-type folds that permit it to change length. The boot must be able to change length because the axle shafts are coupled together by a sliding yoke that enables the axles to change length. The axle assembly changes length as the car goes over bumps. As the axle length increases, the boot stretches an equal amount. The length of the boot must be adjusted to factory specifications, and the clamps tightened firmly. If the boot is not properly adjusted, it can tear. A torn boot will allow dirt and moisture to contaminate the CV joint and induce early failure of the new part.

Charging for New CV Joint When Only a New Boot is Needed

A CV joint boot can be torn without immediately resulting in destruction of the CV joint itself. You should have the CV joint boots inspected every time your car is lubricated. Any damaged boot must be replaced as soon as possible. If there are no clicking

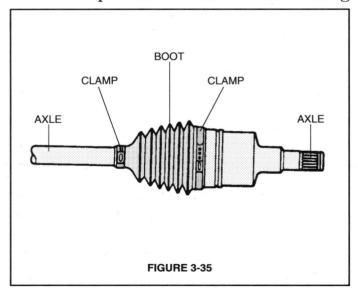

BOOT

CLAMP

CLAMP

AXLE

AXLE

FIGURE 3-35

noises, clunks, or unusual vibrations from the front of the car, you can assume the CV joints are functioning normally.

Mechanics sometimes tell their customers that a torn CV joint boot necessitates replacement of the entire joint. This is not true. If the joint is working normally, replacing the affected boot alone is adequate.

Maintenance Tips

The following maintenance tips will help ensure maximum CV joint life and minimal cost of repair:

- Have the CV joint boots checked at every lubrication.

- Have torn or damaged boots replaced immediately.

- Do not authorize replacement of a CV joint solely because its boot is torn. If the joint is working normally, only a new boot is required.

Diagnostic Checkup

(See also Carbon Removal
and Tune-up)

Symptoms

Any time your car's engine does not run properly a diagnostic checkup is called for. As explained in the section entitled tune-up, most cars manufactured since 1981 can only receive simple maintenance tune-ups that usually have no significant effect on the performance of the engine. When an engine in a late-model, computerized car does not run as it should, it usually means there is a malfunction in one or more of the computer's sensors or in an emission-control device.

Locating the offending part can be time consuming and difficult. This process is referred to as a diagnostic checkup. Routine diagnostic checkups can be done in less than 30 minutes and usually cost between $30 and $60. Many auto repair shops are equipped with sophisticated engine analyzers to expedite the job. These machines can quickly perform dozens of electronic tests to isolate defects. The lay person usually refers to the process of testing an engine with one of these devices as "putting the engine on the scope." Scope is a shortened form of the word "oscilloscope," which is only one of the many testing devices built into a complete engine analyzer.

One of the larger companies manufacturing engine analyzers is Sun Electric Corpo-

ration. This company builds a computerized analyzer that performs extremely sophisticated tests on a modern engine and the various computer sensors and controls that help it run. Figure 3-36 shows a typical state-of-the-art computer analyzer. Unfortunately, all of these machines, which can cost more than $20,000, are only fully effective when the mechanics using them understand the capabilities of the analyzer and are familiar with the engine control systems on the car being analyzed. Furthermore, sophisticated computerized engine analyzers are not really necessary to do a diagnostic checkup. They

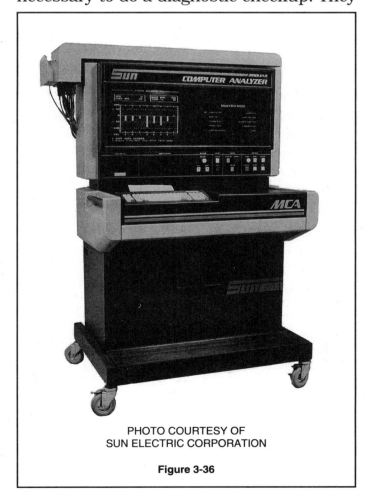

PHOTO COURTESY OF
SUN ELECTRIC CORPORATION

Figure 3-36

just make the job a lot easier, a lot faster, and a bit more accurate.

Nevertheless, essentially the same tasks can be accomplished by a good mechanic with an inexpensive digital multimeter (cost, approximately $100) and a special hand-held tool called a scanner, which can be obtained for approximately $1000. For this reason, you should not make the mistake of assuming that only those shops that possess large, exotic-looking engine analyzers have the ability to troubleshoot computerized cars. There is no substitute for knowledge and skill on the part of the mechanic. A "smart" diagnostic machine cannot offset the ineptitude of an inexperienced, poorly trained mechanic. Frequently, a problem in a car can be caused not by a computer sensor or other electronic device, but by a flaw in the wiring connecting the device to the on-board computer. It requires real knowledge and technical skill to locate such a problem. Engine analyzers generally cannot accomplish this on their own. Additionally, there are many situations in which an engine analyzer can at best narrow a problem down to two, three, or more possible causes. It is up to the mechanic to identify the actual offending part. This takes knowledge of how the car works.

Here are some of the indications that point to the need for a diagnostic checkup:

1. Instrument panel "check engine" or "service engine soon" light comes on.

2. Hard starting.

3. Stalling.

4. Engine pings even though fuel of the correct octane is being used.

5. Rotten egg smell from exhaust pipe.

6. Engine surges or bucks.

7. Rough idle.

8. Poor gas mileage.

9. Intermittent performance complaints, that is, engine problems that seem to come and go unpredictably.

Typical Causes and Corrections

Here are some of the most common causes of the aforementioned symptoms listed in numerical order. If you see a term printed in *italics*, it means that a definition of that term (and possibly an illustration) is found in the section entitled Parts and Terms. If you see a triangle symbol (▲) next to the number of the symptom you are reading, it means that additional information is contained in Mistakes and Ripoffs.

Here are some of the topics covered in detail in Mistakes and Ripoffs:

• Misinterpretation of trouble codes.

• Failure to employ scanner in "snapshot" mode during troubleshooting.

• Failure to reference technical service bulletins before performing engine analysis.

- Tampering with ignition timing to correct engine pinging.

- Tampering with exhaust gas recirculation (EGR) valve to make engine run smoother.

- Charging for fuel injector cleaning without verifying a partially clogged injector.

- Failure to perform exhaust system back-pressure test before replacing catalytic converter.

Instrument Panel "Check Engine" or "Service Engine Soon" Light Comes On (1) ▲

If the "check engine" or "service engine soon" light on the instrument panel illuminates temporarily, it does not always indicate a defect that requires correction. If the light comes on with the ignition key turned to the "on" position and the engine is not running, this merely verifies that the "service engine soon" light works. As soon as the engine starts, the light should go out. If it doesn't, it indicates a problem with the car's computer.

Under certain driving conditions, such as ascending a long grade, it is possible for this light to come on temporarily without necessarily indicating a serious problem. If the light comes on briefly and then goes out and you do not notice any unusual performance problems, you can ignore the condition. In this case a diagnostic checkup is not really necessary. If the light comes on intermittently and you do notice something unusual about the way the engine runs, a diagnostic checkup is required.

Often, the "check engine" or "service engine soon" light can come on and stay on, or come on and then go out later. If the light stays on, a diagnostic checkup is absolutely required; however, you do not immediately have to stop the car and turn off the engine. If the light comes on and then goes out when you restart the engine, a diagnostic checkup is required if you notice some performance problem, especially if the light keeps coming on repeatedly.

As part of the diagnostic checkup, your mechanic will examine the car's computer system for stored *trouble codes.* A car's computer can often identify malfunctioning parts in the ignition system, fuel system, and emission control system. A unique two-digit trouble code is associated with each malfunctioning part or system capable of being monitored by the car's computer. For example, on a General Motors car a code 13 indicates a defective *oxygen sensor,* while a code 15 suggests a bad *coolant temperature sensor.*

The trouble code may be stored in memory even though the "check engine" light may have gone out. Generally, the codes are stored for a predetermined number of engine restarts subsequent to the computer's having detected the malfunction. The codes are then erased if the malfunction does not recur. To read stored trouble codes, a test device called a scanner is plugged into an electrical connector under the dash or in some cases under the hood. If a scanner is not available, a jumper wire can be placed in a special electrical connector that causes the "check engine" light or "service engine soon" light to flash in a sequence corresponding to the trouble codes. Reading trouble codes this way can be difficult and easy to misinterpret. Using a scanner eliminates the possibility of misreading the codes. Even though trouble codes are accurately read, they are often misinterpreted, resulting in a lot of unnecessary replacement of normally functioning parts. Refer to Mistakes and Ripoffs for details.

Sometimes the "check engine" light or "service engine soon" light can come on for a few seconds and then go out. This is referred to as an intermittent problem or *soft failure* as mechanics put it, as opposed to so-called *hard failures* which result in the light staying on. Intermittent problems are usually caused by wiring defects, not failed parts. A dirty or loose connection can be jarred by driving over a bump, causing the service engine soon light to come on temporarily. Examples of intermittent problems are unpredictable stalling of the engine, after which it restarts and runs fine; occasional surging or bucking of the engine; occasional hard starting, abrupt shutting off of the engine at highway speed for a split second; etc. In these cases, consumers are sometimes cheated either deliberately or inadvertently by mechanics who don't know how to isolate intermittent problems. Mechanics might randomly replace parts hoping to solve the problem or might do a lot of useless, unnecessary work. The proper solution is a complete dynamic engine analysis or the use of a scanner in the "snapshot" mode. You must ask your mechanic if he has the equipment to perform a *snapshot test*. Refer to Mistakes and Ripoffs for details.

Hard Starting (2) ▲

Modern fuel-injected cars should start quickly under all conditions. Failure to do so requires a diagnostic checkup. Some of the items you should ask your mechanic to check are as follows:

- Condition of ignition wires.

- Engine compression.

- Fuel injector duty cycle or "on time" during cranking.

All the above items can be quickly checked with an engine analyzer. There are some situations in which it will be impossible for a mechanic to locate the problem using diagnostic tests. This is especially true if your car experienced the difficulty even while it was new. In this case, the vehicle could have a design problem only the manufacturer knows about. The only way for a mechanic to discover this would be to obtain a technical service bulletin issued by the manufacturer.

A technical service bulletin describes the problem and the corrective action required. Many repair shops have computerized libraries of technical service bulletins for many makes and models of cars. Ask your mechanic to check for relevant technical service bulletins before he spends a lot of time and a lot of your money fishing for problems he would otherwise never be able to identify. One of the more common corrective actions described in technical service bulletins involves the replacement of computer microchips called *proms.* These devices store information in the form of computer binary code on how much fuel the engine will receive under various operating conditions, ignition timing, and so forth. There is no way for a mechanic to examine the computer code stored in proms. Only the manufacturer knows whether the code works properly. Frequently, manufacturers supply replacement proms containing revised code to make certain engines run better. The details about the proms and the problems they will correct are outlined in technical service bulletins. Proms are covered by your vehicle's 5-year/50,000-mile emission controls warranty.

Stalling (3)

Stalling is usually an intermittent problem that can be isolated in a diagnostic checkup. To make it easier for your mechanic to find the problem you have to tell him when it occurs. Does the engine stall only when it is cold? Does it run normally when cold and only stall when it is hot? If the problem occurs only when the engine is cold, there is the possibility of heavy carbon buildup in the engine's intake manifold (see the section entitled Carbon Removal). Remind your mechanic of this possibility. If the engine stalls when it is fully warmed up and it seems to idle too slowly, it could be due to a defective idle air control motor in the fuel injection system. On certain cars, engine stalling can occur if the speedometer cable is broken or disconnected. The car's on-board computer depends on an electrical speed signal that is not produced if the cable is inoperative. The speed signal is used by the computer to reset the idle air control motor, which in turn regulates idle speed. Make sure your mechanic checks for a correct speedometer speed signal if your car is experiencing a peculiar stalling problem.

Engine Pings Even Though Fuel of the Correct Octane is Being Used (4) ▲

Pinging is an abnormal form of combustion that creates a metallic rattling noise in the engine under certain driving conditions. Left uncorrected, pinging can destroy an engine. Many car owners notice that when their cars were new they ran well on 87 octane fuel but required higher octane to avoid pinging after several thousand miles of driving. If you can eliminate pinging by changing from 87 octane regular unleaded to 89 octane gasoline, it is not worth spending money on a diagnostic checkup. However, a car designed to run on 87 octane fuel should not require 92 or 93 octane premium to eliminate pinging. Any engine will experience an increase in "octane appetite" as it ages, that is, it requires higher octane fuel to run without pinging. A jump from an 87 octane to 89 octane is not unusual; however, a jump in octane requirement from 87 to 92 is unacceptable and indicates an abnormal condition. Reducing an engine's tendency to ping used to be as simple as retarding ignition timing a few degrees. For reasons covered in Mistakes and Ripoffs this is no longer true. Ask your mechanic to check your car's *exhaust gas recirculation system* if you are forced to use very high octane fuel to reduce pinging. On some engines, particularly those equipped with a turbocharger, there is a device called a *knock sensor*. Failure of this part can also cause pinging, so make sure your mechanic checks it.

Some mechanics disconnect the exhaust gas recirculation (EGR) system to resolve customer complaints about a surging engine in some cars when they are driven at part throttle cruising speed. Although disabling the EGR system can eliminate some perceived engine roughness, it can also cause heavy pinging and poor gas mileage, as well as increased emission of dangerous oxides of nitrogen.

Rotten Egg Smell From Exhaust Pipe (5) ▲

An odor similar to rotten eggs coming from your car's exhaust indicates a fuel mixture that is too rich, that is, too much fuel and too little air. A diagnostic checkup including an exhaust gas analysis can identify the cause of the problem. Typical causes are a defective *coolant temperature sensor*, a malfunctioning *manifold absolute pressure sensor* or *mass airflow sensor*, a defective *oxygen sensor* or leaking fuel injectors, all of which are covered by your vehicle's 5-year/ 50,000-mile emission controls warranty.

Engine Surges or Bucks (6) ▲

Surging is a variation in engine power while the car is under steady throttle or cruising. A car with fuel injection should never surge or buck under any conditions. You may sometimes notice this problem when you are driving at steady speed with the accelerator pedal only slightly depressed, at which time you can feel the car "pulsing" or "holding back" from time to time. A diagnostic checkup may be required if your car has this problem. Typical causes of surging are a partially clogged or leaking fuel injector, a defective EGR valve, a clogged EGR filter, a vacuum leak, a defective oxygen sensor, or a defective engine coolant temperature sensor.

Before you spend any money on diagnostic services to locate the cause of a surging engine, change the brand of gasoline you use. Try three tanks of a brand that meets the BMW fuel detergency standard (see the section entitled Carbon Removal.) Some refiners put more detergent in their premium grades than their regular unleaded gas, so it could be worth it to use premium for a while. The detergent action of the fuel may clean a partially clogged injector.

Rarely, if ever, should it be necessary to pay for fuel injector cleaning. Gasolines meeting the BMW fuel detergency standard do a good job of cleaning injectors that are partially clogged by deposits. Always try changing brands of gasoline (use a major brand) before paying for cleaning of the fuel injector to correct a surging engine. Furthermore, you should keep in mind that fuel injectors that have become obstructed by deposits are covered by your vehicle's 5-year/ 50,000-mile emission controls warranty. Many mechanics do not know how to verify a partially clogged fuel injector before performing a fuel injector cleaning service. Refer to Mistakes and Ripoffs for additional information.

Rough Idle (7)

Rough idle can be caused by a partially

clogged or leaking fuel injector or a defective ignition wire. Either condition can be quickly identified in a diagnostic checkup. Another cause of rough idle that frequently goes undiagnosed is a defective charcoal cannister purge system, which is part of the emission controls system and is covered by the 5-year/50,000-mile warranty.

A defective purge valve (on cars equipped with one) can cause an overly-rich fuel mixture and can even result in the discharge of black smoke from the tail pipe. Make sure you remind your mechanic to check the charcoal cannister purge system if you have a rough idle.

Poor Gas Mileage (8)

Poor gas mileage without any other noticeable drop in engine performance symptoms usually indicates a defective *oxygen sensor* or a bad *manifold absolute pressure sensor*. These parts help control the mixture of the fuel. A mechanic can easily locate a malfunctioning oxygen sensor or manifold absolute pressure sensor during a diagnostic checkup. Both parts are covered by your vehicle's 5-year/50,000-mile emission controls warranty.

Occasionally, poor gas mileage can be caused by a partially clogged *catalytic converter*. Before your mechanic charges you for expensive diagnostic time on other vehicle systems, ask him to do a *four-gas exhaust gas analysis* followed by an *exhaust system back-pressure test*. The four-gas exhaust analysis measures the percentage or quantity of hydrocarbons, carbon monoxide, carbon dioxide, and oxygen in the exhaust gases emitted from the tail pipe. On cars equipped with a catalytic converter, the carbon monoxide and hydrocarbon readings will not be relevant; however, the carbon dioxide and oxygen readings can be used to confirm that the fuel mixture is too rich (there is too much fuel and not enough air). An excessively rich fuel is indicated by a reading in which the carbon monoxide percentage exceeds the percentage of oxygen in the exhaust.

If an overly-rich fuel mixture is not the cause of poor gas mileage, a clogged catalytic converter may be the culprit. In this case, your mechanic can do a back-pressure test on the catalytic converter. Many catalytic converters are replaced unnecessarily because mechanics fail to verify obstruction of the part by performing a back-pressure test. Catalytic converters are covered by your vehicle's 5-year/50,000-mile emission controls warranty.

Intermittent Performance Complaints, that is, Engine Problems that Seem to Come and Go Unpredictably (9) ▲

Intermittent engine performance problems are the most difficult to isolate. Often problems of this nature do not set off any trouble codes in the vehicle's computer. If your car is experiencing intermittent problems, ask your mechanic to do a complete diagnostic checkup. While performing the checkup, the mechanic should wiggle the wiring harnesses under the hood and tap on the computer sensors and relays to see if the disturbance induces the problem to occur. This technique often uncovers loose electrical connections and defective parts that otherwise seem to work normally. Additionally, you should ask your mechanic to hook up a scanner to your car and operate it in the snapshot mode. See Mistakes and Ripoffs for information about the snapshot mode.

Parts and Terms

If your car requires a diagnostic checkup, your mechanic will probably mention one or more of the following terms or components. Remember to refer to the section entitled Mistakes and Ripoffs for the detailed information you need to help control the cost of diagnostic work.

Catalytic Converter The catalytic converter is located in the exhaust system and is a component of the vehicle's emission controls system. In appearance, the catalytic converter looks very similar to a muffler. It reduces the amount of hydrocarbons, carbon monoxide and oxides of nitrogen emitted into the atmosphere. Catalytic converters can become obstructed, causing loss of engine power and reducing gas mileage. Catalytic converters are covered under emissions warranty for five years or 50,000 miles.

Coolant Temperature Sensor Figure 3-37 shows a typical coolant temperature sensor. This part relays to the computer the temperature of the engine. In responses, the computer varies the amount of fuel supplied to the engine and may alter the ignition timing. A defective temperature sensor can cause hard starting.

Exhaust Gas Recirculation System The purpose of exhaust gas recirculation (EGR) is to recirculate a portion of the burned exhaust gases back into the engine for another burning. This process reduces nitrogen oxides emission, which are dangerous pollutants. Some mechanics disable the EGR system on certain cars in an effort to produce a more smoothly running engine. This is a dangerous action that can lead to destructive pinging, poor gas mileage, and increased air pollution.

Four-gas Exhaust Gas Analysis Using an exhaust gas analyzer, a mechanic can check the percentage or quantity of hydrocarbons, carbon monoxide, carbon dioxide, and oxygen in the exhaust gases emitted from the tail pipe. The data can be used to evaluate the condition of the catalytic converter, the fuel system, and the ignition system. If the percentage of carbon monoxide exceeds the percentage of oxygen, the fuel mixture is too rich and poor gas mileage is likely.

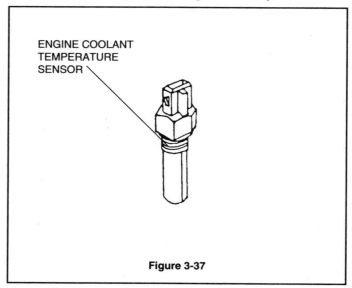

ENGINE COOLANT TEMPERATURE SENSOR

Figure 3-37

Hard Failure A hard failure in a computerized car refers to a malfunction that sets a two digit trouble code in computer memory and causes the "check engine" light or "service engine soon" light to come on and stay on.

Knock Sensor A knock sensor is a device that monitors the engine for pinging. If pinging is evident, the sensor transmits a signal to the computer, and the computer in turn retards ignition timing until pinging ceases. Knock sensors are common on cars equipped with turbochargers.

Manifold Absolute Pressure Sensor Also called MAP sensor, the manifold absolute pressure sensor (Figure 3-38) tells the computer how much load the engine is operating under, that is the MAP sensor tells the computer whether you are accelerating, cruising, or decelerating. A defective MAP sensor can cause poor gas mileage, surging, hesitation, and other engine performance problems. MAP sensors are covered by a 5-year/50,000-mile emission controls warranty.

Mass Airflow Sensor This device measures the amount of air entering the engine and transmits this information to the computer. The computer adjusts the amount of fuel injected in accordance with the amount of air entering as reported by the mass airflow sensor. A defective mass airflow sensor can cause poor gas mileage and various engine performance problems. The part is covered by a 5-year/50,000-mile emission controls warranty.

Oxygen Sensor After an engine has warmed up, the oxygen sensor (Figure 3-39) constantly monitors the amount of oxygen present in the engine's exhaust. If it detects too much oxygen, the fuel mixture is too "lean" and it signals the computer to inject more fuel into the engine. If the oxygen sensor detects too little oxygen, the fuel mixture

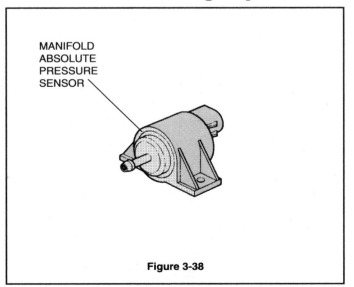

MANIFOLD ABSOLUTE PRESSURE SENSOR

Figure 3-38

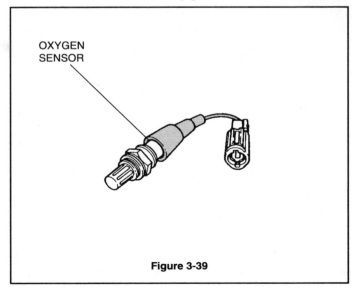

OXYGEN SENSOR

Figure 3-39

is too "rich," so it signals the computer to inject less fuel. In this way, the oxygen sensor always ensures that the engine receives the ideal air/fuel mixture for best gas mileage and lowest emission of air pollutants. Failure of the oxygen sensor results in poor gas mileage and various engine performance problems.

Pinging Pinging (also called spark knock, knocking, preignition, or detonation) is an abnormal form of combustion that causes shock waves in the engine's cylinders. The shock waves result in a metallic rattling noise that is most audible during light acceleration. Left uncorrected, pinging can destroy an engine, or at least reduce its useful life. Sometimes a higher octane fuel can prevent pinging. In other cases, repair of the vehicle's exhaust gas recirculation system is required, or replacement of the knock sensor if the car is equipped with one.

Prom Prom stands for programmable read only memory. Prom microchips installed in a car's computer contain information about fuel mixture, ignition timing, and other data. Frequently, auto manufacturers issue replacement proms containing a revised computer code. The revised code can correct various problems in an engine's performance.

Snapshot Test A device called a scanner is connected to a car's computer to read trouble codes, which represent various malfunctions in the car. In the snapshot mode, a scanner is connected and allowed to read the trouble codes while the car is operating. When a malfunction occurs, the scanner takes a "snapshot" of various engine operating parameters and records the data. By reviewing the "snapshot," the mechanic can see which abnormal conditions existed immediately before the malfunction occurred, while it was occurring, and after it occurred. This test is particularly useful in diagnosing intermittent problems.

Soft Failure A car's computer system experiences a "soft failure" when the problem causes the "check engine" light or "service engine soon" light to come on temporarily.

Surging Surging is a condition in which a car during cruising feels like it is bucking or "holding back" from time to time. Surging can be caused by a malfunctioning EGR system and various other defects.

Trouble Codes Trouble codes are two-digit numerical codes set in computer memory when the computer notes a malfunction in one of the systems it is designed to monitor. A mechanic can read trouble codes with a device called a scanner. Replacing parts solely on the basis of trouble codes can be a mistake. Often a single malfunction can set many trouble codes that have nothing to do with the real cause of the problem.

Mistakes and Ripoffs

The following information will help you control the cost of engine diagnostic checkups and repair. The topics covered are limited to those that are most likely to be associated with errors commonly made by mechanics or deliberate attempts to defraud the consumer.

Misinterpretation of Trouble Codes

Many mechanics mistakenly assume that computer trouble codes always accurately define the location of malfunctions in a car's electronic engine controls. This is not the case. Trouble codes usually help pinpoint the general area of a failure, but frequently then do not isolate a defective part. Even worse, one defective part can often cause the computer to set off several trouble codes, which erroneously indicate additional malfunctioning parts.

Any time your mechanic tells you that several parts require replacement because of multiple trouble codes, you should be suspicious. You should suggest to him that he individually test the suspected parts before replacing them. Generally, once the real culprit is found, all the other trouble codes can be cleared and will not reappear. The bottom line is that, trouble codes give your mechanic clues about what parts he should test. The codes do not eliminate the need for specific testing to confirm defects.

Failure to Employ Scanner in "Snapshot" Mode During Troubleshooting

Nothing is more frustrating to a car owner than complaining to a mechanic about a problem, only to have the mechanic insist that the problem does not occur when he examines the car. This is frequently the case with so-called intermittent problems—mal-

functions that come and go unpredictably and may not set any trouble codes in computer memory. Many mechanics either throw up their hands and express their regret at not being able to help the customer or replace parts randomly hoping to solve the problem.

There is a better alternative. It's called a snapshot test. In this test, your mechanic connects a device called a scanner to your car's computer. The car is then driven with the scanner activated. The scanner is set to trigger as soon as it "sees" some abnormal condition. When a malfunction occurs, the scanner takes a "snapshot" of the computer data being generated just before the malfunction, during it, and for a short period after. Malfunctions that don't occur long enough to set a failure code in computer memory are nevertheless detected and stored in the scanner. The scanner locks the trouble code into its own memory and preserves the data that existed just before the trouble code was set. By reading the scanner's memory, the mechanic can see what abnormal conditions led up to the occurrence of the malfunction and can isolate most intermittent problems.

Failure to Reference Technical Service Bulletins Before Performing Engine Analysis

Some of the problems that arise in computerized cars are so complex that even the most talented mechanic with the best test equipment could never solve them. Often, only the manufacturer of your car knows how to fix certain engine performance problems. Without access to the manufacturer's technical information, even a sophisticated diagnostic checkup could be useless.

Fortunately, all car manufacturers make, to car dealers and independent repair shops alike, technical solutions available in the form of technical service bulletins, also called TSBs in the auto repair trade. You should remind your mechanic to check his library of TSBs before he spends a lot of time examining your car to find a cause for an engine performance problem.

Tampering with Ignition Timing to Correct Engine Pinging

Too many mechanics rush into tampering with the factory-specified ignition timing to solve a pinging problem. On those cars in which ignition timing is still adjustable, many mechanics simply retard the basic ignition timing to get rid of pinging. This could work, but it could also reduce power, fuel economy, and greatly increase pollution emitted from the engine.

Before your mechanic retards the ignition timing beyond that specified by the car manufacturer, the mechanic should verify the correct operation of the EGR system. He should also check for a restricted catalytic converter using a back-pressure test.

For some cars, the manufacturer might have issued new proms for use in the on-board computer. These proms (computer chips) contain ignition timing information in the form of a computer code. The replacement proms could solve the problem of pinging. Ask your mechanic to check for a manufacturer's technical service bulletin on

the subject of pinging before he alters the basic ignition timing.

Tampering with the Exhaust Gas Recirculation (EGR) Valve to Make the Engine Run More Smoothly

A small amount of engine surging, also described as bucking, galloping, loping, and "holding back," is sometimes the unavoidable by-product of exhaust gas recirculation in an engine. To eliminate the symptoms, some mechanics disconnect or disable the EGR valve, a part that controls the amount of exhaust gases recirculated into the engine for reburning.

This is not only unwise, it is illegal. First, EGR reduces the tendency of an engine to ping. Disabling the valve can cause severe pinging and engine damage. Second, EGR reduces emissions of nitrogen oxides, which pollute the air. Never allow your mechanic to disable your car's EGR system!

Charging for Fuel Injector Cleaning Without Verifying a Partially Clogged Injector

Some auto repair shops jump at every opportunity to sell their customers fuel injector cleaning. If you use a good grade of gasoline, injector cleaning is almost never necessary. Even if your car's fuel injectors become somewhat obstructed by deposits, a few tanks of a good grade of gasoline will clean the injectors.

If your car does have one or more partially obstructed fuel injectors, a test that few mechanics bother to do can confirm the problem. If your mechanic has an engine analyzer such as the Sun MCA Analyzer or a four-gas exhaust gas analyzer, he can do a test called the *percentage of carbon dioxide change.* In this test, the mechanic disables your car's fuel injectors one at a time and observes the change in carbon dioxide output in the engine's exhaust. A fuel injector that is partially obstructed will show minimal change in carbon dioxide emissions when disabled.

Failure to Perform an Exhaust System Back-pressure Test Before Replacing the Catalytic Converter

Car owners are sometimes told by mechanics that their cars don't run well because of a partially clogged catalytic converter. This is quite possible; however, there is a test for a clogged catalytic converter that many mechanics don't do. You should ask your mechanic to do it before you allow him to replace the catalytic converter on your car.

A hole is drilled into the exhaust pipe in front of the catalytic converter and just behind it. A fitting on which a pressure gauge is mounted is installed in the hole. Pressure in front of and behind the catalyst is compared. If the pressure drop across the catalyst is too high (usually greater than one pound per square inch), it is considered obstructed and must be replaced. The holes in the exhaust pipe are repaired with special screws after the test has been completed.

Maintenance Tips

The following maintenance tips will help ensure a smoothly running engine that requires a minimal number of diagnostic checkups and minimal cost:

- Use major brands of gasoline containing adequate fuel injector detergent. Fuels that meet the BMW detergency standard work fine.

- Occasionally use a premium grade. Some gasoline companies put more detergent in their premium grades than in regular unleaded.

- If your car's engine does not run properly, find a mechanic who has a scanner or an engine analyzer and a library of technical service bulletins.

- If your car's problem is intermittent and your mechanic cannot locate the problem within one hour, ask him to perform a snapshot test using a scanner. If he doesn't know what a snapshot test is or doesn't have the equipment to do it, find another mechanic.

Distributor Cap and Rotor
(See also Diagnostic Checkup and Tune-up)

Symptoms

Rotors rarely fail, but distributor caps sometimes do. When the cap fails, the cap and rotor are replaced together. Failure of a distributor cap is accompanied by the following symptoms:

1. Rough idle, misfiring, hard starting, engine backfiring.

Typical Causes and Corrections

Here are some of the most common causes of the aforementioned symptoms listed in numerical order. If you see a term printed in *italics*, it means that a definition of that term (and possibly an illustration) is found in the section entitled Parts and Terms. If you see a triangle symbol (▲) next to the number of the symptom you are reading, it means that additional information is contained in Mistakes and Ripoffs.

Here are some of the topics covered in detail in Mistakes and Ripoffs:

• Unnecessary replacement of cap and rotor to improve gas mileage and general engine performance.

• Failure to replace cap and rotor when rotor tip or distributor cap electrodes appear burned or corroded.

Rough Idle, Misfiring at Low Speed, Hard Starting, Engine Backfiring (1) ▲

These symptoms can be caused by a cracked distributor cap or a distributor cap that is *carbon tracking*. Carbon tracking provides a cross-circuiting path inside the distributor cap. Figure 3-40 shows carbon-track lines running from the center electrode of the distributor cap to one of the side electrodes. Carbon-track lines are also shown connecting adjacent side electrodes. Carbon tracks permit a short circuit of high-voltage electrical energy.

Normally, the electrical energy is distributed from the ignition coil to the center elec-

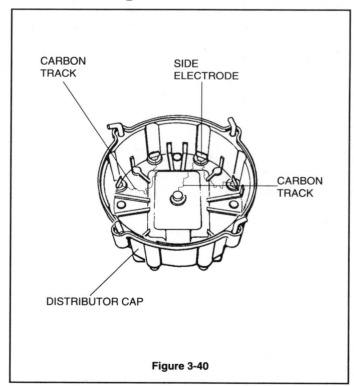

CARBON TRACK

SIDE ELECTRODE

CARBON TRACK

DISTRIBUTOR CAP

Figure 3-40

trode on the distributor cap, to the rotor, and then to each side electrode one at a time as the rotor rotates. From the electrodes the electrical energy is sent to the spark plugs (Figure 3-41). When carbon tracking occurs, electricity bypasses the rotor and goes directly from the center electrode on the cap to one of the side electrodes. If there is a carbon track between side electrodes, electrical current can short-circuit between these electrodes. Either circumstance causes engine misfiring, rough idling, hard starting, and possibly backfiring.

Some mechanics claim that the distributor cap and rotor should be replaced periodically regardless of their condition. A distributor cap and rotor should last for at least 50,000 miles. Arbitrary replacement from time to time can be a waste of money. The only reasons to replace these parts are the presence of cracks, carbon tracks, or burned or corroded metal conductors. Figure 3-42 shows a burned rotor tip. This condition justifies replacing the rotor. Burning of the side electrodes (see Figure 3-40) in the distributor cap justifies replacing the cap.

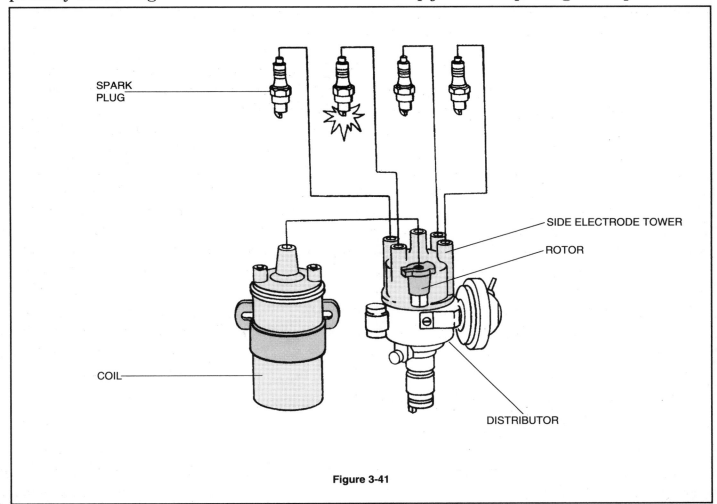

SPARK PLUG

SIDE ELECTRODE TOWER

ROTOR

COIL

DISTRIBUTOR

Figure 3-41

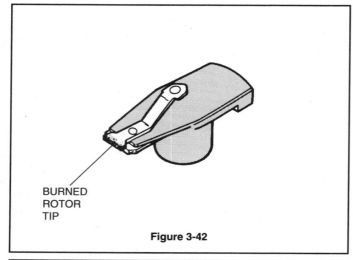

BURNED
ROTOR
TIP

Figure 3-42

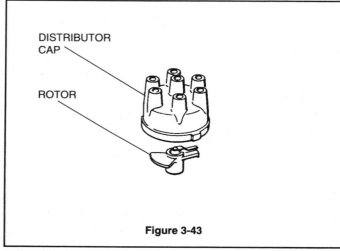

DISTRIBUTOR
CAP

ROTOR

Figure 3-43

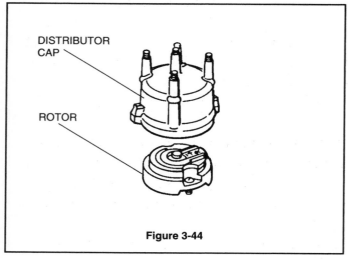

DISTRIBUTOR
CAP

ROTOR

Figure 3-44

Parts and Terms

If your car needs a distributor cap and rotor, your mechanic could mention one or more of the following terms:

Carbon Tracking Carbon tracking is one or more short circuits in a distributor cap. The passage of high-voltage electrical energy leaves a fine line of carbon along the inside of the cap as shown in Figure 3-40.

Cross Firing Cross firing occurs when two cylinders in an engine are receiving a spark at the spark plug at the wrong time. This is usually caused by carbon tracking (Figure 3-40) in the the distributor cap. Carbon tracking causes a short circuit between adjacent electrodes in the distributor cap.

Dielectric Grease Dielectric grease is a substance used on the distributor rotor and the distributor cap side electrodes in certain cars. Dielectric grease helps reduce television and radio interference and reduces the inclination to cross fire.

Rotor A rotor is a device used to distribute electrical energy to the spark plug wires. Rotors come in various shapes and sizes, which can affect their price. A typical small rotor is shown in Figure 3-43. A larger and often more expensive rotor is shown in Figure 3-44. Many modern cars with so-called distributorless ignition do not use rotors.

Rotor Gap The tip of the rotor (see Figure 3-41) does not actually touch the electrodes (see Figure 3-40) in the distributor cap as the rotor spins. There is a gap of several thousandths of an inch. This is called rotor gap, which is not ordinarily measured in distance. Instead, it is described in terms of the number of volts required for a spark to jump from the tip of the rotor to the electrodes in the distributor cap. Typically the figure is 3000 volts, but as many as 9000 volts may be required in some cars. The voltage is measured by an oscilloscope in an engine analyzer.

Mistakes and Ripoffs

The following information will help you control the cost of distributor service. The topics covered are those most likely to be associated with errors commonly made by mechanics or deliberate attempts to defraud the consumer.

Unnecessary Replacement of Cap and Rotor to Improve Gas Mileage and General Engine Performance

If the engine in your car is not misfiring, a new distributor cap and rotor will not make it run any better. You should expect at least 50,000 miles of use from a distributor cap and rotor. Generally, these parts should not be replaced more frequently.

Failure to Replace Cap and Rotor When Rotor Tip or Distributor Cap Electrodes Appear Burned or Corroded

Some mechanics use an engine analyzer to measure the voltage required to jump the gap between the rotor tip and the distributor cap side electrodes. Often they assume that an acceptably low voltage requirement indicates that the parts are in good working order. This conclusion may not be true in every case. A visual inspection of the distributor cap and rotor should be made at every maintenance tune-up. If the rotor tip is burned or corroded (Figure 3-42) or if the side electrodes (Figure 3-40) in the distributor cap are similarly burned, both the cap and rotor should be replaced.

Maintenance Tips

The following maintenance tips will help ensure maximum distributor cap life and minimal cost of maintenance:

- Have the exterior surface of the distributor cap cleaned with spray solvent every year. Grease and oil on the cap can cause carbon tracking and other problems. A mechanic can clean most distributor caps without removing any parts in two or three minutes.

- Do not routinely have the distributor cap and rotor replaced. These parts should last at least 50,000 miles. Ask your mechanic to check for burned or corroded rotor tip and cap electrodes at every maintenance tune-up.

- When a new distributor cap is required, have the rotor replaced too.

Fuel Injector Cleaning

(See also Carbon Removal,
Diagnostic Checkup, and Tune-up)

CLEANING FUEL injectors is almost never necessary, although many auto repair shops charge their customers for this service. Some mechanics insist such cleaning should be done during every maintenance tune-up. This argument had some merit during the mid-1980s, when clogging of electronic fuel injectors became a big problem on cars equipped with multiport fuel injection systems. This problem was solved when the oil companies put in special gasoline additives that could actually clean the injectors with the engine operating in normal use. These additives are now found in all good quality gasolines.

In rare cases you may purchase fuel that is deficient in deposit control additives. If that happens, multiport injectors can begin to clog after only a few hundred miles of driving. Running the engine on gasoline containing the proper additives will clean the deposits very quickly, however. If you are not willing to wait for the cleaning action of high-detergent gasoline to solve your problem, cleaning fuel injectors can provide a quick fix.

Symptoms

Here are some of the symptoms you may notice that indicate the need for cleaning the fuel injectors:

1. Rough idle, engine surges.

2. Engine misfires.

Typical Causes and Corrections

Here are some of the most common causes of the aforementioned symptoms listed in numerical order. If you see a term printed in *italics*, it means that a definition of that term (and possibly an illustration) is found in the section entitled Parts and Terms. If you see a triangle symbol (▲) next to the number of the symptom you are reading, it means that additional information is contained in Mistakes and Ripoffs.

Here are some of the topics covered in detail in Mistakes and Ripoffs:

• Charging for injector cleaning on cars equipped with throttle body injection.

• Failure to confirm clogged injectors using proper diagnostic tests.

Rough Idle, Engine Surges (1) ▲

Rough idle and engine surging at cruising speed can result from a partially clogged fuel injector. Before you have any repair service performed on your car, try three tanks of a different brand of gasoline. Use the premium grade. Some oil companies blend more detergent into their premium grades than into their lower octane grades.

If a different gasoline does not work and fuel injector cleaning is recommended by your mechanic, you must determine the kind of injection system your car uses before you allow him to proceed. Fuel injector cleaning can be useful on cars equipped with *multiport injectors*, but is generally of no use at all on *throttle body injectors*.

Figure 3-45 shows a typical throttle body injection system. Basically, a throttle body injector takes the place of the old-fashioned carburetor. A single electronic injector is mounted in a throttle body assembly. One injector provides fuel for all the cylinders in the engine. The fuel is distributed to each cylinder through a standard intake manifold. Throttle body injectors are not prone to clogging with fuel deposits because the injector is located far enough away from the engine to keep it relatively cool.

On the other hand, multiport fuel injectors (Figure 3-46) are located closer to engine

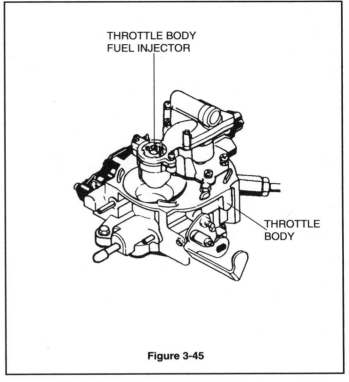

THROTTLE BODY
FUEL INJECTOR

THROTTLE
BODY

Figure 3-45

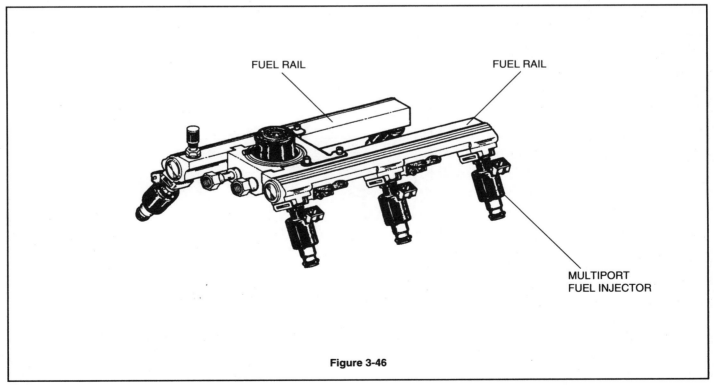

FUEL RAIL

FUEL RAIL

MULTIPORT
FUEL INJECTOR

Figure 3-46

heat. This heat contributes to the formation of deposits on the injectors. The fuel injector assembly shown in Figure 3-46 is designed for use in a V6 engine. There is one electronic injector for each cylinder. A fuel rail distributes gasoline to all the injectors. Figure 3-47 shows how each of the multiport injectors is positioned relative to its respective cylinder. The multiport injector sprays fuel into the manifold just behind the intake valve.

You can find out what kind of injection system your car has in a number of ways. Look under the hood. If the engine is equipped with multiport injection, you will probably see "multiport injection" or "port fuel injection" written on the air cleaner housing or on some other decal somewhere in the engine compartment. You can also check your owner's manual. If your car is equipped with multiport injection, there is a

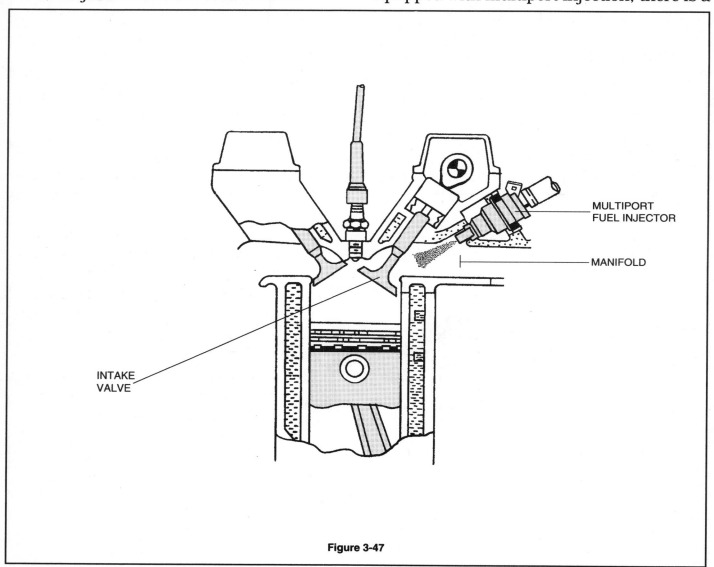

MULTIPORT FUEL INJECTOR

MANIFOLD

INTAKE VALVE

Figure 3-47

greater likelihood that an injector will clog than if it has a throttle body injector system.

If your mechanic insists that injector cleaning is necessary (remember, try a different brand of gas first), ask him how he made that determination. Few mechanics bother to do specific tests to corroborate their diagnosis. For additional information about this, refer to Mistakes and Ripoffs.

Engine Misfires (2) ▲

A partially clogged or leaking fuel injector can cause the engine to misfire. If your car is equipped with *throttle body fuel injection* (Figure 3-45), the single electronic injector should be replaced. If your engine is fitted with multiport fuel injection (Figure 3-46), replacing the affected injector alone should correct the problem.

Some mechanics will tell you that a general fuel injector cleaning is called for. This is usually not true. Your best strategy is to have the defective injector replaced. Thereafter, try a different brand of high-detergent gasoline. Use three tanks of the premium grade to help clean out all the injectors, after which you can resume use of the octane level normally required by your car.

Parts and Terms

If your car needs fuel injector work, your mechanic could mention one or more of the following terms:

Multiport Fuel Injection Also called port fuel injection. With multiport injection, a single injector is used for each cylinder. Figure 3-46 shows a multiport configuration for a V6 engine.

Port Fuel Injection See Multiport Fuel Injection.

Throttle Body Injection In this system, a single fuel injector supplies fuel to all the cylinders. The throttle body takes the place of the carburetor. A throttle body system is shown in Figure 3-45. Some cars are equipped with duel throttle bodies; however, this system is rare.

Mistakes and Ripoffs

The following information will help you control the cost of servicing your fuel injectors. The topics covered are those most likely to be associated with errors commonly made by mechanics or deliberate attempts to defraud the consumer.

Charging for Injector Cleaning on Cars Equipped with Throttle Body Injection

Throttle body fuel injection systems are not prone to deposit formation, as is the case with multiport injection systems. If there is any trouble with the single injector (Figure 3-45) used in most throttle body systems it should be replaced.

Multiport injection systems (Figure 3-46) use a separate injector for each cylinder. The proximity of the injector to heat from the combustion chamber makes it prone to deposit formation.

If your mechanic tells you your car requires cleaning of the fuel injectors, you should seriously doubt him if your car has a multiport system and totally disbelieve him if it has a throttle body system.

Failure to Confirm Clogged Injectors Using Proper Diagnostic Tests

Some mechanics convince their customers that fuel injector cleaning is necessary because injectors can become partially clogged and can cause poor engine performance without actual misfiring. It is true that partially clogged injectors can do this, but so can a lot of other components. The question is, How does the mechanic really know that partially clogged injectors are making the engine run poorly?

Many mechanics just guess. Nevertheless, there are specific tests that can and should be done. If your mechanic does not have an engine analyzer, he can hook up a special pressure testing unit that measures the pressure drop at each fuel injector. An injector that has a much greater or lesser pressure drop than average is considered defective. An engine analyzer can be used to measure the change in the relative percentage of carbon dioxide while the fuel injectors are temporarily disabled one at a time. The fuel injector that produces little or no change relative to the others is considered defective.

The important point to keep in mind is that you should not allow your mechanic to clean your fuel injectors unless he has done specific tests that verify the need for this service.

Maintenance Tips

The following maintenance tips will help ensure clean fuel injectors:

- Use major brands of gasoline containing adequate amounts of additives that control deposits.

- Occasionally use a premium grade of gasoline because it often has higher concentration of deposit control additives than do lower octane grades.

- If your engine runs rough, try three tanks of a premium grade of a major brand of gasoline before you think about servicing your fuel injection system. There is one caution, however. If your engine is misfiring, the problem must be corrected immediately or there could be damage to the catalytic converter.

- Do not waste your money on fuel injection cleaners sold in auto stores. These products are generally worthless.

Head Gasket

- Failure to properly torque cylinder head.

- Failure to check for cause of engine overheating.

- Failure to machine cylinder head.

Engine Runs Rough, Idles Rough, Misfires (1) ▲

Rough idle and misfiring can be due to a *blown head gasket.* Figure 3-48 shows a typical cylinder head, head gasket, and engine block for a four-cylinder engine. The head gasket seals the combustion chamber of each cylinder. Each of the four combustion chambers is sealed by the edges of the large circular opening in the gasket. If the gasket fails at the narrow area between cylinders, cylinder compression is lost and engine misfiring results. Figure 3-49 shows a blown cylinder head gasket. Notice that in the gasket depicted, a passageway has opened between adjacent cylinders.

Also shown in Figure 3-49 are coolant passages and oil passages in the head gasket. These openings allow engine coolant and motor oil to circulate to the cylinder head from the engine block. Occasionally, a defect in the head gasket near one of these passages can cause the loss of coolant or motor oil.

A blown head gasket is usually caused by engine overheating or localized cylinder head overheating, which causes the head to *warp.* Sometimes improperly *torqued head bolts* can also cause a blown head gasket. If your car has a blown head gasket, make sure you ask your mechanic to locate the cause of the

Symptoms

Here are some of the symptoms you will notice that indicate the need for a new engine cylinder head gasket:

1. Engine runs rough, idles rough, misfires.

2. White smoke from exhaust pipe even after engine warms up.

3. Motor oil present in radiator or water/antifreeze mixture present in motor oil.

Typical Causes and Corrections

Here are some of the most common causes of the aforementioned symptoms listed in numerical order. If you see a term printed in *italics,* it means that a definition of that term (and possibly an illustration) is found in the section entitled Parts and Terms. If you see a triangle symbol (▲) next to the number of the symptom you are reading, it means that additional information is contained in Mistakes and Ripoffs.

Here are some of the topics covered in detail in Mistakes and Ripoffs:

- Failure to check engine deck flatness.

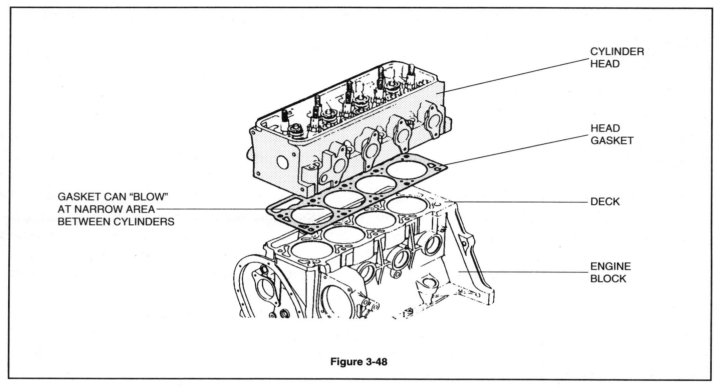

CYLINDER HEAD

HEAD GASKET

GASKET CAN "BLOW" AT NARROW AREA BETWEEN CYLINDERS

DECK

ENGINE BLOCK

Figure 3-48

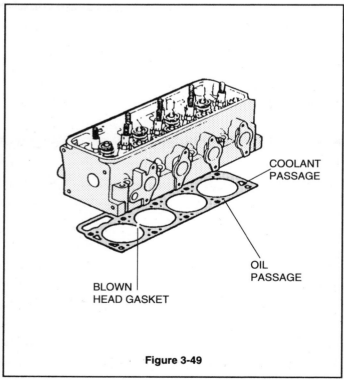

COOLANT PASSAGE

OIL PASSAGE

BLOWN HEAD GASKET

Figure 3-49

general overheating of the engine or the localized overheating of the cylinder head. Localized overheating of the cylinder head can be caused by obstructed coolant passages in the head gasket, the engine block, or the head itself. If overheating is localized, the radiator may not boil over and the engine temperature warning light may not come on. Many mechanics fail to adequately inspect an engine for the cause of overheating during replacement of a head gasket. The result is often a repeat failure of the part a few thousand miles later.

Another frequent cause of repeat failure of a cylinder head gasket is failure to *retorque* the cylinder head bolts. Some manufacturers recommend that their cylinder head bolts be retorqued a short time after replacement of the head gasket. Make sure you ask your mechanic whether this advice applies to your car, and be sure to have the service done if it does.

White Smoke from Exhaust Pipe Even After Engine Warms Up (2)

A cold engine normally emits white smoke from the exhaust pipe as condensation is burned off. If white smoke continues to billow from the exhaust pipe even after the engine warms up, it could indicate an internal leak in the head gasket.

Figure 3-49 shows a coolant passage in the head gasket. If the surface of the cylinder head has become distorted because of overheating, the pressure on the gasket may not be adequate to ensure a tight seal. In this case, coolant could leak from the coolant passage into the combustion chamber. The water and antifreeze mixture entering the combustion chamber is responsible for the white smoke at the tail pipe.

The solution to this problem is a new head gasket. See symptom number one for additional details.

Motor Oil Present in Radiator, or Water/Antifreeze Mixture Present in Motor Oil (3)

Oil in the radiator or water in the motor oil could indicate a blown head gasket. If the cylinder head warps, the integrity of the coolant passages and oil passages shown in Figure 3-49 can be compromised. Crossflow between the oil and coolant passages can cause intermixing of both fluids. The solution to this problem is to install a new head gasket. See symptom number one for additional details.

Parts and Terms

If your car needs a head gasket, your mechanic could mention one or more of the following terms:

Blown Head Gasket A blown head gasket is one that results in crossflow of fuel/air mixture and exhaust gases between adjacent cylinders. Sometimes a blown head gasket refers to one that results in intermixing of oil and coolant because of leakage between oil and coolant passages in the gasket.

Milling the Cylinder Head Milling a cylinder head refers to machining or grinding the surface that mates to the head gasket to make the mating surface flat.

Retorque Cylinder Head After a cylinder head gasket has been replaced, it is sometimes necessary to retighten the bolts attaching the head to the engine block. The amount each bolt is tightened is referred to as "torque."

Torque the Cylinder Head Bolts This phrase refers to the process of precisely tightening the bolts that attach the cylinder head to the engine block.

Warped Head A cylinder head is warped when the surface that mates to the head gasket is not perfectly flat.

Mistakes and Ripoffs

The following information will help you

control the cost of replacement of a head gasket. The topics covered are those most likely to be associated with errors commonly made by mechanics or with deliberate attempts to defraud the consumer.

Failure to Check Engine Deck Flatness

Figure 3-48 shows the deck of the engine block. This surface must be flat to ensure a tight seal between the block, the head gasket, and the cylinder head. If your car's engine experiences repeated failure of the head gasket, a warped deck is possible. Although the condition is rare, it does account for some failures of the head gasket. Sometimes a warped deck can be corrected by *milling* in a machine shop. In extreme cases, a new engine block is necessary. If an engine deck is warped, there is usually ancillary distortion of the cylinders and high oil consumption.

Failure to Properly Torque Cylinder Head

The bolts that attach the cylinder head to the engine block must be tightened in a sequence specified by the manufacturer and to a specified tightness or torque. Torque is measured with a special tool called a torque wrench. Sometimes mechanics don't bother to use a torque wrench. Their failure to do so can result in a repeat failure of the head gasket.

Failure to Check for Cause of Engine Overheating

Most head gasket failures are due to general or localized overheating of the engine. Sometimes mechanics simply replace the head gasket and don't bother to explore the cause of overheating. Their neglect can result in another blown head gasket after a few thousand miles of driving. If your mechanic bills you for the replacement of a blown head gasket and doesn't charge you for associated work on the cooling system, you should question his thoroughness.

Generally, when a head gasket blows, there is a related cooling problem such as a broken water pump belt, an inoperative engine fan, a clogged radiator, or a leaking coolant hose. Occasionally a clogged coolant passage in the cylinder head or head gasket can cause localized overheating in the head and a blown head gasket. If no reference is made to any of these difficulties on your repair bill, question your mechanic to determine whether he even bothered to look for any of them. If he didn't and the head gasket blows again (within 12,000 miles of driving), you can reasonably blame your mechanic. You should remember, though, that certain cars have a built-in tendency to blow head gaskets because of design flaws. If your mechanic asserts there is a design flaw in your car, ask him to substantiate the claim with a technical service bulletin or other evidence.

Failure to Machine Cylinder Head

When a cylinder head gasket blows due to overheating, it nearly always *warps*. Warping means the surface of the head that mates to the gasket is bowed instead of flat. The only correction for this problem entails restoring flatness of the head by *milling* or grinding it. This work is done on special equipment in a machine shop. Sometimes mechanics fail to have this work done, and the head gasket blows again shortly after the repair has been completed.

One of the unfortunate drawbacks associated with milling a cylinder head is an increase in the compression ratio of the engine. Usually this has no discernible effect on engine performance. In some cases, however, it can cause pinging. If this happens, you should use a higher octane gasoline. If that doesn't eliminate pinging, a thicker head gasket sometimes works, or a new cylinder head might be necessary. If you are confronted with such a problem, your mechanic may be at fault.

Some cylinder heads warp so badly that a lot of material has to be milled from the head to make it flat. Car manufacturers specify the maximum amount of metal that can be milled from a cylinder head before the head must be replaced. It is your mechanic's responsibility to verify the amount of metal milled from your car's cylinder head when it is returned by the machine shop. A typical maximum amount of metal that can be removed safely is 0.010 inch. Removing more than that can cause problems in addition to pinging. Sometimes so much metal is removed from the head that the timing chain tensioner cannot take up the slack in the timing chain. This results in engine noise caused by timing chain "slap."

Maintenance Tips

The following maintenance tips will help ensure maximum life of your engine's cylinder head gasket and minimal cost of repair if your engine experiences head gasket failure:

- Have your car's cooling system checked annually.

- Check the maintenance schedule in your owner's manual. If the manufacturer recommends retorquing the cylinder head bolts, make sure you have this important service done on time.

- If your car's engine temperature light comes on, stop the car immediately and turn off the engine. Do not use the car until the problem is corrected.

- If your car requires a new cylinder head gasket and the head must be milled, ask your mechanic to write down on your repair bill the amount of material that was removed from the head to restore flatness.

- If your car's engine has a blown head gasket, make sure your mechanic checks out the cooling system thoroughly.

Ignition Wires

(See also Distributor Cap and Rotor, and Spark Plugs)

IGNITION WIRES should last at least 50,000 miles on any car; however, it is possible for failure to occur sooner.

Symptoms

Ignition wires should last at least 50,000 miles on any car, although failure may occur before that mileage is reached. Failure of an ignition wire is accompanied by the following symptoms:

1. Rough idle, engine misfiring, especially at high speed.

Typical Causes and Corrections

Here are some of the most common causes of the aforementioned symptoms listed in numerical order. If you see a term printed in *italics*, it means that a definition of that term (and possibly an illustration) is found in the section entitled Parts and Terms. If you see a triangle symbol (▲) next to the number of the symptom you are reading, it means that additional information is contained in Mistakes and Ripoffs.

Here are some of the topics covered in detail in Mistakes and Ripoffs:

- Failure to properly route ignition wires to prevent cross firing.

- Failure to use wires having correct resistance value, which can result in incorrect operation of the on-board computer.

- Failure to coat the spark plug ceramic insulators with dielectric grease when installing ignition wires.

Rough Idle, Engine Misfiring, Especially at High Speed (1) ▲

These symptoms can be caused by a gradually failing ignition wire. A defective wire can be confirmed quickly using an automotive oscilloscope (engine analyzer). If an ignition wire fails completely and becomes open circuited electrically, voltage in the ignition system can build up to the point where it destroys the ignition coil or ignition module. For that reason, you must have defective ignition wires replaced immediately. Also, engine misfiring caused by bad ignition wires will rapidly ruin the car's catalytic converter.

Ignition wires have a certain resistance value designed into them by the car manufacturer. Factory original equipment replacement wires will have the correct resistance value. Some wires purchased in parts stores may not. This can cause problems with the operation of the car's computer. Ask your mechanic to verify that the resistance value of the ignition wires he intends to install in your car matches factory specifications.

Parts and Terms

If your car needs ignition wires, your mechanic may mention one or more of the following terms:

Resistor Wire All production cars use ignition wires that have electrical resistance built into them. The resistance reduces radio and television interference. It also reduces electromagnetic radiation that can interfere with the operation of the car's onboard computer. Resistor wire comes in seven-millimeter and eight-millimeter diameters. The thinner seven-millimeter wire must never be used on a car originally equipped with eight-millimeter wire.

Solid Wire A solid ignition wire is one having a solid metal conductor. This type of wire is only used in some racing cars.

Mistakes and Ripoffs

The following information will help you control the cost of ignition wire service. The topics covered are those most likely to be associated with errors commonly made by mechanics or deliberate attempts to defraud the consumer.

Failure to Properly Route Ignition Wires to Prevent Cross Firing

A mistake commonly made by some mechanics involves incorrect routing of new ignition wires. The result can be a rough running engine, with surging, bucking, and poor gas mileage. No two ignition wires for successive cylinders in the engine's firing order should be routed next to each other. This is shown in Figure 3-50. A bank of four of the cylinders of an eight-cylinder engine is shown. The firing order of this engine is 1-5-4-2-6-3-7-8. This means that ignition occurs in cylinder one, followed by cylinder five, and so on. Notice that in Figure 3-50, the wires to cylinders seven and eight are not placed immediately adjacent to each other in the bracket. In this engine's firing order, cylinder seven fires, followed by cylinder eight. Consequently, the wires to these cylinders must not be routed next to each other. The wires to cylinders five and six are not critical because these two cylinders do not fire suc-

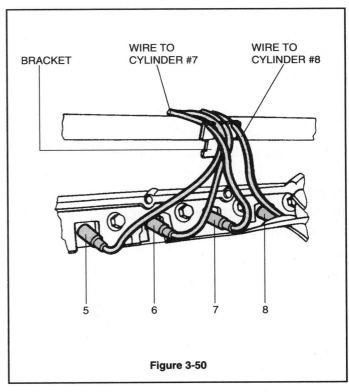

Figure 3-50

cessively in the 1-5-4-2-6-3-7-8 firing order.

The reason that wires seven and eight can't be adjacent involves a phenomenon called electromagnetic induction. The voltage in ignition wires can exceed 40,000 volts. At that high a level, the voltage in one wire can induce a current flow in an adjacent wire. If this "induced" current flows to a cylinder that is in its combustion stroke, that cylinder can fire prematurely. It is this premature firing that causes rough engine operation and poor fuel economy. If your car experiences this problem after the installation of a new set of wires, you should remind your mechanic to check the ignition wire's routing.

Failure to use Wires Having Correct Resistance Value, which can Result in Incorrect Operation of the On-Board Computer

Sometimes a computerized car can experience unusual performance problems after new ignition wires are installed, even though the wires check out fine on an engine analyzer. The factory original wires have a certain built-in resistance value. Replacement wires may not have the same resistance. If they do not, electromechanical interference can upset the operation of the on-board computer. If your car experiences bizarre engine performance problems after a new set of ignition wires has been installed, ask your mechanic to check the resistance of the wires against factory specifications.

Failure to Coat the Spark Plug Ceramic Insulators with Dielectric Grease When Installing Ignition Wires

The area of a spark plug that comes into contact with the ignition wire should be coated with a substance called dielectric grease when the new wire is installed. This substance prevents the wire's seizing to the spark plug, thereby facilitating removal of the wire at some later time. Ask your mechanic to apply dielectric grease when he installs new ignition wires in your car.

Maintenance Tips

The following maintenance tips will help ensure maximum ignition wire life:

- When motor oil is added to the engine, wipe off any oil that spills onto ignition wires immediately. Oil destroys the insulation on the wires.

- Check the ignition wires from time to time to make sure they are affixed to their routing clips or brackets.

- When new wires are installed, remind your mechanic to apply dielectric grease to the spark plugs to prevent seizure of the wires.

Ring Job

Symptoms

Here are some of the symptoms you will notice that indicate the need for a ring job:

1. Hard starting in cold weather, no power going up hills.

2. Blue smoke from exhaust.

Typical Causes and Corrections

Here are some of the most common causes of the aforementioned symptoms listed in numerical order. If you see a term printed in *italics*, it means that a definition of that term (and possibly an illustration) is found in the section entitled Parts and Terms. If you see a triangle symbol (▲) next to the number of the symptom you are reading, it means that additional information is contained in Mistakes and Ripoffs.

Here are some of the topics covered in detail in Mistakes and Ripoffs:

• Failure to properly hone cylinder walls.

• Failure to stagger piston rings.

• Failure to check dimensions of cylinders.

• Charging for a ring job when only valve stem seals have been replaced.

Hard Starting in Cold Weather, No Power Going Up Hills (1) ▲

An engine that will not start quickly when it is cold and lacks power could have worn piston rings. Figure 3-51 shows a cross section of an engine. The rings are circular components that fit in the grooves in the pistons. Figure 3-52 shows a more detailed, exploded view of piston rings. The rings are shown in the order in which they are installed in the piston grooves.

Worn piston rings can be confirmed by a compression test. If the test determines that a ring job is required, you should compare

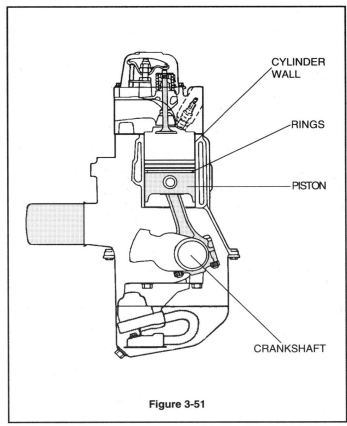

Figure 3-51

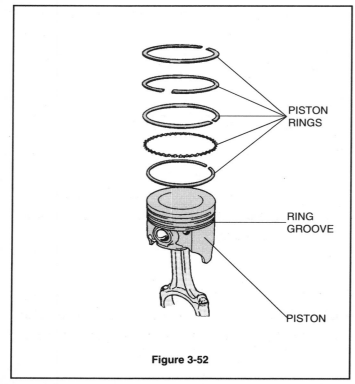

PISTON RINGS

RING GROOVE

PISTON

Figure 3-52

the cost of a factory-rebuilt engine or one rebuilt by a machine shop with the cost of a ring job. Factory-rebuilt engines are available through authorized new car dealers. It is possible for an independent shop to purchase a factory-rebuilt engine from a dealer.

Most dealers refuse to do major repairs on an engine in a car that has been driven more than 80,000 miles. Instead, they would rather sell you a factory-rebuilt motor or a new one—and with good reasons. First, a factory unit comes with a warranty. If anything goes wrong with it, the dealer can fix it and bill the factory. This protects the dealer and benefits you because your engine warranty is good at any dealer having the same franchise.

Second, the factory engine is usually more completely rebuilt than the one repaired at an independent garage. The engine block is specially cleaned to prevent cooling problems. Cylinders (Figure 3-51) are rebored to restore perfect roundness, thereby ensuring maximum compression, power, and control of oil consumption. The crankshaft (Figure 3-51) is machined to restore a perfect fit. These are only a few of the important features of a factory-rebuilt engine that you may not get in one that has been repaired.

The important issue for you to decide is whether asking for a ring job is to be preferred to buying a remanufactured engine. Good mechanics can take careful measurements of most engine components while doing a ring job to determine how serviceable they are. If the crankshaft has not worn excessively, if the camshaft bearings are in good shape, and if many other important parts are okay, simply *honing* the cylinders and replacing the rings might suffice. Nevertheless, you should be aware that there is a good chance your engine will not run like new or sound like new if a ring job alone is done on a engine with 80,000 miles. If a patch job on the engine is good enough, the ring job is reasonable. Opt for a remanufactured engine, however, if you want like-new performance.

Blue Smoke from Exhaust (2) ▲

Blue smoke from the tail pipe and high oil consumption could indicate worn piston rings (Figures 3-51 and 3-52). Although worn valve stem seals could also cause the same symptoms, there is a way to distinguish between the two. Worn rings usually result in the constant emission of blue smoke from the tail pipe. Bad valve stem seals generally cause blue smoke mostly during deceleration.

If your mechanic tells you your car needs a ring job to correct emission of blue smoke and high oil consumption, ask him whether he thinks new valve stem seals might correct the problem. Replacing valve stem seals costs a fraction of the price of a ring job and could be worth the chance. You should also ask your mechanic if he confirmed worn rings using a *wet compression test.*

Parts and Terms

If your car needs a ring job, your mechanic could mention one or more of the following terms:

Crosshatch Pattern When a ring job is performed, the engine cylinders are refinished with a hone, which is a device containing grinding stones. The hone is attached to a drill and is passed up and down each cylinder as the drill rotates the hone at high speed. The stones have an abrasive effect and apply fine scratches to the walls of the cylinders. The hone should be passed up and down each cylinder at a speed that produces scratches intersecting each other at a 60-degree angle. This is called the 60-degree crosshatch pattern (Figure 3-53). The fine scratches ground into the cylinder walls ensure that the new piston rings will seat properly. Seating means wearing into the cylinder walls perfectly so that there is little oil consumption and no loss of compression. New rings have microscopic scratches in the surfaces that come into contact with the cylinder walls. The high spots on the ring scratches are worn off by the high spots on the cylinder wall scratches. This results in a perfect mating surface between the rings and the cylinder walls. After the mating surface has been established, the roughness is gone and excessive wear will stop.

Cylinder Rebore After thousands of miles of use, the cylinders of an engine begin to wear out-of-round. They can also become tapered, that is, wider at the top than at the bottom. This results in loss of compression and power as well as oil consumption. Reboring a cylinder entails machining it to a wider diameter, thereby restoring perfect roundness. When cylinders are rebored, oversized pistons must be used.

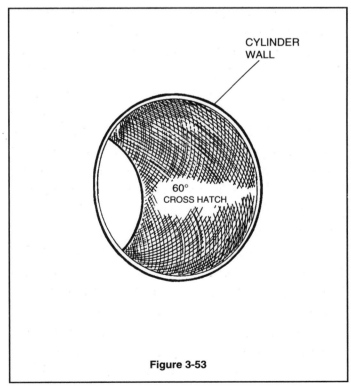

Figure 3-53

Honing   Honing involves the use of grinding stones to apply a special finish to an engine's cylinder walls. Refer to the section on Crosshatch Pattern for details.

Wet Compression Test   During a wet compression test the engine is cranked with a compression gauge screwed into the cylinder being tested, and the compression is recorded. Then some motor oil is squirted into the cylinder and the test is repeated. Again the compression is recorded. If the wet compression increases significantly, low compression is due to bad piston rings, not a burnt valve.

Mistakes and Ripoffs

The following information will help you control the cost of a ring job. The topics covered are those most likely to be associated with errors commonly made by mechanics or deliberate attempts to defraud the consumer.

Failure to Properly Hone Cylinder Walls

When a ring job is done, the cylinders walls must be *honed* to a 60-degree *crosshatch pattern*. Sometimes mechanics fail to do this, or they apply the wrong crosshatch pattern. A mistake can result in failure of the new rings to seat and high oil consumption.

Failure to Stagger Piston Rings

See Figure 3-52. You will notice that the end gap (opening) of each piston ring is rotated several degrees with respect to any other ring in the set. This is called staggering the end gaps. Sometimes mechanics fail to stagger new rings properly when they are installed on a piston, leaving all gaps in alignment. This causes loss of compression and high oil consumption.

Failure to Check Dimensions of Cylinders

If your mechanic does a ring job on your car's engine and it continues to burn oil, it is possible that the mechanic failed to measure the dimensions of each cylinder. Each cylinder must be checked for roundness and taper. The term "taper" refers to the tendency of a cylinder to wear more at the top than at the bottom. Sometimes mechanics merely *hone* each cylinder without verifying whether the cylinder wear is oval or tapered. Oval or tapered cylinders must be *rebored* and fitted with oversized pistons. Before your mechanic does a ring job on your car's engine, ask him to record the dimensions of each cylinder on the repair bill. This will ensure that he doesn't forget to take the measurements.

Charging for a Ring Job when Only Valve Stem Seals have been Replaced

Complaints of high oil consumption often lead to the recommendation of a ring job as the cure. Sometimes new rings are the solution. In many cases, though, worn valve stem seals are the culprits. There is a quick test you can do that can help distinguish between worn valve stem seals and worn rings. If you see blue smoke coming from the tail pipe constantly, worn rings are the probable cause. If you see puffs of blue smoke only on deceleration (when you take your foot off the gas pedal), worn valve stem seals are the problem.

Some mechanics charge for a ring job even when they are merely replacing the valve stem seals, a repair that costs about one-tenth as much as a ring job. If your mechanic suggests a ring job, ask him to return the old parts to you, particularly the cylinder head gasket. Also, ask him to record the dimensions of each cylinder on the repair bill. Chances are your scrutiny will discourage him from attempting to bilk you.

Maintenance Tips

The following maintenance tips will help ensure that your engine's piston rings will have a maximum life and that the cost of repair, if your engine does need a ring job, is minimal:

- Have oil changes performed at least as often as recommended by the car manufacturer.

- Always have the oil filter changed when the oil is changed.

- Have the engine air filter checked and changed at least as often as recommended by the car manufacturer.

- Do not use synthetic motor oil or Teflon-based oil additives immediately after a ring job. These products can prevent the new rings from seating. First drive a few thousand miles using ordinary motor oil.

- Before you authorize a ring job, try to determine whether oil consumption is due to wear on the valve stem seal.

- If your car has been driven more than 80,000 miles, compare the cost of a factory-rebuilt engine or a machine shop-rebuilt engine with the cost of a ring job. Choose the rebuilt engine if you plan to keep your car a long time and want like-new engine performance.

- Ask your mechanic to return old parts to you if he does a ring job on your car. Also, ask him to record the dimensions of each cylinder on the repair bill.

Shock Absorbers

(See also Ball Joints, Wheel Alignment, and Wheel Balancing)

Symptoms

Here are some of the symptoms indicating the need for new shock absorbers:

1. Car bounces uncontrollably after going over a bump or while moving on a wavy surface.

2. Front end of car "dives" when brakes are applied.

3. Unusual wear patterns on rear tires on certain small cars with independent and semi-independent rear suspensions, such as Plymouth Horizon, Dodge Omni, and others.

Typical Causes and Corrections

Here are some of the most common causes of the aforementioned symptoms listed in numerical order. If you see a term printed in *italics*, it means that a definition of that term (and possibly an illustration) is found in the section entitled Parts and Terms. If you see a triangle symbol (▲) next to the number of the symptom you are reading, it means that additional information is contained in Mistakes and Ripoffs.

Here are some of the topics covered in detail in Mistakes and Ripoffs:

- Unnecessary replacement of shock absorbers to correct steering wheel vibration.

- Unnecessary replacement of shock absorbers to correct uneven tire wear on front tires.

Car Bounces Uncontrollably After Going Over a Bump or While Moving on a Wavy Surface (1) ▲

When the front end of a car seems to float up and down several times after going over a bump, worn-out shock absorbers (also called shocks) are the probable cause. A typical shock absorber is shown in Figure 3-54.

There is an easy test you can do yourself to confirm that new shocks are required; lean on one side of the front bumper, and bounce the car up and down a few times and

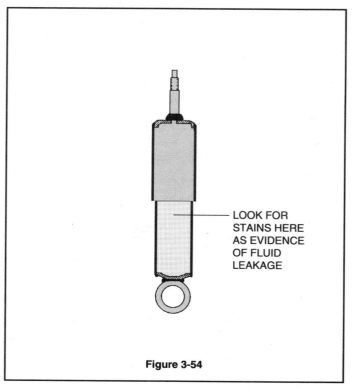

LOOK FOR STAINS HERE AS EVIDENCE OF FLUID LEAKAGE

Figure 3-54

release it. If the car continues to bounce more than once before it stops, the shock on that side of the car is worn out. The same test can be done with the rear bumper to verify worn-out rear shocks.

Before actually failing completely, a shock absorber can gradually deteriorate because its hydraulic fluid is leaking. Leakage is made evident by the appearance of stains on the shock housing. No leakage is acceptable in a shock absorber. You should inspect your car's shocks for fluid stains (Figure 3-54) before the warranty expires, and demand new shocks if you find evidence of leakage.

If your car is under warranty and requires a single new front shock because one has leaked, it is not necessary to replace both front shocks in matched sets—if the dealership uses factory-manufactured original parts. The replacement shock will closely match the dampening characteristics of the remaining good shock, and handling of the car will not suffer. If an aftermarket (a nonfactory original part) shock absorber is used, you should request replacement of shocks in matched sets. You should also have shocks replaced in matched sets whenever shocks are required out-of-warranty.

Your mechanic may suggest the option of installing *adjustable shocks* or *gas-filled shocks*. Adjustable shocks can be set so that the ride of your car is soft, medium, or firm. It is not worth the extra cost of adjustable shocks unless you were dissatisfied with the ride of your car when it was new. If you want a somewhat stiffer suspension than the car originally had, then adjustable shocks can

be a good investment. Gas-filled shocks, which contain hydraulic fluid pressurized by nitrogen gas, may not be a wise choice unless your car was originally equipped with them. Because they can have an effect on the *spring rate* of the vehicle, it is generally best to use them only on cars designed to accommodate them.

Front End of Car "Dives" When Brakes are Applied (2)

If the front end of your car seems to dive or dip sharply downward when the brakes are lightly applied, the cause is probably excessive shock absorber (shock) wear. The only cure is new front shocks. Refer to symptom number one for details.

Unusual Wear Patterns on Rear Tires on Certain Small Cars Such as Plymouth Horizon, Dodge Omni, and Others (3)

Some cars can develop flat spots on the rear tires when the rear shocks have worn out. The tendency for flat spots to develop is aggravated by even the slightest imbalance of the rear wheels. If your mechanic suggests new rear shocks to correct the problem, he is probably telling you the truth.

Parts and Terms

If your car needs shocks, your mechanic could mention one or more of the following terms:

Adjustable Shocks Adjustable shocks are designed with variable hydraulic valving to allow for soft, medium, or firm ride settings.

Gas-filled Shocks Gas-filled shocks contain hydraulic fluid pressurized by nitrogen gas. These shocks should only be used on cars having suspensions designed for them.

Spring Rate Spring rate is the increase in the upward force a car's springs exert for every unit of additional compression of the springs. In other words, the more the springs are pressed down by the car's weight, the more the springs try to force the car back up. Normal hydraulic shock absorbers do not appreciably alter the spring rate of a car's suspension; however, gas-filled shocks can. Because gas-filled shocks can do this, they can significantly change the handling characteristics of a car as determined by its original factory calibration.

Mistakes and Ripoffs

The following information will help you control the cost of shock absorber replacement. The topics covered are those most likely to be associated with errors commonly made by mechanics or deliberate attempts to defraud the consumer.

Unnecessary Replacement of Shock Absorbers to Correct Steering Wheel Vibration

Side-to-side vibration of the steering wheel is usually caused by incorrect wheel balance. Have your car's wheels balanced if it is af-

fected by this problem, and ascertain the condition of the shocks by doing the test described in symptom number one.

Unnecessary Replacement of Shock Absorbers to Correct Uneven Tire Wear on Front Tires

Worn-out shock absorbers virtually never cause abnormal front tire wear. If your car's front tires are wearing unevenly, have the wheel balance and alignment checked.

Maintenance Tips

The following tips will help extend the life of your car's shock absorbers and minimize the cost of replacing them.

- Make sure that your car's wheels are always properly balanced.

- Replace shock absorbers in matched sets when you use any brand other than original equipment from the factory.

- Check shocks for leakage of hydraulic fluid before your car's warranty expires. Leaking shocks should be replaced under warranty.

- Do not use gas-filled shocks unless your car was designed for them.

Spark Plugs

(See also Diagnostic Checkup,
Ignition Wires, and Tune-up)

SPARK PLUGS can last at least 30,000 miles in many cars. Platinum-tip spark plugs can operate for 60,000 miles or more. Most consumers have spark plugs replaced too frequently. Check your owner's manual for the recommended replacement interval. More frequent replacement will not improve engine performance or fuel economy. Never allow a mechanic to clean the spark plugs in your engine using abrasive blasting methods. After a plug has been cleaned this way, it requires more voltage to fire. Fouled spark plugs should be replaced.

Symptoms

Failure of a spark is accompanied by the following symptoms:

1. Rough idle, engine misfire.

Typical Causes and Corrections

Here are some of the most common causes of the aforementioned symptoms listed in numerical order. If you see a term printed in *italics*, it means that a definition of that term (and possibly an illustration) is found in the section entitled Parts and Terms. If you see a triangle symbol (▲) next to the number of the symptom you are reading, it means that additional information is contained in Mistakes and Ripoffs.

Here are some of the topics covered in detail in Mistakes and Ripoffs:

- Failure to allow an aluminum cylinder head to cool off before removing the spark plugs.

- Failure to clean the spark plug recesses before removing the plugs.

- Failure to put antiseize compound on the spark plug threads.

- Failure to coat the spark plug ceramic insulators with dielectric grease.

Rough Idle, Engine Misfire (1) ▲

These symptoms can be caused by a fouled or otherwise defective spark plug. A bad spark plug can be identified very quickly with an engine analyzer. In many cases, it is not necessary to replace all the spark plugs if only one is defective. If the set of spark plugs have been in the engine for more than half the distance of their recommended useful life, it is best to replace the entire set if one goes bad. For example, suppose your car calls for new spark plugs every 30,000 miles. One plug fails at 10,000 miles. In this case, only the failed plug should be replaced. The entire set can then be replaced 20,000 miles later. If the failure occurred at 16,000 miles, it would be wise to replace the entire set and then replace them again at 46,000 miles.

Parts and Terms

If your car needs spark plugs, your mechanic could mention one or more of the following terms:

Copper Core Spark Plugs These plugs have a copper segment in the center electrode (Figure 3-55). The copper segment extends heat range and reduces fouling and misfiring.

Heat Range Heat range refers to a spark plug's ability to dissipate heat. Car manufacturers specify a particular heat range for the spark plugs of all engines. The spark plug must run with enough heat to burn off deposits from the tip of the plug, but not with so much heat as to damage the plug. How

hot the plug runs is determined by its internal design. For any engine, spark plugs of many possible heat ranges are available. The manufacturer of the car suggests a heat range that works best under average driving conditions, but sometimes a spark plug with a heat range hotter or colder than that of the standard factory equipment is appropriate. If you do mostly high-speed driving, a slightly colder plug could reduce the tendency of the plug to burn out. If you do mostly low-speed, stop-and go-driving, a hotter plug could prevent the formation of carbon deposits. The maximum deviation from a recommended heat range is two heat ranges above or below the factory standard.

Platinum-tip Spark Plugs Platinum-tip spark plugs use a platinum center electrode (Figure 3-55) which is very resistant to wear and corrosion. These plugs also have less of a tendency to misfire than ordinary plugs. Although they are more expensive than copper-core plugs, platinum-tip plugs last twice as long.

Resistor Plug The resistor plug is a type of spark plug containing built-in electrical resistance in the center electrode (see Figure 3-55) to help suppress television and radio interference. Most cars come from the factory equipped with resistor plugs.

Mistakes and Ripoffs

The following information will help you control the cost of servicing spark plugs. The topics covered are those most likely to be

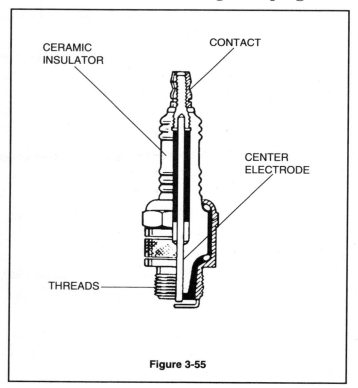

CERAMIC INSULATOR
CONTACT
CENTER ELECTRODE
THREADS

Figure 3-55

associated with errors commonly made by mechanics or deliberate attempts to defraud the consumer.

Failure to Allow an Aluminum Cylinder Head to Cool Off Before Removing the Spark Plugs

If the engine in your car has an aluminum cylinder head, never permit a mechanic to remove the spark plugs when the engine is hot. Doing so can tear out the threads in the cylinder head and necessitate a very expensive repair.

Failure to Clean the Spark Plug Recesses Before Removing the Plugs

A substantial amount of dirt and debris can accumulate in the recess in the cylinder head in which a spark plug is installed (Figure 3-56). This debris must be blown out with compressed air before the spark plug is removed. If the mechanic fails to do this, dirt and grit can enter the engine when the plug is taken out.

Furthermore, dirt can get into the threads in the cylinder head, making it difficult to install the new spark plug. This is a frequent cause of stripped threads in the cylinder head. Additionally, dirt in the threads in the cylinder head causes poor contact between the spark plug shell and the head. This results in reduced heat transfer from the spark plug to the head and overheating of the plug. If you happen to be watching your mechanic replace the spark plugs in your car, remind him to blow out the dirt around the plugs before removing them.

Failure to Put Antiseize Compound on the Spark Plug Threads

When new spark plugs are installed in an engine that has an aluminum cylinder head, it is a good idea to coat the threads (see Figure 3-55) with antiseize compound. Failure to coat the threads can make it extremely difficult to remove the spark plugs thereafter, and it is possible that damage to the cylinder head may occur.

Remind your mechanic to use antiseize compound when he installs new spark plugs in your car. Antiseize compound is not the same as thread lubricant, so make sure your mechanic understands the difference. Also, the compound used must be compatible with aluminum. Some antiseize compounds are not, so your mechanic must use the right product.

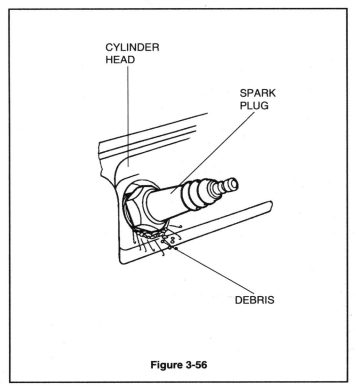

CYLINDER HEAD

SPARK PLUG

DEBRIS

Figure 3-56

Failure to Coat the Spark Plug Ceramic Insulators and Contacts with Dielectric Grease

A special dielectric grease should be applied to the contact (see Figure 3-55) and ceramic insulator of a spark plug when it is installed. This substance prevents the ignition cable from seizing onto the spark plug. If dielectric grease is not used, it may not be possible to remove the ignition cable later on without damaging the cable. Ask your mechanic if he routinely uses dielectric grease when installing ignition cables.

Maintenance Tips

The following maintenance tips will help ensure maximum spark plug life and minimal maintenance cost:

- Never use fuel additives that are not approved by the vehicle manufacturer.

- Do not have spark plugs routinely replaced more frequently than is recommended by the car manufacturer.

- When replacement of spark plugs is required, have the job done by a competent mechanic. It is easy to cause $500 worth of damage by improperly installing a spark plug.

Starter

(See also Battery)

Symptoms

Starters are often replaced unnecessarily. In many cases, what seems to be a malfunction in the starter is really caused by a rundown battery or bad connections. Failure of a starter is accompanied by the following symptoms:

1. Engine cranks very slowly with a fully charged battery.

2. Engine does not crank at all with a fully charged battery; no clicking noise heard from starter.

3. Starter spins, but engine does not crank.

4. Loud grinding noise from starter.

Typical Causes and Corrections

Here are some of the most common causes of the aforementioned symptoms listed in numerical order. If you see a term printed in *italics*, it means that a definition of that term (and possibly an illustration) is found in the section entitled Parts and Terms. If you see a triangle symbol (▲) next to the number of the symptom you are reading, it means that additional information is contained in Mistakes and Ripoffs.

Here are some of the topics covered in detail in Mistakes and Ripoffs:

• Failure to perform tests of starter cranking voltage, circuit resistance, and current draw to confirm bad starter.

• Failure to check condition of ring gear.

Engine Cranks Very Slowly with a Fully Charged Battery (1) ▲

This symptom can be caused by a shorted starter. There are, however, other possible causes, including fuel system problems that cause excessive fuel to enter the cylinders, and ignition problems that cause excessive spark advance. Either condition will make it difficult for the starter to crank the engine.

In many cases, slow cranking is due to bad electrical connections. Make sure your mechanic has performed starter *cranking voltage, circuit resistance,* and *current draw* tests to confirm the starter is defective. Refer to Mistakes and Ripoffs for details.

Engine Does Not Crank At All with a Fully Charged Battery; No Clicking Noise Heard from Starter (2) ▲

This symptom can be caused by bad electrical connections to the starter or a bad starter *solenoid* (Figure 3-57). If the solenoid is bad, it can be replaced as a separate component; however, when the cost of labor is considered, it is often cheaper to replace the entire starter with a rebuilt unit. If your mechanic suggests replacing the solenoid, ask for a price on a completely rebuilt starter assembly.

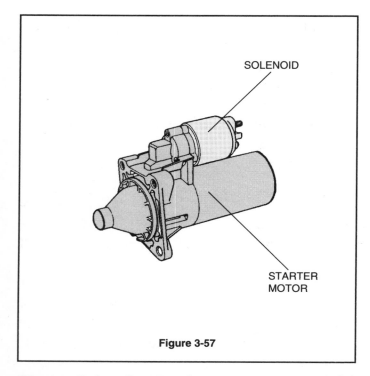

SOLENOID

STARTER
MOTOR

Figure 3-57

Starter Spins, but Engine Does Not Crank (3)

This symptom usually indicates that the starter *clutch drive* (often called Bendix drive) is defective. It is not worth replacing this part. Tell your mechanic you want a rebuilt starter assembly if the clutch drive has failed.

Loud Grinding Noise from Starter (4) ▲

This symptom usually indicates a bad *clutch drive* (often called Bendix drive), but a worn or damaged *ring gear* is also likely. If there is damage to the ring gear, a new starter may work well for a short time and then fail again. Remind your mechanic to check the ring gear if you have a starter replaced to correct a grinding noise.

Parts and Terms

If your car needs a starter, your mechanic could mention one or more of the following terms:

Bendix Drive   See Clutch Drive.

Circuit Resistance Test   High resistance in the starter circuit resulting from loose or corroded connections can cause the starter to turn very slowly. A circuit resistance test identifies high resistance to current flow in the circuit from the starter to the battery and from the starter to ground. To check for resistance in the battery's positive circuit, a voltmeter is connected to the positive terminal of the battery and to the battery terminal on the starter. While the engine is cranking the reading on the voltmeter should not exceed 0.6 volt. This reading is called the positive circuit's voltage drop. To check for resistance in the ground circuit, the voltmeter is connected to the battery's negative terminal and the starter housing. The voltmeter should not indicate more than 0.3 volt with the engine cranking. This reading is called the negative circuit's voltage drop. High negative circuit voltage drop is often due to a loose or missing ground strap connecting the engine to the body. This strap is disconnected when the engine is removed or sometimes during body repairs after an accident.

Clutch Drive   The clutch drive (Figure 3-58) is a device that permits the starter to engage the engine's flywheel ring gear. The solenoid (Figure 3-58) is energized when the ignition key is turned to the crank position. The solenoid is connected to the clutch drive by a lever. During cranking, the solenoid pulls the lever back, thereby forcing the clutch drive forward. The pinion gear on the clutch drive engages the ring gear on the engine. As the starter motor turns, it turns the engine through the engagement of the ring and pinion gears.

Cranking Voltage Test This test measures the voltage available at the starter during cranking. A voltmeter is connected to the battery terminal on the starter and to ground, and the engine is cranked (the battery must be fully charged). While cranking, the voltmeter must read at least 9.6 volts. If it indicates less, there could be high circuit resistance or excessive starter current draw. In either case, the starter will turn too slowly.

Current Draw Test A starter that has an

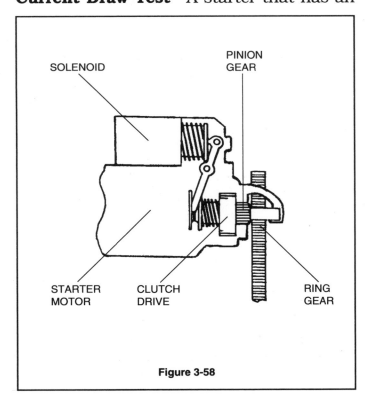

Figure 3-58

internal short will draw too much current and crank the engine slowly. If it draws too little current, there could be high circuit resistance. This test can be done in less than a minute with a device called an inductive ammeter. This device measures current flow without disconnecting any wires. The battery must be fully charged when the test is performed. A large eight-cylinder engine will normally draw approximately 300 amps of current. A six-cylinder engine can be expected to draw 225 amps, whereas four-cylinder engines draw 150 to 175 amps.

Ring Gear The ring gear (see Figure 3-58) is a large toothed gear attached to the engine crankshaft. The starter turns the ring gear, which in turn cranks the engine.

Solenoid A solenoid is an electromechanical device that moves when it is energized. In a starter, the solenoid (see Figure 3-58) causes the clutch drive to engage the ring gear.

Mistakes and Ripoffs

The following information will help you control the cost of starter service. The topics covered are those most likely to be associated with errors commonly made by mechanics or deliberate attempts to defraud the consumer.

Failure to Perform Tests of Starter Cranking Voltage, Circuit Resistance, and Current Draw Tests to Confirm Bad Starter

Many starters are replaced unnecessarily

because mechanics do not bother to perform proper electrical system tests. If your mechanic tells you your car requires a new starter, ask him if he has performed these three tests. Each of these tests is described in detail in Parts and Terms.

Failure to Check Condition of Ring Gear

If your car requires a new starter to correct a grinding noise, make sure you remind your mechanic to check the ring gear (Figure 3-58) on the engine. Damaged teeth on the ring gear can hasten the failure of the new starter. Many mechanics fail to check the ring gear. The engine may crank fine until the starter pinion gear (Figure 3-58) meshes with some worn-out or chipped teeth on the ring gear. When this happens you may hear a lot of grinding noise but the engine will not crank.

Maintenance Tips

The following tips will help ensure maximum starter life and minimal cost of repair:

- Have battery terminals checked annually. Battery terminals must be clean and tight.

- Do not crank the engine any longer than the period recommended in the owner's manual. Prolonged cranking can overheat the starter.

- If a mechanic recommends replacement of your car's starter, ask him whether he performed the appropriate electrical tests to confirm that the starter is defective.

Struts

(See also Ball Joints, Shock Absorbers, and Wheel Balancing)

Symptoms

Here are some of the symptoms that indicate the need for strut service:

1. Car bounces uncontrollably after going over a bump or a while moving on a wavy surface.

2. Front end of car "dives" when brakes are applied.

Typical Causes and Corrections

Here are some of the most common causes of the aforementioned symptoms listed in numerical order. If you see a term printed in *italics*, it means that a definition of that term (and possibly an illustration) is found in the section entitled Parts and Terms. If you see a triangle symbol (▲) next to the number of the symptom you are reading, it means that additional information is contained in Mistakes and Ripoffs.

Here are some of the topics covered in detail in Mistakes and Ripoffs:

• Unnecessary replacement of entire strut assembly.

• Unnecessary replacement of strut dampers to correct steering wheel vibration.

• Unnecessary replacement of strut dampers to correct uneven tire wear.

Car Bounces Uncontrollably After Going Over a Bump or While Moving on a Wavy Surface (1) ▲

When the front end of a car seems to float up and down several times after going over a bump, worn out *struts* are the probable cause. There is an easy test you can do yourself to confirm that strut service is required. To verify that your car needs new front struts, lean on one side of the front bumper and bounce the car up and down a few times and release it. If the car continues to bounce more than once before it stops, the strut on that side of the car is worn out. The same test can be done at the rear bumper to verify worn-out rear struts.

If defective struts are indicated, it is sometimes possible to replace just the worn-out *damper* (the shock-absorbing mechanism inside the strut) instead of the entire strut. Figure 3-59 shows a fully assembled strut. Figure 3-60 shows a strut that has been removed from a car. The lock ring can be unscrewed to remove the shock absorber section of the strut from the strut housing. Instead of replacing the seals and fluid in the shock absorber section, a sealed replacement *cartridge* is simply screwed into the strut housing. For those cars that don't have replaceable cartridges, there are aftermarket struts available that come equipped with replaceable units, making subsequent service less expensive.

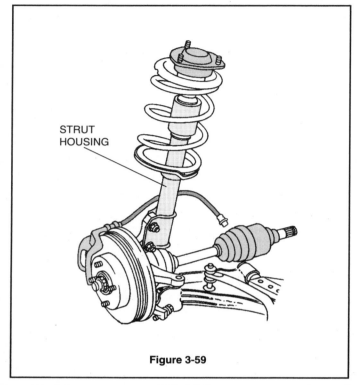

STRUT
HOUSING

Figure 3-59

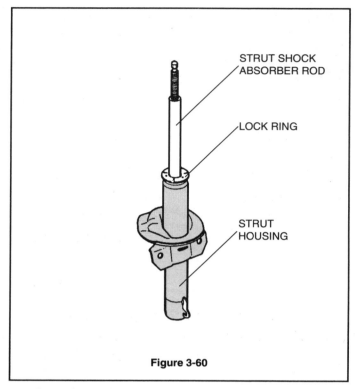

STRUT SHOCK
ABSORBER ROD

LOCK RING

STRUT
HOUSING

Figure 3-60

Struts can give 75,000 or more miles of useful service. If your car is under warranty and requires a single new front strut because one has leaked and is inoperative, it is not necessary to replace both front struts if the dealership uses factory original parts. The replacement strut will closely match the dampening characteristics of the remaining good strut, and handling of the car will not suffer. If an aftermarket strut cartridge is used, you should request replacement of strut cartridges in matched sets. You should also have strut cartridges replaced in matched sets whenever strut service is required out-of-warranty.

Front End of Car "Dives" When Brakes are Applied (2)

If the front end of your car seems to dive or dip sharply downward when the brakes are applied lightly, the cause is probably excessive strut wear. The only cure is new struts or new strut *cartridges*. Refer to symptom number one for details.

Parts and Terms

If your car needs struts, your mechanic could mention one or more of the following terms:

Cartridge Also called a strut damper, the cartridge is a shock absorber insert installed in the strut housing. Figure 3-60 shows a strut housing. The lock ring is unscrewed to removed the shock absorber section. A replacement shock absorber cartridge is then screwed in.

Damper   See Cartridge.

Strut   Also called MacPherson strut. A fully assembled strut is shown in Figure 3-59. The strut supports the coil spring and shock absorber as an integral assembly.

Mistakes and Ripoffs

The following information will help you control the cost of strut replacement. The topics covered are those most likely to be associated with errors commonly made by mechanics or deliberate attempts to defraud the consumer.

Unnecessary Replacement of Entire Strut Assembly

Unless a strut has been bent in an accident it is rarely necessary to replace the entire unit. Most struts have a replaceable shock-absorber section called a strut *damper* or *cartridge*. If your car's struts require service, ask your mechanic to install replacement cartridges.

Unnecessary Replacement of Strut Dampers to Correct Steering Wheel Vibration

Side-to-side vibration of the steering wheel is usually caused by incorrect wheel balance. Have your car's wheels balanced if you have this problem, and ascertain the condition of the struts by doing the test described in symptom number one.

Unnecessary Replacement of Strut Dampers to Correct Uneven Tire Wear

Worn-out strut dampers virtually never cause abnormal tire wear. If your car's tires are wearing unevenly, have wheel balance and alignment checked.

Maintenance Tips

The following tips will help extend the life of your car's struts and minimize the cost of replacing them.

- Make sure that your car's wheels are always properly balanced.

- Replace strut dampers instead of entire strut assembly.

- Do not replace strut dampers in an attempt to correct uneven tire wear.

Transmission Tune-up

SERVICING A car's automatic transmission has been one of the major areas of automotive repair, where incompetence, deceit, and outright fraud have been commonplace. Many automatic transmission shops have charged consumers for major repairs when only minor service would do. In many cases, consumers are sold minor service when no service is required at all!

Ordinarily, major transmission service entails a complete overhaul. Minor service involves a change of fluid and filter and a band and linkage adjustment on those transmissions that have adjustable bands. This minor service is referred to as a transmission tune-up. Some transmission shops advertise tune-ups at prices as low as $14.95. Before you succumb to this enticing price, you must first determine whether the transmission in your car even requires periodic service. Many cars do not, unless they are used to tow a trailer or are driven in extremely hot climates or in frequent stop-and-go traffic. In many cases transmission fluid will last the life of a car with absolutely no maintenance service at all. Check your owner's manual to determine the manufacturer's recommended schedule for transmission maintenance.

Some car experts advocate changing the automatic transmission fluid periodically,

even if the manufacturer does not require it. Here is their rationale. Automatic transmission fluid is designed to provide proper lubrication for the life of a car if its temperature does not exceed 175°F. Unfortunately, there are many times when transmission fluid temperature will get much higher. These situations include towing a trailer, heavy stop-and-go driving, rocking a car back and forth when it is stuck in snow, and driving a car with a defective cooling system that causes abnormally high temperature of the engine coolant. The higher transmission fluid temperatures caused by these conditions induce progressive breakdown of the fluid over time and wear of transmission clutches, bands, and other parts.

Some transmission experts claim that normal driving raises the transmission fluid's operating temperature well above 175°F to an average of 195°F. This supposedly causes its gradual deterioration and therefore justifies replacement every 15,000 miles or so. This argument seems self-serving as regards to the transmission service industry, which would like to stimulate additional business. If replacing transmission fluid is to be done periodically under driving conditions that are not severe, doing so every 60,000 miles is far more realistic than at 15,000-mile intervals. With the exception of cars used to tow trailers, most cars do not have sufficient transmission fluid deterioration to justify replacing it before 60,000 miles. Besides, there are easy ways for the average car owner to evaluate the condition of the fluid at any time. The method for checking your transmission fluid is discussed later on in this article.

Regarding periodic band adjustments as part of regular maintenance, many transmissions do not have bands, and those that do generally do not require attention except in when a trailer is towed. Auto manufacturers specify certain precise techniques for adjusting transmission bands with special tools. These techniques are virtually never utilized by mechanics. In fact, an experienced mechanic can do a satisfactory band adjustment without special tools. If you pay for a band adjustment, you are not likely to get what you pay for. Instead your mechanic will do a quick check of band clearance by hand. It is rare to find a transmission band that needs an adjustment anyway, so if you aren't having problems with your transmission, you will almost never gain anything by having a band adjustment done.

In connection with the often advertised $14.95 transmission tune-up "specials," you should be aware that no automotive shop can make a profit doing the work at that price. It costs a shop that much money simply to put your car on a lift. There are two motives for advertising this ridiculously low price. One involves attracting customers who might have legitimate transmission problems and selling them the extensive repairs that are actually required. The other motive is not so ethical. The low price is intended to lure customers into the shop for the purpose of selling them major services that are not required. How you might defend against this chicanery is discussed in Mistakes and Ripoffs.

Symptoms

Here are some of the symptoms that could indicate the need for a transmission tune-up:

1. Transmission slips during upshifts.

2. Fluid on dipstick looks dark and smells burned.

3. Fluid on dipstick has a milky pink color.

4. Shifts at the wrong speed or no passing gear.

Typical Causes and Corrections

Here are some of the most common causes of the aforementioned symptoms listed in numerical order. If you see a term printed in *italics*, it means that a definition of that term (and possibly an illustration) is found in the section entitled Parts and Terms. If you see a triangle symbol (▲) next to the number of the symptom you are reading, it means that additional information is contained in Mistakes and Ripoffs.

Here are some of the topics covered in detail in Mistakes and Ripoffs:

- Using metal particles and/or sludge in the oil pan to justify the need for a transmission overhaul.

- Failure to drain the torque converter if the transmission is equipped with a converter drain plug.

- Charging the customer for major repair

work when simple adjustment of the throttle valve linkage would suffice.

• Use of wrong transmission fluid.

Transmission Slips during Upshifts (1) ▲

If your car's transmission slips when it shifts into a higher gear, a transmission overhaul may not be necessary. A transmission tune-up costing anywhere from $30 to $50 may be all that is required. Before getting a tune-up done, of course you should first verify that the transmission fluid is at the correct level.

The cause of the slippage could be a partially clogged transmission *filter* or *screen*. Figure 3-61 shows a partially disassembled view of a typical automatic transmission. The *oil pan* must be removed to access the filter, which is attached to the *valve body* and is sealed by a gasket. Shown in Figure 3-62 is a more detailed view of a transmission filter as seen from the underside of the transmission.

Filters can be made of disposable felt or paper or reusable wire screen. Sediment can plug up both paper and screen filters and lower the hydraulic pressure within the transmission. This causes slipping. Sometimes just cleaning or replacing the filter and adding new fluid can restore normal transmission operation; however, there is a good chance the transmission will fail sometime thereafter. A filter clogged with soft sludge indicates substantial wear of the friction material on the transmission bands and clutches. After the filter has been cleaned or replaced, the transmission could operate well for a long time, depending how much

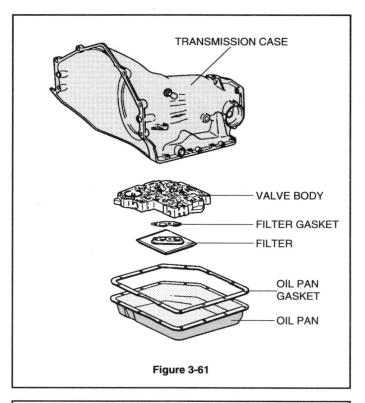

TRANSMISSION CASE

VALVE BODY

FILTER GASKET

FILTER

OIL PAN GASKET

OIL PAN

Figure 3-61

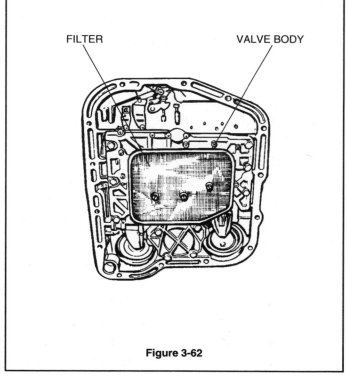

FILTER

VALVE BODY

Figure 3-62

friction material remains on the clutches and bands. If large flakes (and not just soft sludge) are trapped in the filter, it indicates that the clutches and bands are disintegrating, in which case complete overhaul of the transmission is needed. If your mechanic tells you he found large flakes in the filter, encourage him to do a major transmission overhaul immediately.

Sometimes, mechanics show the customer the transmission oil pan (Figure 3-61) and point to the presence of some metal dust and a small amount of sludge as evidence that a transmission overhaul is absolutely necessary. Virtually every automatic transmission will show a small accumulation of metal and sludge in the oil pan. This is normal. See Mistakes and Ripoffs for details.

When your mechanic performs a transmission tune-up on your car, ask him to drain the *torque converter*. Some transmissions have a torque converter drain plug, as shown in Figure 3-63. If there is no drain plug, unfortunately the converter cannot be drained.

Fluid on Dipstick Looks Dark and Smells Burned (2) ▲

The condition of the fluid on the transmission oil dipstick can tell you a lot about its condition. Most automatic transmission fluids (ATFs) should look reddish and clear. To examine it, place a few drops from the dipstick on your fingers. The fluid should not appear reddish-brown, brown, or black. There are exceptions; Dexron II ATF, used in many cars, turns a bit reddish-brown as it ages. This color is normal as long as the fluid

does not smell burned. Synthetic and partially synthetic transmission fluids turn black very quickly and always smell burned. This is normal for these kinds of fluid.

Nonsynthetic ATF that smells burned has an odor resembling old dishwater, rotten eggs, or burned popcorn. This odor indicates overheating of the transmission fluid. If the fluid has overheated, it must be changed promptly. Sometimes a transmission tune-up that simply changed the fluid and cleans or replaces the filter (Figures 3-61 and 3-62) can ensure proper operation and reasonably long life. If large flakes are found deposited in the filter, a transmission overhaul may be necessary. See symptom number one for more details.

Fluid on Dipstick has a Milky Pink Color (3)

If the transmission fluid on the dipstick has a milky pink color, water has entered the transmission. The most likely source of the water is a leak in the *transmission cooler* at the engine radiator. Make sure your me-

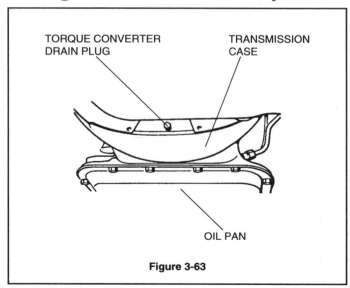

TORQUE CONVERTER DRAIN PLUG

TRANSMISSION CASE

OIL PAN

Figure 3-63

chanic fixes this problem before any work is done on the transmission.

If water in the transmission is attributable to a radiator problem, antifreeze has also entered the transmission. Antifreeze destroys the glue that bonds the friction material to the *bands* and *clutches*. Depending on how long the transmission has been exposed to the antifreeze, a simple transmission tune-up might not suffice. If exposure has been minimal, the transmission oil filter or screen (see Figures 3-61 and 3-62) should be cleaned or replaced. The fluid should be changed twice to flush out any water/anti-freeze mixture. If the transmission operates normally thereafter, an overhaul might not be necessary.

Shifts at the Wrong Speed or No Passing Gear (4) ▲

When a transmission does not upshift at the proper speed or no longer goes into passing gear with the throttle wide open, an adjustment of the throttle valve cable *(TV cable)* is often necessary. The TV cable or linkage connects the gas pedal to a pressure valve in the transmission. If the cable is kinked or improperly adjusted, shifts can occur at the wrong speeds, and it may be impossible for the transmission to go into passing gear. Some cars use a *detent cable* or linkage that affects passing gear but does not influence shift speeds. Many late-model cars use electronically controlled transmissions incorporating electric solenoids and switches to engage the passing gear.

If the transmission in your car is not electronically controlled and you experience loss of passing gear or incorrect shift speeds, you should be very wary of permitting a mechanic to perform a major transmission overhaul to correct the problem. Adjustment of a TV cable or detent cable is a simple ten-minute task. Always suggest to your mechanic that he check the cable or linkage adjustment before doing an overhaul.

Parts and Terms

If your car needs a transmission tune-up, your mechanic could mention one or more of the following terms:

ATF An abbreviation for automatic transmission fluid.

Bands A band (Figure 3-64) is a friction element in an automatic transmission. It is a band of metal containing a glued-on strip of material similar to a brake lining. Transmissions that use bands generally use one band to engage second gear and a different band when low or reverse gear is selected. Other transmission designs do not use bands at all.

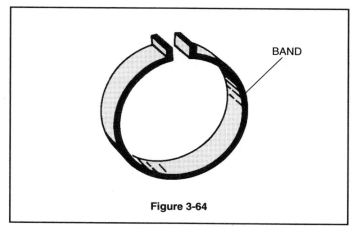

BAND

Figure 3-64

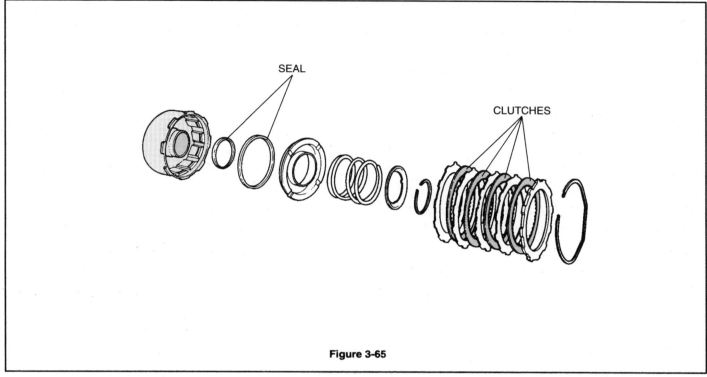

SEAL

CLUTCHES

Figure 3-65

Clutches Clutches are the friction elements in an automatic transmission. Clutches are squeezed together under hydraulic pressure to engage various gear ranges. Typical clutches are shown in Figure 3-65. Unlike the clutches in a standard transmission, which operates without fluid, automatic transmission clutches are constantly bathed in lubricating fluid (automatic transmission fluid).

Cooler Automatic transmission fluid is cooled by passing it under pressure through a separate compartment in the car's radiator (Figure 3-66). The radiator cools the transmission fluid in the same way it cools the engine's water/antifreeze mixture. It is possible to install an auxiliary transmission cooler in a car. An auxiliary cooler contains

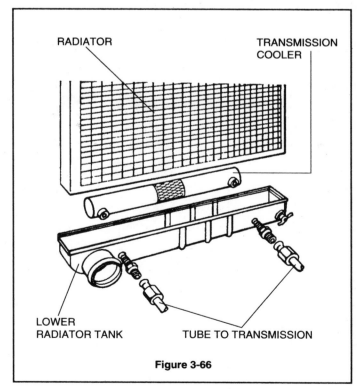

RADIATOR

TRANSMISSION COOLER

LOWER RADIATOR TANK

TUBE TO TRANSMISSION

Figure 3-66

fins that provide air cooling of the transmission fluid. If a transmission requires a major overhaul, the cooler(s) must be flushed to clean them out. Failure to do so will result in contamination of the transmission with metal particles and sludge, and the life of the rebuilt transmission will be shortened.

Detent Cable   See TV Cable.

Filter   An automatic transmission has a filter to remove particles from the transmission fluid. Transmission filters are made of felt, paper, or wire mesh. The filter is attached to the transmission valve body. A typical filter is shown in Figure 3-62.

Kickdown Rod   See TV Cable.

Oil Pan   The transmission oil pan (Figure 3-67) is mounted to the bottom of the transmission case. It stores a quantity of transmission fluid.

Screen   A screen is a form of transmission filter.

Torque Converter   The torque converter (see Figure 3-67) connects the engine to the transmission. It is a hydraulic device that multiplies engine torque during acceleration. If a transmission requires a major overhaul, the torque converter must be flushed to clean it out. Failure to do so will result in contamination of the transmission with metal particles and sludge, and the life of the rebuilt transmission will be shortened.

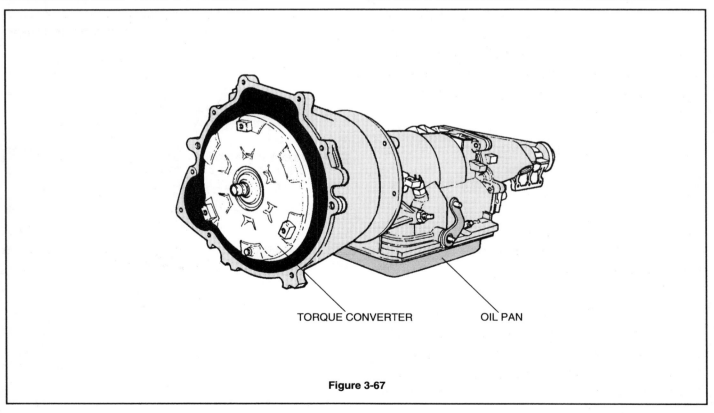

TORQUE CONVERTER   OIL PAN

Figure 3-67

TV Cable The TV cable is an abbreviation for throttle valve cable. The throttle valve cable or linkage connects the gas pedal to a pressure valve on the transmission that influences shift speed and engagement of passing gear. A detent cable works essentially the same way, except that it affects the engagement of the passing gear only. TV and detent linkages are sometimes called kickdown rods.

Varnish Varnish is a light- to dark-brown sticky substance that forms in an automatic transmission due to overheating and oxidation of the fluid.

Mistakes and Ripoffs

The following information will help you control the cost of transmission service. The topics covered are those most likely to be associated with errors commonly made by mechanics or deliberate attempts to defraud the consumer.

Using Metal Particles and/or Sludge in the Oil Pan to Justify the Need for a Transmission Overhaul

Every automatic transmission accumulates a small amount of metal particles and sludge in the oil pan (see Figure 3-67) after a period of use. Some repair shops exploit this fact to induce unwary customers to spend a lot of money on transmission overhauls that are not necessary. If your transmission has been operating normally and you are having it tuned-up as a matter of routine maintenance, do not be concerned

about any debris in the oil pan. Just ask your mechanic to change the filter and the transmission fluid.

If your mechanic finds varnish in the oil pan, some action beyond a simple tune-up might be necessary. Varnish is light to dark brown and feels sticky when touched. The presence of varnish indicates overheating of the transmission. Overheating can damage many of the internal seals in the transmission, especially the clutch assembly seals (see Figure 3-65). Exposure to excessive heat can cause these seals to harden, thereby reducing their ability to seal fluid under pressure. This problem in turn causes the clutches to slip, resulting in slippage during upshifts. Damage to the seals can be evaluated by performing a pressure test. A pressure test can be done in about 30 minutes. If your mechanic finds varnish in the transmission, ask him to do a pressure test before he undertakes any major transmission work. A new filter and fresh fluid could be all the transmission needs to restore correct operation.

Failure to Drain the Torque Converter if the Transmission is Equipped with a Converter Drain Plug

When a tune-up is performed on an automatic transmission, the torque converter should be drained if it is equipped with a drain plug. Remind your mechanic to drain the converter.

Charging the Customer for Major Repair Work When Simple Adjustment of the Throttle Valve Linkage Would Suffice

Consumers are sometimes bilked by unscrupulous transmission shops that do a major transmission overhaul to correct a shift timing problem or to fix the absence of passing gear. Frequently, these performance difficulties can be corrected by a simple adjustment of cable or linkage. Many transmissions have a cable or link rod that connects the accelerator pedal to the transmission. If the cable or rod is out of adjustment, the transmission may not shift at the right speed, or it may not go into passing gear at wide-open throttle.

Many late-model cars use electronically controlled transmissions. Some of these designs incorporate a device called a kickdown switch. This device sends an electrical signal to the transmission when the accelerator pedal is pressed to the floor. The signal energizes a downshift solenoid on the transmission that engages passing gear. Sometimes even a minor electrical problem can result in failure of the transmission to go into passing gear. Make sure your mechanic checks the kickdown switch and downshift solenoid before he jumps to the conclusion that a transmission overhaul is necessary.

Use of Wrong Transmission Fluid

Not all automatic transmission fluid is the same. Using the wrong fluid in your car's transmission can cause shifting problems and premature failure of clutches and bands. There are basically two distinct types of automatic transmission: friction-modified and nonfriction-modified. Each requires a unique fluid.

Nonfriction-modified transmissions are designed so that the bands and clutches engage very quickly to avoid excessive slippage and wear. These transmissions use Type F and Type G automatic transmission fluid. Type G is usually specified by the manufacturers of certain imported cars. Type F is often used in certain Fords. Using friction-modified fluid such as Dexron II or Mercon in a transmission designed for Type F or G fluid will cause early wear of the clutches and bands and the need for frequent overhauls.

Friction-modified transmissions are designed to engage very smoothly. Use of a friction-modified fluid helps ensure smoother shifting. This kind of transmission fluid is more "slippery" than is nonfriction-modified fluid and causes less abrupt engagement of the clutches and bands. To compensate for extra heat generated by the slippage, friction-modified transmissions use bigger bands and more clutches. These transmissions typically use Dexron II or Mercon fluid. If Type F or Type G fluid is mistakenly used, the transmission will shift more abruptly and with some harshness, but its life expectancy will not be reduced. Most cars built by General Motors are equipped with friction-modified transmissions.

Whenever any work is done on your car's transmission, make sure your mechanic uses the correct fluid specified in the owner's manual. If he tells you he uses "universal" transmission fluid, you have something to be concerned about if you own a Ford. The makers of some brands of synthetic automatic transmission fluids claim these fluids work well in every car. Ford says no! According to Ford, a transmission fluid cannot be friction-modified and nonfriction-modified at

the same time. Ford does not acknowledge that these universal fluids meet all specifications for Ford transmissions.

Maintenance Tips

The following maintenance tips will help ensure maximum automatic transmission life and minimal cost of service:

- Have the fluid and filter changed every 60,000 miles. If you subject your car to severe service as defined by the owner's manual, have this service performed more frequently.

- Use the kind of transmission fluid specified by the vehicle manufacturer.

- If the transmission does not shift at the correct speed or does not engage passing gear, ask for a TV cable or linkage adjustment before paying for a complete overhaul.

- Have the engine cooling system drained and flushed periodically. This will ensure maximum efficiency of the transmission cooler.

Tune-up

(See also Carbon Removal, Diagnostic Checkup, Distributor Cap and Rotor, Ignition Wires, and Spark Plugs)

Symptoms

Very few late-model cars with engine performance problems can benefit from a tune-up. This comes as a surprise to most consumers, who have grown accustomed to the annual tune-up of the engine as preventive maintenance. It is also surprising to those who have gotten used to the idea that when a car doesn't run well, the solution is simply to have it tuned-up at the local garage.

Because most cars built since 1981 have computerized fuel and ignition systems, the solution to their engine performance problems is usually much more complex and expensive than a simple tune-up. Late-model cars that don't run well usually require sophisticated testing procedures referred to as a diagnostic checkup. So, if your car doesn't run well, it is important to remember that chances are a tune-up will not solve the problem, particularly if you have had the spark plugs replaced at the time recommended by the vehicle's manufacturer.

So what is a tune-up these days, and what will it do for your car? Modern cars require a simple procedure referred to as a maintenance tune-up, which differs drastically from the old-fashioned "complete tune-up." Maintenance tune-ups usually are done every three years or 30,000 miles. On some cars equipped with platinum spark plugs, the replacement interval is 60,000 miles.

Basically the procedure includes replacing the spark plugs, air filter, and fuel filter and testing the spark plug wires. Additional important services performed during a maintenance tune-up include cleaning or replacing the PCV valve (not all cars have a PCV valve) and PCV filter, and checking belts and hoses, battery condition, and fluid levels. On many cars the timing is not checked because it cannot be adjusted. The idle speed cannot be adjusted on many cars either, nor can the fuel mixture. Thanks to computer technology, very little remains to be adjusted by a mechanic as far as engine performance is concerned.

Some people in the automobile repair industry advocate that maintenance tune-ups be performed more frequently than suggested by the vehicle manufacturers, citing environmental benefits such as reduced exhaust emissions. The United States Environmental Protection Agency has performed studies in this area. The results prove conclusively that replacing spark plugs and ignition wires on high-mileage vehicles that are running well produces no significant lowering of tail pipe emissions.

What all this means is that you should have a maintenance tune-up performed on your car periodically before symptoms of malfunction are apparent. Use the manufacturer's guidelines in your owner's manual to determine how often a maintenance tune-up is needed. If your car is not running properly, a tune-up may not help because the need for a maintenance tune-up rarely produces noticeable symptoms of poor engine performance. In this case, a diagnostic checkup is required.

As a rule, you should not pay for a basic maintenance tune-up unless your car calls for one according to the maintenance schedule in the owner's manual. If your car is not running properly and it is not scheduled for a maintenance tune-up, ask for a diagnostic checkup. This kind of service costs much more than a tune-up, but you'll save the money you would have spent for an unnecessary tune-up.

Occasionally you may detect a few conditions attributable to the need for a maintenance tune-up. These symptoms are as follows:

1. Loss of fuel economy (poor gas mileage).

2. Rotten egg smell from the exhaust pipe.

3. Engine misfires (car feels like it bucks).

4. Rough idle and stalling.

5. Oil leaks from engine.

There are many other causes for the above symptoms. The only ones considered here will be those attributable to deficiencies that can be corrected during a maintenance tune-up.

Typical Causes and Corrections

Here are some of the most common causes of the aforementioned symptoms listed in numerical order. If you see a term printed in *italics*, it means that a definition of that term (and possibly an illustration) is found in the section entitled Parts and Terms. If you see a triangle symbol (▲) next to the number of the symptom you are reading, it means that additional information is contained in Mistakes and Ripoffs.

Here are some of the topics covered in detail in Mistakes and Ripoffs:

- Unnecessary replacement of air filter and PCV valve.

- Charging for points and condenser replacement.

- Unnecessary replacement of distributor cap, rotor, ignition wires, and ignition coil.

- Unnecessary fuel injector cleaning.

- Unnecessary tune-ups to restore temporary loss of performance resulting from disconnection of battery.

- Charges for work that should be done free under your car's 5-year/50,000-mile emission controls warranty.

- Forcing a consumer to spend more money on emission-related repairs than the law requires.

Loss of Fuel Economy (1) ▲

There are dozens of possible causes of poor gas mileage, most of which have nothing to do with a routine maintenance tune-up. The only items replaced during a maintenance tune-up that can cause poor gas mileage (generally without simultaneously causing engine misfiring) are the *air filter* and the *PCV valve.*

A clogged air filter starves the engine for air, sometimes resulting in excessive enrichment of the fuel mixture. Not only will loss of fuel economy result from a clogged air filter, but there is a strong possibility that a rotten egg smell will emanate from the tail pipe. The pungent odor is caused by the presence of hydrogen sulfide in the exhaust gases.

For these conditions to occur, an air filter must be severely restricted. Computerized cars are equipped with fuel management systems referred to as closed loop systems. In a closed loop system, the composition of the exhaust gases is constantly monitored by a device called an oxygen sensor. By "examining" the oxygen content of the exhaust gases, the sensor knows whether the fuel mixture is too rich (not enough gasoline and not enough air) or too lean (too little gasoline and too much air). After the engine has warmed up, the oxygen sensor begins reporting the status of the fuel mixture to the computer. If the mixture is a bit too rich because of a slightly clogged air filter, the computer automatically reduces the amount of fuel supplied to the engine. Because the computer is capable of compensating for inadequate air supply to the engine within certain limits, a partially clogged air filter will not necessarily produce symptoms.

An obstructed PCV valve can also result in excessive enrichment of the fuel mixture and hydrogen sulfide emissions. Some cars use a fixed PCV orifice instead of a valve. In either case, the computer can to a certain extent compensate for a partially obstructed PCV system. Consequently, no adverse symptoms may be apparent.

Rotten Egg Smell from the Exhaust Pipe (2)

The smell of rotten eggs from the tail pipe is caused by the presence of hydrogen sulfide in the exhaust gases. This condition results from excessive enrichment of the fuel mixture, that is, the engine is getting too much fuel and not enough air. A clogged *air filter* can be responsible for this condition. Left uncorrected, it will lead to destruction of the catalytic converter. If the *catalytic converter* fails, the vehicle will probably fail an emissions test during a routine state inspection.

Engine Misfires (3) ▲

Engine misfire usually produces noticeable surging or bucking. In many cases, however, misfiring may not be felt by the driver. Nevertheless, it can cause serious damage to the engine and *catalytic converter*. Misfiring can be caused by one or more defective *spark plugs* or *ignition wires*.

Rough Idle and Stalling (4) ▲

Rough idle and stalling can be caused by an obstructed *PCV valve*.

Oil Leaks from Engine (5)

A clogged *PCV valve* and *PCV filter* can cause excessive pressure to build up in an engine's crankcase. This pressure can result

in oil leakage from various locations on the engine.

Parts and Terms

When your car requires a maintenance tune-up, your mechanic will probably mention one or more of the following components. Remember to refer to the section entitled Mistakes and Ripoffs for detailed information you need to help control the cost of engine performance repairs on your car.

Air Filter The air filter prevents dust and other particles from entering the engine. If the filter is clogged, the engine will be starved for air. This is referred to as excessive enrichment of the fuel mixture. Air filters usually are round, but they can also be oval, cylindrical, or rectangular. The filter is located in a housing called the air cleaner assembly. A typical air filter is shown in Figure 3-68.

When a vehicle is used in very dusty areas, it is wise to replace the air filter at least every year. Under normal driving conditions, however, replacement after three years is reasonable.

Catalytic Converter The catalytic converter (Figure 3-69) is located in the exhaust system. Externally, it looks like a muffler. Internally, it is quite different. Catalytic converters are designed to reduce emissions of dangerous pollutants from automobile engines. Most modern cars use a so-called three-way catalyst—that is, one that reduces emission of hydrocarbons, carbon monoxide, and oxides of nitrogen. Catalytic converters are covered under a 5-year/50,000-mile emission control systems warranty on every automobile and light truck. If a car's engine is kept running properly and only unleaded fuel is used, the catalytic converter should last the life of the car.

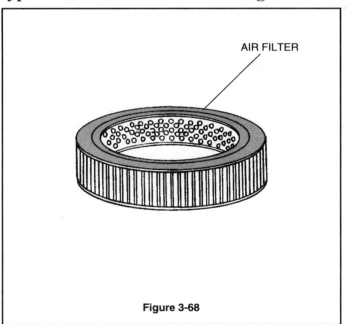

AIR FILTER

Figure 3-68

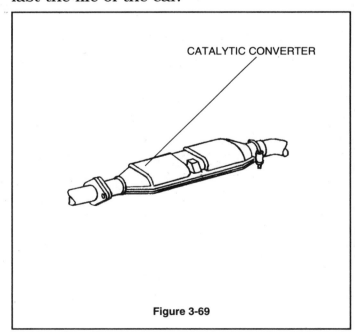

CATALYTIC CONVERTER

Figure 3-69

Ignition Wires Also called spark plug cables, ignition wires deliver high-voltage electrical energy from the distributor to the spark plugs (shown in Figure 3-70). Although they may look fine externally, ignition wires can have internal problems that necessitate replacement. On most cars built since 1981, ignition wires can be expected to last a minimum of 50,000 miles. It is not uncommon for them to remain perfectly functional for 100,000 miles.

PCV Filter The PCV filter (Figure 3-71) removes road dust and grit from the fresh air flow entering the engine crankcase. This step prevents contamination of the motor oil. The PCV filter usually is located inside the air cleaner assembly (it is only a fraction of the size of the air filter). It also can be found inside the oil filler cap of some cars.

PCV Valve PCV stands for positive crankcase ventilation. Every time a cylinder fires, some of the combustion gases leak past the piston rings into the engine's crankcase (where the motor oil is stored). The PCV

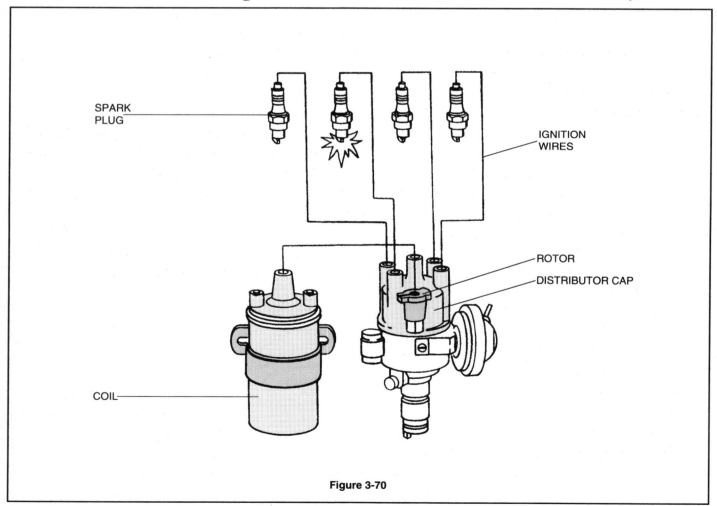

SPARK
PLUG

IGNITION
WIRES

ROTOR

DISTRIBUTOR CAP

COIL

Figure 3-70

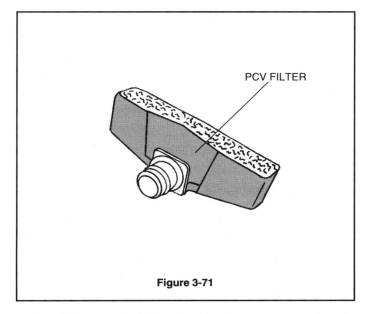

Figure 3-71

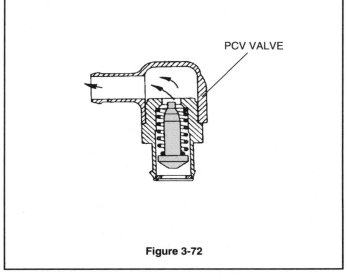

Figure 3-72

valve (Figure 3-72) admits these gases back into the engine's combustion chambers to be reburned, thereby reducing air pollution.

Spark Plugs Spark plugs (Figure 3-70) ignite the fuel mixture in the engine's combustion chambers. On cars built before 1981, a maximum of 12,000 miles of service could be expected from most spark plugs. Because of the use of unleaded fuel, superior ignition systems, and other factors, spark plugs last a minimum of 30,000 miles in most modern cars. Platinum plugs can last 60,000 miles or more.

Mistakes and Ripoffs

The following information will help you control the cost of tune-up work done on your car. The topics covered are limited to those most likely to be associated with errors commonly made by mechanics or deliberate attempts to defraud the consumer.

Unnecessary Replacement of Air Filter and PCV Valve

Unless you drive your car in an extremely dusty environment, it is a waste of money to replace the air filter more often than the interval suggested by the vehicle manufacturer. Assuming that the engine oil is changed on schedule, a clogged PCV valve is a rarity.

There are many "quick lube" shops that aggressively merchandise new air filters and PCV valves during a routine oil change. Usually the service people who recommend these parts receive a commission for each part sold. Their suggestions for replacement service are more often motivated by personal profit than by an interest in ensuring a well-maintained car. If you have had the air filter and PCV valve replaced during a maintenance tune-up, resist the pressure to replace them again during an oil change at a quick lube shop.

Charging for Points and Condenser

Thousands of car owners still believe their vehicles require periodic replacement of ignition points and condenser. Because there are practically no cars left in operation that have these parts, few mechanics overtly bill a customer for them. Nevertheless, some unscrupulous mechanics perpetuate the myth that replacement of points and condenser is still part of a tune-up. Here's why points and condensers no longer play a role in your car's maintenance requirements.

Until 1970 almost all automobile engines required complete tune-ups—as often as every 6000 miles. Few cars could be driven more than 12,000 miles without a noticeable deterioration in performance. The primary cause of loss of performance was wear and tear on the distributor points (Figure 3-73).

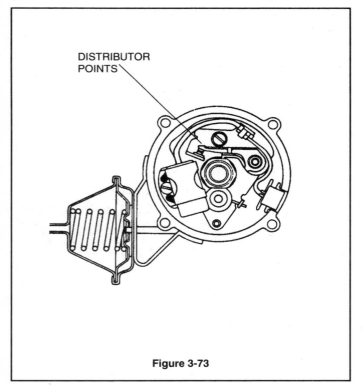

DISTRIBUTOR POINTS

Figure 3-73

Because of inevitable deterioration of the distributor points, car owners grew accustomed to the need for an annual tune-up. Right now, however, it is almost impossible to find a car on the road that has distributor points. Many cars don't even have distributors. Even so, some mechanics exploit the belief held by many car owners (particularly elderly drivers) that the annual replacement of points and plugs is necessary to avoid breakdowns. Some automotive service advertisements still promote tune-ups with pricing based on replacement of the distributor points and condenser.

Virtually every domestic car manufactured since 1971 has an electronic ignition system that does not include points. The same holds true for nearly all imported cars built since 1976. Therefore, you don't need an annual tune-up to replace distributor points because your car probably does not have them. Most likely your car was manufactured with one of three systems: transistorized ignition, computerized electronic ignition, or computerized distributorless ignition.

Transistorized Ignition In the early 1970s ignition points and condensers were replaced by breakerless transistorized ignition systems containing magnetic pulse generators (Figure 3-74). These electromagnetic ignition parts do not function in any way like points and condensers, but since they are located in approximately the same position in the distributor, many mechanics have mistakenly replaced them anyway, even though no routine service is actually required.

Computerized Electronic Ignition In the late 1970s and early 1980s computerized electronic ignition systems appeared, further altering the role played by the old-fashioned distributor. Not only were points and condensers eliminated, but the traditional mechanisms, the centrifugal and vacuum spark advance, were done away with too. As an engine speeds up, ignition timing must be advanced. This used to be accomplished by a set of centrifugal weights mounted in the distributor and an external vacuum advance diaphragm. These mechanical devices controlled ignition timing advance imprecisely, so they have been replaced by a computer. Unlike centrifugal weights and vacuum advance devices, computers don't need periodic maintenance. Moreover, thanks to the computer, it is generally not necessary to ever adjust basic ignition timing.

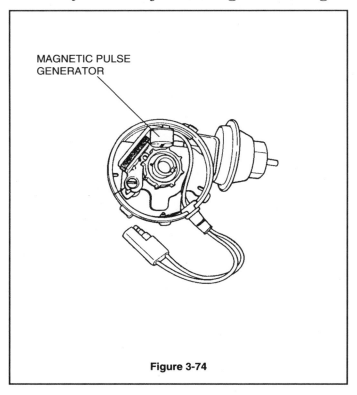

MAGNETIC PULSE GENERATOR

Figure 3-74

Computerized Distributorless Ignition In the two systems described above, a rotating rotor distributes high voltage (supplied by a spark coil) to the spark plug at each cylinder via a distributor cap and ignition wires (Figure 3-70). The distributor can wear out, and the distributor cap and rotor require periodic replacement because they burn out. In modern distributorless ignition systems the distribution of electrical energy to the spark plugs is handled by a coil pack and an electronic control unit, which is really a computer. The entire distributor is eliminated, and with it, the need to service the cap and rotor.

Unnecessary Replacement of Distributor Cap, Rotor, Ignition Wires, and Ignition Coil

Any good quality distributor cap and rotor should provide at least 50,000 miles of trouble-free service. These items should be checked but not necessarily replaced during a routine maintenance tune-up. Many mechanics recommend replacing them frequently as insurance against a possible breakdown. To do so would waste money.

Usually, the only justification for replacing a distributor cap is a condition known as carbon tracking (also called flashover). Carbon tracking is characterized by the presence of fine black lines on the inside surface of the distributor cap. These lines result from electrical leakage and cross firing inside the cap. Poor engine performance is the result, and the only cure is a new cap and rotor. Another legitimate reason to replace a distributor cap is the presence of burned electrodes.

Similarly, a burned rotor tip justifies replacing the rotor.

Like the distributor cap and rotor, ignition wires should not be replaced at every maintenance tune-up. The wires are capable of providing 100,000 miles of service in some instances, and 50,000 miles of useful life is quite common. A defective ignition wire can be identified very quickly using an engine analyzer.

Some repair shops replace only the wire that has failed. This is not advisable. If one ignition wire has failed, others in the set are likely to follow soon thereafter. It is best to replace ignition wires in complete sets.

Ignition coils never should be replaced as a routine maintenance item. Unless your car's coil has failed, a new one will not make the engine run any better.

Unnecessary Fuel Injector Cleaning

Cleaning the fuel injector is almost always a waste of money. Nevertheless, many auto repair shops advertise this service as though it were the answer to most complaints about engine performance. Many mechanics claim that cleaning the fuel injector should be a part of a routine maintenance tune-up. But if you regularly use a major brand of gasoline, it almost always contains all the additives necessary to keep your car's fuel injectors clean and operating perfectly.

In the mid-1980s clogging of electronic fuel injectors became a big problem on cars equipped with multiport fuel injection systems. Systems of this type have an individual injector (Figure 3-75) to supply fuel to each cylinder in the engine. On some cars, the part of the injector known as the pintle can accumulate deposits that restrict the flow of fuel out of the injector. These deposits cause rough idle in less severe cases and engine misfire and poor gas mileage in extreme cases.

Chemists in the petroleum industry went to work on the problem and quickly came up with a solution—special gasoline additives that could actually clean the injectors with the engine operating in normal use. These additives are now found in all good quality gasolines.

Dishonest mechanics attempt to persuade owners of all types of fuel-injected cars that regular cleaning of the fuel injector is a good idea. Even in the days before additives were blended into gasoline to solve clogging, not all types of fuel injectors even experienced the problem. Many cars are equipped with a type of fuel system called throttle body injection. In this system, a single injector, or sometimes a pair of injectors, replaces the carburetor found on older cars. Throttle body injectors are not subject to the sort of clogging problems that used to plague multiport injectors. Furthermore, the same gasoline additives that keep multiport injectors clean ensure the cleanliness of throttle body injectors.

In rare cases you may purchase fuel deficient in additives that cut deposits. If that happens, multiport injectors can begin to clog after only a few hundred miles of driving. Running the engine on gasoline containing the proper additives will clean the deposits very quickly, however. Occasionally a fuel injector can become obstructed due to conditions that fuel additives are unable to prevent. In other cases a fuel injector can leak fuel into the combustion chamber. This does not mean that a general cleaning of the fuel injector is called for. All that is needed is to locate the malfunctioning injector and replace it. Any good mechanic can identify a clogged fuel injector very easily.

Unnecessary Tune-ups to Restore Temporary Loss of Performance Resulting from Disconnection of Battery

Sometimes a consumer is persuaded to pay for a tune-up after the replacement of the vehicle's battery or after a repair that required disconnecting of the battery. On many computerized cars, the computer stores information about the engine's fuel mixture requirements in its memory. This information, called block learn, controls the amount of fuel injected into the engine.

No two engines require exactly the same quantity of fuel under identical operating conditions because of various production tolerances and other variables. Once block learn "learns" your engine's unique requirements, it adjusts the fuel delivery to meet those requirements. If the battery is disconnected for any reason, all the information in block learn is lost. The computer reverts to standard fuel delivery values that are not ideal for your car's engine. After a short pe-

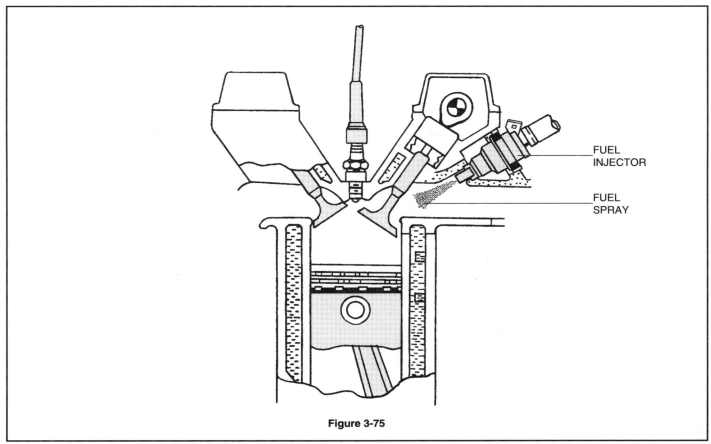

FUEL
INJECTOR

FUEL
SPRAY

Figure 3-75

riod, the computer "relearns" your engine's peculiar running requirements and puts that information back into the block learn memory. Until that happens, the engine can run poorly.

If you bring your car into a repair shop for a new battery and the car enters the shop running fine but leaves running terribly, drive it a few miles after it warms up. It will begin to run normally again. Don't let a mechanic fast-talk you into a tune-up to correct something that will correct itself.

Charges for Work that Should Be Done For Free Under Your Car's 5-year/50,000-mile Emission Controls Warranty

Many consumers who purchase tune-ups to correct engine performance problems wind up paying for much more expensive repairs to correct the malfunctions. A substantial percentage of all these repairs could be obtained for free under the terms of your vehicle's 5-year/50,000-mile emission controls warranty.

Many motorists have been unnecessarily charged for PCV valves, new carburetors, fuel injectors, ignition wires, and dozens of other items that should have been fixed for free under the terms of the 5-year/50,000-mile Vehicle Emission Controls' *Design and Defect Warranty* mandated by the Federal Clean Air Act. Every car and light truck sold in America has this warranty, regardless of whether the vehicle was bought new or used.

If your car's engine is not running correctly, and the vehicle is less than 5 years old and has been driven less than 50,000 miles,

there's a good chance you can get the problem fixed for nothing. Just about anything that can go wrong with a late-model engine generally is covered under the emission controls warranty.

Unfortunately, most drivers are accustomed to getting an annual engine tune-up because cars used to require regular tuning. It is assumed that a tune-up is the solution to an engine performance problem on a late-model car. A basic maintenance tune-up will not correct most engine performance problems.

On many cars, the spark plugs can be used for 30,000 miles and therefore don't need annual replacement. Check your owner's manual for the suggested replacement interval. The spark plugs are covered as emission-control items up to the first suggested replacement interval. So if your car calls for a 30,000-mile spark plug replacement, the plugs are warranted as emission-control items for at least the first 30,000 miles.

In many states, motor vehicle exhaust emissions are tested periodically. If your car fails such a test, you may be entitled to free repairs under the terms of the 2-year/24,000-mile *performance warranty*. This warranty supplements the 5-year/50,000-mile *design and defect* warranty.

Basically, the warranty provides special provisions in those areas where the state or local government has implemented an emissions *inspection/maintenance* program conforming to federal guidelines. If your car fails an emissions test and you are required by state or local law to fix it, the manufacturer must absorb the entire cost for the first

2 years or 24,000 miles. The carmaker has a somewhat more limited liability for 5 years or 50,000 miles. However, repairs not covered under the *performance warranty* may still be covered under the *design and defect warranty.*

Most consumers are surprised at the large number of under-the-hood components covered by the emissions warranty. Here are a few of them:

- Oxygen sensor
- Dual-walled exhaust pipe
- Catalytic converter
- PCV valve
- Fuel injectors
- Carburetor
- On-board computer
- Turbocharger
- Intake manifold
- Exhaust manifold
- Distributor
- Ignition wires
- Spark plugs

Once again, this is only a partial list of covered parts. Unfortunately, it is not always easy to get these items replaced under the emissions warranty. Unwary consumers frequently are charged for these parts by independent repair shops as well as franchised car dealers.

Independent repair shops do not have the authority to bill auto manufacturers for warranty work. Consequently, if such a shop discovers an emissions-related defect, they may not apprise you of your option to go to a car dealership, where the problem can be corrected without charge under the emissions warranty. If you select that option, an independent shop legitimately can charge you for diagnostic time, but car dealerships are not permitted to do so as far as the Environmental Protection Agency is concerned. *No charges for diagnostic time are allowed in connection with work required under the emissions warranty.*

Although new car dealers can get reimbursed by the auto manufacturers for emissions warranty work, the amount the manufacturers are willing to pay is often substantially less than what the dealer normally charges for nonwarranty work. So the dealer has an incentive to attempt to make you pay for emissions warranty work. Your knowledge of your rights under the warranty and your persistence in demanding fair treatment are your best defenses against inappropriate charges.

Both emissions warranties are described in detail in two brochures printed by the Environmental Protection Agency. One is entitled *What You Should Know About Your Auto Emissions Warranty*, and the other is called *If Your Car Just Failed An Emission Test You May Be Entitled To Free Repairs.* To obtain them call (202) 382-2640, or write to: Warranty Complaint, Field Operations and Support Division, U.S. Environmental Protection Agency, Washington, D.C. 20460. You can also contact the Field Operations and Support Division to register a complaint if you think your mechanic has charged you for repairs that should have been done under the emission controls warranty. However, before you grumble, try first to resolve the problem with the management of the car dealership; if that doesn't work, contact the auto manufacturer's zone office and give them an opportunity to intercede on your behalf.

As a footnote to the coverage afforded by the emissions warranty, it should be pointed out that 1990 Clean Air Act Amendments will change the scope of warranty coverage. Beginning with 1995 models, the 5-year, 50,000-mile warranty on most emission parts will be reduced to 2 years/24,000 miles. The exceptions are the catalytic converter, which will be covered for 8 years/80,000 miles, and the on-board computer, which will have similar coverage.

Forcing a Consumer to Spend More Money on Emission-Related Repairs than the Law Requires

If your vehicle fails a state inspection because of excessive exhaust emissions, the law limits the amount of money you are required to spend on repairs to have the car pass the inspection. After the dollar limit has been reached, you do not have to spend any more money, and the vehicle must be considered as having passed the emissions test.

Currently, in California, the limit is $300. In many other areas it averages $100. Consequently, in California a repair shop that fails your vehicle for excessive emissions cannot force you to spend more than $300 to correct the problems.

Beginning in 1995, the liability limit to the consumer will increase to $450, as defined in the 1990 Clean Air Act Amendments.

Maintenance Tips

The following maintenance tips will help ensure a smoothly running engine and help keep maintenance service to a minimum.

- Replace the engine air filter and PCV filter and spark plugs at the interval recommended by the vehicle manufacturer.

- Avoid spilling motor oil on spark plug wires. Motor oil causes the wires to deteriorate and should be wiped off immediately if spilled while oil is being added to the engine.

- Maximize the value of your car's 5-year, 50,000-mile emission control systems warranty. If your engine does not run properly, the malfunction may be covered by the emissions warranty.

- Don't pay for a tune-up every time your car's engine does not run properly. Tune-ups almost never correct engine performance problems. Generally a poorly running engine requires a diagnostic check-up.

Valve Adjustment

(See also Valve Job)

MANY MECHANICS are aware that "tight" valves, that is, valves operating at clearances less than the specified by the carmaker, can burn out prematurely. Some mechanics, however, are not aware of the damage that can be caused by valves that are too loose. Extremely loose valves will be unduly noisy, but noise isn't the biggest problem. When valves are operated with clearances that are too wide, damage to the valve faces can result. The valves are literally pounded into their respective seats, causing distortion of the valve and reduced sealing ability. This problem is more likely in engines that are operated at a high rpm. If your engine is exceptionally noisy and has adjustable valves, get them adjusted right away to avoid valve damage!

Symptoms

Here are some of the symptoms you will notice that indicate the need for a valve adjustment:

1. Loud ticking noise from engine that increases in frequency as engine speed increases.

2. Ticking noise from engine that subsides as engine heats up.

Typical Causes and Corrections

Here are some of the most common causes of the aforementioned symptoms listed in numerical order. If you see a term printed in *italics*, it means that a definition of that term (and possibly an illustration) is found in the section entitled Parts and Terms. If you see a triangle symbol (▲) next to the number of the symptom you are reading, it means that additional information is contained in Mistakes and Ripoffs.

Here are some of the topics covered in detail in Mistakes and Ripoffs:

• Failure to adjust valves with engine at temperature specified by the car manufacturer.

• Charging for a valve adjustment that is not done.

• Mistaking a leaking exhaust manifold for a loose valve or a defective lifter.

Loud Ticking Noise from Engine that Increases in Frequency as Engine Speed Increases (1) ▲

A ticking or clicking noise in the engine compartment is usually caused by a loose valve. On a *pushrod* engine (Figure 3-76) with adjustable valves, the adjustment procedure is very simple. To ensure correct adjustment your mechanic must perform the task with the engine either fully warmed up or cold as specified by the car manufacturer. When valve clearances are specified for a hot

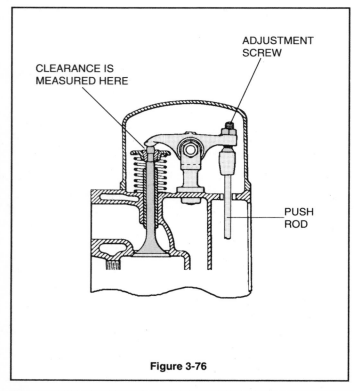

CLEARANCE IS
MEASURED HERE

ADJUSTMENT
SCREW

PUSH
ROD

Figure 3-76

engine, the most accurate valve adjustment is performed with the engine running. If your car has a pushrod engine, ask your mechanic if he is willing to do a valve adjustment with the engine running.

On engines with an overhead camshaft (Figure 3-77), adjusting the valves can be much more difficult. Because clearances are usually measured directly at the base of the camshaft lobe, the valve adjustment cannot be performed with the engine running. Furthermore, because many overhead cam engines use separate camshafts for intake and exhaust valves, accessing the adjustment screws and measurement points can be difficult; consequently, the cost of a valve adjustment is higher than it would be for a pushrod engine. Overhead cam engines with four valves per cylinder cost the most to ad-

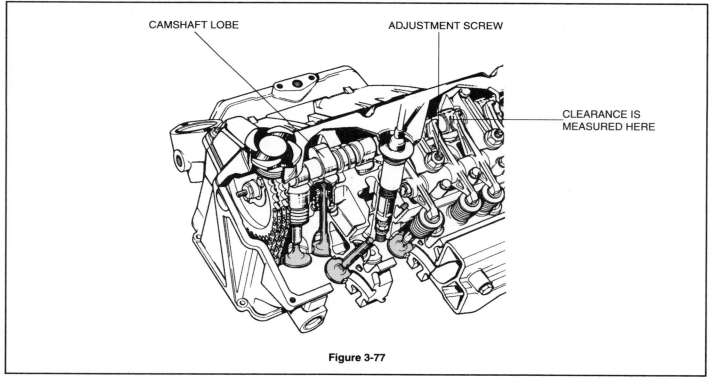

CAMSHAFT LOBE

ADJUSTMENT SCREW

CLEARANCE IS
MEASURED HERE

Figure 3-77

just because there are twice as many adjustments to perform.

Engines having adjustable valves generally have *solid lifters* and may be expected to produce more noise than those designed with *hydraulic lifters*. As the engine wears, the valves tend to get much more noisy than they were when new. Some mechanics try to reduce this noise by reducing valve clearances during an adjustment. This procedure is not wise. Valves that are operated at less than specified clearance will run more quietly, but they will also tend to burn out more quickly. Never encourage your mechanic to tighten your engine's valve adjustments to less than specified dimensions merely to reduce noise.

Ticking Noise from Engine that Subsides as Engine Heats Up (2) ▲

A clicking or ticking noise from the engine that gradually goes away as the engine warms up can be due to a noisy *hydraulic lifter*. A valve lifter is depicted in Figure 3-78. The camshaft lobe pushes the lifter upward, which in turn forces the pushrod in the same direction. The pushrod rotates the rocker arm, which forces the valve downward against its spring, thereby opening the valve. In an engine equipped with solid mechanical lifters, a small amount of clearance is required between the valve stem and the rocker arm as shown in Figure 3-78.

In engines equipped with hydraulic lifters, there should be no clearance. The inside of the lifter is filled with motor oil, which acts as a cushion that gently forces the pushrod upward and opens the valve. The oil in the

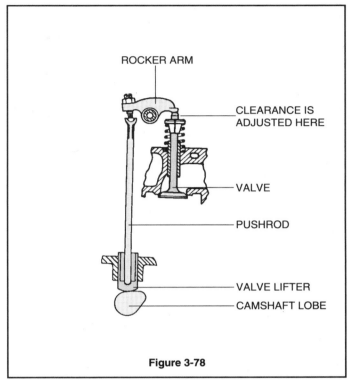

Figure 3-78

lifter takes up any play or clearance between the valve stem and the rocker arm; however, if the lifter leaks oil, clearance can develop and a ticking noise will be heard. The ticking noise is caused by the rocker arm tapping on the valve stem.

Typically, a defective hydraulic lifter leaks oil when the engine is turned off. The instant the engine is started, the excessive clearance between the rocker arm and the valve stem causes a lot of noise. As the engine warms up, the lifter fills with motor oil and gradually reduces the stem-to-rocker clearance, and the noise abates.

Some hydraulic valve systems are adjustable. If you hear a lot of valve noise when the engine is cold, an adjustment could eliminate the problem. On other engines there is no adjustment possible. In this case replacement of one or more lifters may be required.

Before you allow your mechanic to replace the lifters in your engine to correct a ticking noise, find out if the lifters are adjustable and ask him to try an adjustment first. Replacing hydraulic valve lifters is a difficult and expensive job—adjusting the valves is not.

Parts and Terms

If your car needs a valve adjustment, your mechanic could mention one or more of the following terms:

Hydraulic Lifter A valve lifter is shown in Figure 3-78. Lifters can be either mechanical (solid) or oil filled (hydraulic). Engines equipped with hydraulic lifters are quieter than those containing solid lifters.

Pushrod Pushrods are used in nonoverhead cam engines. The pushrod acts on the rocker arm to force the valve open. A pushrod is shown in Figure 3-78.

Rocker Arm A rocker arm is a lever that forces an engine valve to open. Pushrod engines always have rocker arms. Such a design is shown in Figure 3-78. Overhead cam engines may or may not have rocker arms. The design shown in Figure 3-77 does, but in some high performance engines the cam lobe may act directly on the valve stem with no rocker arm to assist the valve opening process.

Solid Lifters See Hydraulic Lifter.

Tappet Tappet is a term often used interchangeably with *lifter*.

Mistakes and Ripoffs

The following information will help you control the cost of a valve adjustment. The topics covered are those most likely to be associated with errors commonly made by mechanics or deliberate attempts to defraud the consumer.

Failure to Adjust Valves with Engine at Temperature Specified by the Car Manufacturer

Car manufacturers specify whether engine valves should be adjusted with the engine cold or fully warmed up. Frequently, mechanics don't bother to wait for an engine to cool down before performing a valve adjustment. If your engine sounds unusually noisy after the valves have been adjusted, it could be that your mechanic failed to do the job with the engine at the right temperature.

Charging for a Valve Adjustment that is Not Done

It is fairly common for mechanics to charge customers for valve adjustments that are never done. If your engine does not sound particularly noisy at the time the maintenance schedule calls for a valve adjustment, there is a chance your mechanic may not do it.

If you have any doubts about the honesty of the shop you are doing business with, you can mark the fastener on the valve cover to make sure that a mechanic at least went through the motions of removing the cover to access the valve mechanism.

Put a small dab of paint or colored nail polish on one of the nuts or bolts (Figure 3-79) that fasten the valve cover to the cylinder head. The paint must touch the nut or bolt and a portion of the valve cover itself. Pick an inconspicuous location and make the dab of paint very small so as not to advertise your actions. If the paint has not been disturbed, you know that the hardware was not removed and that the valve adjustment could not have been done. In that case, get your money back and find another shop.

Mistaking a Leaking Exhaust Manifold for a Loose Valve or a Defective Lifter

A leaking exhaust manifold (see Figure 3-79) can mimic the noise produced by a defective hydraulic lifter. Many mechanics fail to tighten the exhaust manifold bolts and mistake the noise for a bad lifter.

Maintenance Tips

The following maintenance tips will help you control the cost of valve adjustments and ensure that accurate adjustments are performed:

- Do not have engine valves adjusted more frequently than the car manufacturer suggests. To do so would waste money. If the valves require more frequent adjustment, there is a defect in the adjustment mechanism or a problem with one or more lifters or the camshaft.

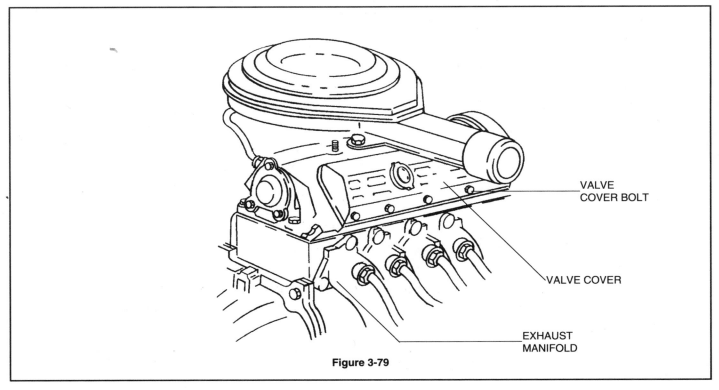

VALVE COVER BOLT

VALVE COVER

EXHAUST MANIFOLD

Figure 3-79

- If your car's engine has hydraulic lifters, a valve adjustment is generally not required. Check your owner's manual.

- Do not race the engine when it is started, particularly in cold weather. Give the hydraulic lifters a minute to pump up fully with oil.

- Mark the valve's cover to verify that it was removed if you have any doubts about the integrity of the repair shop you are dealing with.

Valve Job

(See also Valve Adjustment)

THERE WAS a time in automotive history when the "carbon and valve job" was regularly performed. Now, improved metallurgy and cleaner unleaded gasoline have made the need for valve work far more infrequent than it used to be. With proper maintenance, most cars should not require valve work for more than 100,000 miles of use.

Symptoms

Here are some of the symptoms you will notice that indicate the need for a valve job:

1. Engine runs rough, idles rough, misfires, or backfires.

2. Engine fails emissions test.

Typical Causes and Corrections

Here are some of the most common causes of the aforementioned symptoms listed in numerical order. If you see a term printed in *italics*, it means that a definition of that term (and possibly an illustration) is found in the section entitled Parts and Terms. If you see a triangle symbol (▲) next to the number of the symptom you are reading, it means that additional information is contained in Mistakes and Ripoffs.

Here are some of the topics covered in detail in Mistakes and Ripoffs:

- Failure to check valve adjustment before diagnosing burned valves.

- Failure to test compression with the engine fully warmed up.

- Charging the consumer for a valve job when only valve stem seals are required.

- Charging the consumer for a completely rebuilt cylinder head when only one valve is actually repaired.

Engine Runs Rough, Idles Rough, Misfires, or Backfires (1) ▲

Rough idle, misfiring, and backfiring can be caused by one or more burned valves; however, there are several other causes for these symptoms. To verify valve trouble, a mechanic could perform a *dynamic cylinder compression test* and a *power balance test* using an engine analyzer. If valve problems are indicated, the mechanic can confirm his suspicions by doing an actual *dry compression test* and a *wet compression test* of the cylinder. A compression test determines how much pressure is developed in a cylinder during engine cranking, thereby indicating leakage due to burned valves or bad rings.

Low compression in a cylinder can be due to a burned valve, usually an exhaust valve. Figure 3-80 shows a typical cylinder head as it would appear if you were looking down into it with the valve cover cut away. Exhaust valves are much hotter than intake valves,

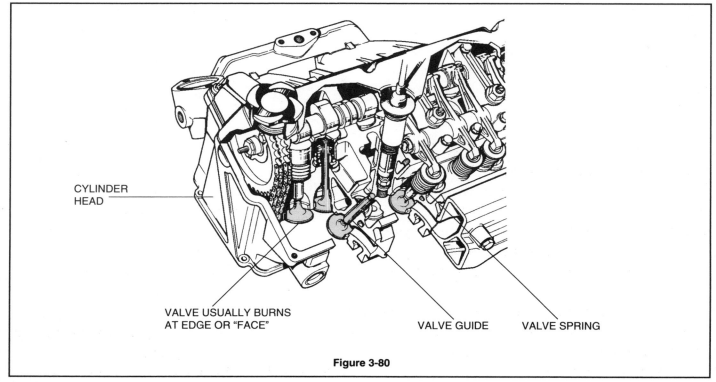

CYLINDER HEAD

VALVE USUALLY BURNS AT EDGE OR "FACE"

VALVE GUIDE

VALVE SPRING

Figure 3-80

and their higher temperature accounts for why they burn more frequently than do intake valves. When a valve burns, it generally burns at its edge or face. A burned valve cannot fully seal the combustion chamber against leakage of compressed gasses. The result is low compression.

If your mechanic tells you your car requires a valve job, ask him how he checked the engine's compression. Both a dry and wet compression test should be performed to confirm a burned valve. In a dry test, the engine is cranked with a compression gauge screwed into the cylinder being tested, and the compression is recorded. Then some motor oil is squirted into the cylinder, and the test is repeated. This is called a wet compression test. The oil put in the cylinder seals the piston rings. If the compression in-

creases significantly during the wet test, low compression is due to bad piston rings, not a burned valve.

Before you allow your mechanic to do a valve job on your car, make sure he checks the valve adjustment first. On an engine with solid lifters, improper adjustment can produce the same low compression readings as do a burned valve. A simple valve adjustment is much less expensive than a valve job. If an engine has been driven for a long period with valves that are too tight, that is, improperly adjusted, the valves can burn. In this case, even after they are adjusted they will leak. Your mechanic must first adjust the valves, then perform another compression test to determine whether they are seating properly. Seating refers to a valve's ability to seal the combustion chamber.

Engine Fails Emissions Test (2)

A burned valve can cause an engine to fail an emission test. Usually, the emission of hydrocarbons will be too high. Refer to symptom number one for additional details about confirming a burned valve.

Parts and Terms

If your car needs valve work, your mechanic could mention one or more of the following terms:

Cylinder Power Balance Test This test is done using an engine analyzer. The engine analyzer turns off the spark to a cylinder and records the drop in the engine rpm that results from disabling the cylinder. The process is repeated for each cylinder of the engine. A cylinder that experiences a lower drop in rpm than all the other cylinders has a power imbalance. In other words, that cylinder is developing less power when its spark plug is firing so it has less effect on the engine's rpm when the spark plug is disabled. A cylinder that appears weak in a test of dynamic power balance could have a burned valve. A power balance test is not conclusive. Additional tests are required to confirm the diagnosis of a burned valve.

Dry Compression Test This test measures the compression in an engine's cylinder. A compression gauge is screwed into the cylinder, and the engine is cranked. The gauge is then read to determine the pressure developed in the cylinder. Low compression can be due to burned valves or worn piston rings. This problem can be confirmed by performing a wet compression test. A dry compression test should be done with the engine fully warmed up.

Dynamic Compression Test A dynamic compression test is performed using an engine analyzer. The engine is cranked, and the amount of current being drawn from the battery by the starter on the compression stroke of each cylinder is precisely measured by the engine analyzer. If current draw is relatively low for a particular cylinder, that cylinder can have a burned valve.

Valve Stem Seal The purpose of a valve stem seal is prevention of oil leakage past the valve stem into the combustion chamber. Figure 3-81 shows where a valve stem seal

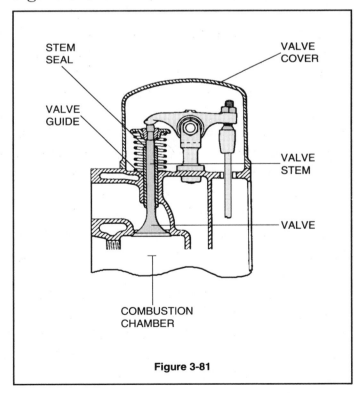

Figure 3-81

is located in a typical engine. The valve cover does just what its name implies—it provides a metal canopy over the valve mechanism. On many cars, the valve cover contains a cap that can be removed to add oil to the engine. The stem seal is a part made from rubber compound that fits over the valve guide and around the valve stem. The seal prevents oil from leaking into the combustion chamber, where it will burn. Many cases of high oil consumption and blue smoke from the exhaust are caused by worn and leaking valve stem seals.

Wet Compression Test During a wet compression test the engine is cranked with a compression gauge screwed into the cylinder being tested, and the compression is recorded. Then some motor oil is squirted into the cylinder and the test is repeated. Again the compression is recorded. If the wet compression increases significantly, low compression is due to bad piston rings, not a burned valve.

Mistakes and Ripoffs

The following information will help you control the cost of valve work. The topics covered are those most likely to be associated with errors commonly made by mechanics or deliberate attempts to defraud the consumer.

Failure to Check Valve Adjustment Before Diagnosing Burned Valves

On many overhead cam engines the valves will become too tight if they are not periodically adjusted. When valves are too tight, they do not seat properly, that is, they do not fully seal the combustion chamber. This causes low compression, the same symptom that would occur if the valves were burned. Seeing low compression, some mechanics jump to the conclusion that a valve job is required when a simple valve adjustment might restore normal engine operation.

Failure to Test Compression with the Engine Fully Warmed Up

Do not be deceived into believing your car's engine needs a valve job because of low compression readings recorded while the engine is cold. To be accurate, compression tests must be done with the engine fully warmed up.

Charging the Consumer for a Valve Job When Only Valve Stem Seals are Required

Worn or damaged valve stem seals will cause high oil consumption and blue smoke from the exhaust. Often consumers are told the only cure for the problem is a valve job. This is not true. Valve stem seals can usually be replaced without removing the cylinder head(s) from the engine, and replacing or grinding of the valves themselves is certainly not required. Refer to Parts and Terms for more information about valve stem seals.

Charging the Consumer for a Completely Rebuilt Cylinder Head When Only One Valve is Actually Repaired

If your car has less than 75,000 miles of use and its engine develops a burned valve, it is often satisfactory to repair the affected valve alone and not disturb the others. Unfortunately, some mechanics charge the consumer for a complete rebuilding of the cylinder head even though they have only fixed one bad valve.

Figure 3-80 shows a typical cylinder head and its components, including the valves. Most engines have two valves per cylinder, one intake valve and one exhaust valve. Engines with four valves per cylinder are becoming more popular, however. Valve failure usually involves burning of an exhaust valve at the valve face. Figure 3-82 shows a typical engine valve. If the face burns, a new valve may be required; however, it can sometimes be repaired by grinding it. If the old valve is ground, the valve stem and tulip (Figure 3-82) are cleaned to remove accumulated carbon. Then the face of the valve is ground on a machine shown in Figure 3-83. Also, the valve seat on the cylinder head is ground with a grinding stone as shown in Figure 3-84.

In a situation in which your engine has a single burned valve, grinding only the dam-

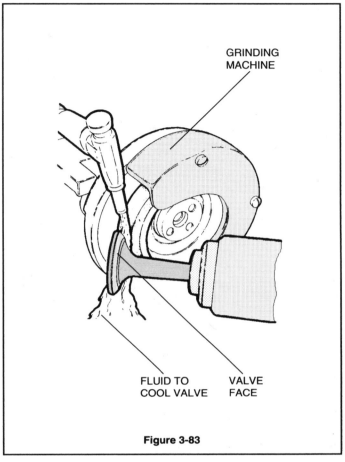

Figure 3-83

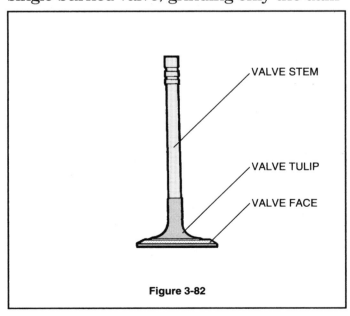

Figure 3-82

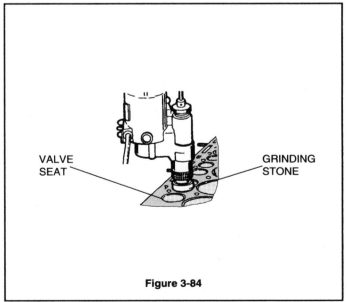

Figure 3-84

aged valve and its seat on the cylinder head could suffice. On engines with less than 75,000 miles this procedure could be a perfectly good solution, assuming that's all you are paying for. Sometimes, though, consumers are charged for a complete cylinder head overhaul instead of repair of the affected valve. A complete overhaul of the cylinder head includes substantial additional work, including reconditioning *all* the valve guides, and *all* the valves and valve seats, testing and replacing weak valve springs, milling the cylinder head to ensure a flat gasket surface, and chemically cleaning the cylinder head and testing it for cracks. This work is usually done in a machine shop. If your mechanic claims a full overhaul was done on your engine's cylinder head, you can ask him to show you his bill from the machine shop if you are not fully confident in his integrity. Keep in mind that some auto repair shops are equipped to do complete machine shop work, so your mechanic may not have needed to send the cylinder head to an outside facility. Also, you must be aware that a machine shop will charge your mechanic a lot less than it would charge you if you brought the cylinder head there yourself. This kind of pricing is called a trade discount and allows your mechanic to make a profit when you are billed for the job. You can expect a fair markup of at least 20 percent on any outside machine shop work your mechanic bills to you.

If your engine has been driven more than 75,000 miles and has a single burned valve, it would be a good idea to recondition all the valves in the cylinder head. If to save money you want to pay only for a temporary patch job, fixing the burned valve would do, but chances are the other valves would have deteriorated sufficiently to justify attention while the cylinder head is removed from the engine. Consequently, when an engine has been used more than 75,000 miles, it is generally best to opt for a complete overhaul of the cylinder head if you intend to keep the car. It will cost you more, but it is worth it.

Maintenance Tips

The following maintenance tips will help ensure maximum life of your engine's valves and minimal cost of repair if your engine experiences valve failure:

- If your car's engine has adjustable valves, make sure they are adjusted at least as frequently as recommended by the manufacturer.

- If your engine has a single burned valve, it is usually satisfactory to repair only the affected valve if the car has been driven less than 75,000 miles. A complete cylinder head overhaul is usually a better choice if the car's been driven more than 75,000 miles.

- If your engine is using a lot of oil and blue smoke is billowing out of the exhaust pipe, the problem could be caused by worn or damaged valve stem seals. Usually, the cylinder head does not have to be removed from the engine to replace valve stem seals. Also, a valve job is not necessary when valve stem seals are required.

Wheel Alignment

(See also Shock Absorbers, and Wheel Balancing)

WHEEL ALIGNMENT is an area of automotive service where consumers are likely to encounter deceitful practices by mechanics and repair shops. Every year countless numbers of motorists are sold wheel alignments on cars that don't need them. Typically, the customer complains about a vibration or shimmy in the steering wheel at speeds over 40 miles per hour. A shop manager or mechanic leads the customer to believe that aligning and balancing the wheels will correct the problem. In fact, balancing the wheels might fix the problem, but alignment is a waste of money. Wheel alignment can correct certain kinds of handling difficulties and tire wear, but it will not rectify vibration problems.

Most cases of steering wheel vibration and front-end shimmy are caused by improper wheel/tire balance or out-of-round tires. More likely than an out-of-round tire is one that is not properly balanced. Left this way over thousands of miles of driving, the tire will wear unevenly, displaying scalloped depressions or cups on the tread. If these depressions get deep enough, the tire becomes so noisy that it can sound as though a wheel bearing were failing.

It is not uncommon for new cars to roll off the assembly line with improperly balanced tires. If you feel a steering wheel vibration in a new car, make sure your dealer checks wheel balance before cups begin to form. On older cars, you should always suspect incorrect wheel/tire balance as the cause of vibration and get this problem tended to before you try new shock absorbers or major repairs of the front suspension. A lot of mechanics mistakenly or deceitfully try to sell their customers new ball joints and shock absorbers, along with a wheel balance and front end alignment as a packaged deal to fix a steering wheel vibration. Unless you trust your mechanic, go for the wheel balancing alone and get a second opinion about the need for additional work.

Symptoms

Here are some of the symptoms you will notice that may indicate the need for a wheel alignment:

1. Car pulls to one side on a flat road.

2. One or more tires worn out on inner or outer edge.

3. Feathered edges on tires.

4. Tires scuff or make screeching sound going around corners.

5. Steering wheel does not tend to return to center on its own after turning a corner.

6. Steering wheel spokes not centered when you are driving straight ahead on a flat road.

Typical Causes and Corrections

Here are some of the most common causes of the aforementioned symptoms listed in numerical order. If you see a term printed in *italics*, it means that a definition of that term (and possibly an illustration) is found in the section entitled Parts and Terms. If you see a triangle symbol (▲) next to the number of the symptom you are reading, it means that additional information is contained in Mistakes and Ripoffs.

Here are some of the topics covered in detail in Mistakes and Ripoffs:

• The performance of a wheel alignment on a car having worn or damaged steering components.

• The performance of a wheel alignment on a car having incorrect riding height.

• Failure to align front wheels to the thrust angle instead of the geometric centerline.

• Failure to check and disable the electronic system controlling the ride height before performing wheel alignment.

• Failure to align vehicle with a full gas tank and its spare tire in trunk, or with miscellaneous heavy objects removed from trunk.

• Unnecessary replacement of ball joints or struts.

• Unnecessary wheel alignment to correct steering wheel vibration.

Car Pulls to One Side on a Flat Road (1) ▲

If your car pulls or drifts to one side as you drive on a flat road, don't immediately assume a wheel alignment is necessary. First, make sure tire pressure is set properly. Then check the tires for uneven wear. If wear is uniform, pulling to one side could be caused by an internal problem in one of the tires. Have the front wheel and tire assemblies interchanged, that is, install the right front tire on the left and the left front tire on the right. If the pull disappears or changes to the opposite direction, you have a tire problem. The only cure is a new set of tires.

Pulling to one side or the other can also be caused by an incorrect steering *caster*, an alignment angle your mechanic can adjust during a wheel alignment. An incorrectly angled caster can cause your car to drift to one side without causing any abnormal tire wear. The side with the wheel that has the most negative caster angle is the side the car pulls to. On some cars this is not adjustable, in which case replacement of some suspension parts is needed.

Cars that have adjustable rear suspensions can be pulled to one side by an incorrect *thrust angle*. The thrust angle must be the same as the geometric centerline of the car. Figure 3-85 shows what is meant by thrust angle. The straight line drawn through the center of the vehicle is the geometric centerline. This forms a 90-degree angle with a line drawn across the front tires when they are steered straight ahead. Notice that an

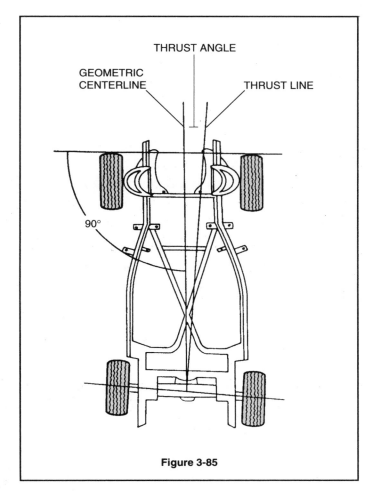

GEOMETRIC CENTERLINE

THRUST ANGLE

THRUST LINE

90°

Figure 3-85

steer in a direction other than that toward which the front wheels are steered. This happens because the rear tires actually establish a direction of their own when a trust angle exists; they don't just follow the front tires.

Ideally, the thrust angle should be 0 degrees. When this is the case, all four wheels form a perfect rectangle. Unfortunately, due to production tolerances, a car may have a built-in thrust angle that can't be changed. If this is true, the front wheels should be aligned not to the geometric centerline, but to the thrust line formed by the rear axle. If a mechanic fails to perform this step, the car may pull to one side even though the front wheels seem to be correctly aligned.

One or More Tires Worn Out on Inner or Outer Edge (2) ▲

One or more tires worn out on the inner or outer edge indicate the need for a camber adjustment, which can be done during a routine wheel alignment. Figure 3-86 shows a typical wear pattern on the edge of its tire that is attributable to improper camber adjustment. Wear on the outside edge is due to

imaginary line drawn through the centers of the back wheels is not parallel with the imaginary line drawn across the face of the front tires. This is because the entire rear axle is skewed, or twisted, a few degrees with respect to the geometric centerline of the vehicle. Notice the line drawn perpendicular (at a right angle) to the rear axle. This is the thrust line. It intersects the horizontal line across the front tires just to the right of the geometric centerline. The angle formed between the geometric centerline and the thrust line is the thrust angle. The thrust angle tends to cause the vehicle to thrust or

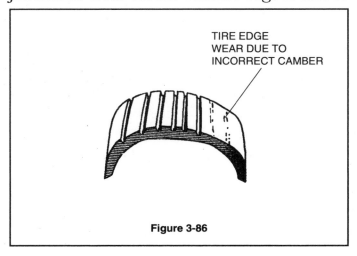

TIRE EDGE WEAR DUE TO INCORRECT CAMBER

Figure 3-86

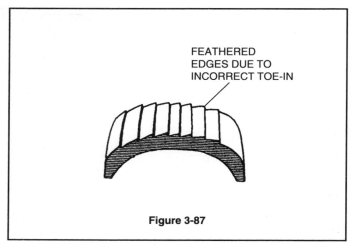

FEATHERED EDGES DUE TO INCORRECT TOE-IN

Figure 3-87

excessive *positive* camber, whereas too much *negative* camber accounts for wear on the inside edge. Either way, resetting camber can be a time-consuming process on many cars, so expect to pay for a complete wheel alignment to restore proper front end geometry.

Often mechanics make the mistake of adjusting camber on cars that have sagging springs. Such an effort will not produce a satisfactory wheel alignment. Another mistake commonly made by some mechanics is the failure to check and then turn off the electronic system controlling the ride height (on cars so equipped) before they perform a camber adjustment.

Feathered Edges on Tires (3)

Feathered edges on front or rear tires indicate an incorrect *toe-in* setting. Figure 3-87 shows a typical wear pattern due to an improperly adjusted toe-in setting. Most cars are aligned so that the front wheels are not perfectly parallel, as shown in Figure 3-88. This illustration greatly exaggerates how much farther apart the back of the tires are as compared with the front tires. In actual-

ity, the difference may only be 1/16 of an inch or so. When the car is driven on the highway, the wheels tend to spread apart, thereby eliminating the 1/16-inch difference and enabling the wheels to become parallel.

Tires Scuff or Make Screeching Sound Going Around Corners (4)

A car's front wheels do not remain exactly parallel in a turn because the outer tire must travel a greater distance than the inner tire. A good way to envision this phenomenon is to picture a running track. To go one lap around the track, the runners on the outside lanes must go a greater distance than those on the inside lanes.

If the front wheels remained parallel in a turn, one tire would drag across the road, causing squeal and excessive scuffing. Con-

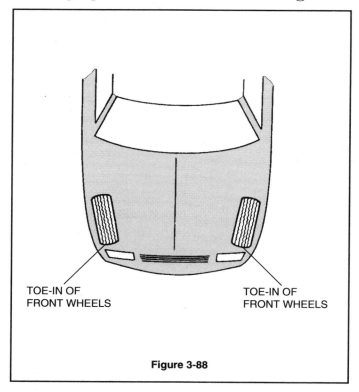

TOE-IN OF FRONT WHEELS

TOE-IN OF FRONT WHEELS

Figure 3-88

sequently, steering systems are designed with a geometry known as *toe-out on turns.* This angle can be checked during a wheel alignment. Sometimes, mechanics fail to check toe-out on turns. It is possible to adjust *toe-in* correctly and still have a problem with toe-out on turns. This happens when certain steering parts are bent. If your car experiences tire scuffing and squealing on turns make sure your mechanic checks toe-out on turns. If toe-out on turns is not at manufacturer's specifications, one or both steering arms are bent and must be replaced. Figure 3-89 shows a typical steering arm on a MacPherson strut front suspension. Toe-out on turns is not adjustable. Never allow your mechanic to heat your car's steering arms with a torch in an attempt to straighten them to correct a toe-out problem. Heating a steering arm could cause it to fracture later on, resulting in loss of steering control.

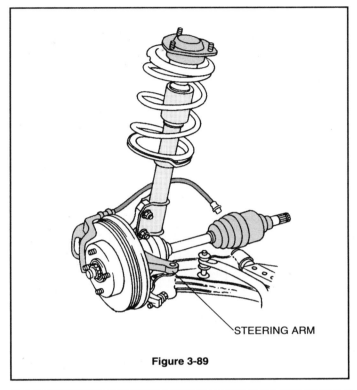

STEERING ARM

Figure 3-89

Steering Wheel Does Not Tend to Return to Center on its Own After Turning a Corner (5)

When you turn a corner, your car's steering wheel should tend to return to the straight-ahead position on its own, with minimal steering effort on your part. This is called self-centering. If the car tends to remain in a turn, it indicates a maladjustment of the *caster angle,* or incorrect *steering axis inclination* due to bent suspension parts.

Figure 3-90 depicts the caster angle. Notice that the upper ball joint is tilted back toward the steering wheel, whereas the lower ball joint is tilted forward toward the front of the car. On a car with a MacPherson strut

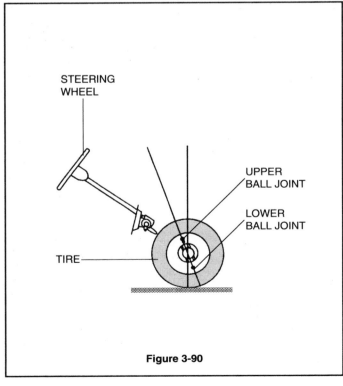

STEERING WHEEL

UPPER BALL JOINT

LOWER BALL JOINT

TIRE

Figure 3-90

suspension, the top of the strut would be tilted back toward the steering wheel. This is called positive caster. An everyday example of positive caster is seen in the design of most bicycles, on which the top of the front fork is angled back toward the rider. Positive caster is what enables a rider to ride without placing his or her hands on the handlebars. The bicycle tends to steer itself straight ahead. Similarly, a car with positive caster tends to steer itself straight ahead. If the steering wheel does not tend to return to the straight-ahead position in a turn, it could be due to an incorrect caster setting. On some cars the caster is not adjustable during a wheel alignment. If the caster setting is wrong, it could be due to bent steering parts, in which case the damaged parts must be replaced.

Another possible cause of the car's failure to self-center is an incorrect steering axis inclination. Steering axis inclination is de-

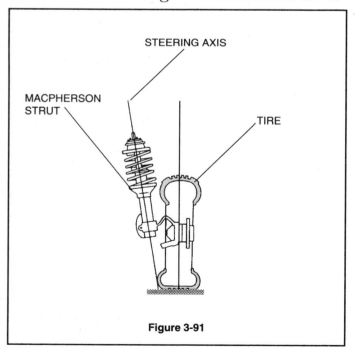

MACPHERSON STRUT

STEERING AXIS

TIRE

Figure 3-91

picted in Figure 3-91. Notice that an imaginary line drawn through the center of the MacPherson strut is inclined a few degrees with respect to true vertical. This imaginary line through the strut is the steering axis, and the number of degrees it is tilted is called the steering axis inclination. Steering axis inclination is not adjustable. If it is not correct, it indicates a bent steering knuckle or a bent spindle (front axle). Mechanics sometimes fail to check the steering axis inclination during a wheel alignment. Advise your mechanic to check this alignment angle if your car does not seem to self-center on turns.

Steering Wheel Spokes Not Centered When You are Driving Straight Ahead on a Flat Road (6) ▲

During a wheel alignment it is possible to adjust toe-in (see symptom three for an explanation of toe-in) correctly without properly centering the steering wheel. This happens when the toe-in is adjusted without ensuring that the front wheels are parallel with the rear wheels with the steering wheel perfectly centered. It is not uncommon for mechanics to make this mistake.

On cars with adjustable rear suspensions, the steering wheel may not be centered if the mechanic fails to align the wheels to the thrust line instead of the geometric centerline of the car. See symptom one for an explanation of thrust line.

Parts and Terms

If your car requires a wheel alignment, your mechanic could mention one or more of the following terms or components. Remember to refer to Mistakes and Ripoffs for the detailed information you need to help control the cost of wheel alignments.

Camber   Camber is a wheel alignment angle. It describes the number of degrees the top of a wheel is tilted out from the car body or in toward the car body. Improper camber causes tire wear on the inner or outer edge of the tire. Figure 3-92 shows negative camber in a MacPherson strut suspension. The amount of negative camber shown will cause wear on the inside edge of the tire.

Caster   Figure 3-90 depicts the caster angle. Notice that the upper ball joint is tilted back toward the steering wheel, whereas the lower ball joint is tilted forward toward the front of the car. On a car with a MacPherson strut suspension, the top of the strut would be tilted back toward the steering wheel. This angle is called positive caster. An incorrect caster angle can cause a car to pull to one side of the road.

Steering Axis Inclination   Steering axis inclination is also called the ball joint angle or king pin inclination. On strut suspensions, the steering axis inclination is the number of degrees of tilt of an imaginary line through the strut and the lower ball joint (see Figure 3-91). On nonstrut suspensions the imaginary line of steering axis inclination intersects the center of the upper and lower ball joint. Steering axis inclination is not adjustable. If it is not correct, it indicates a bent steering knuckle or a bent spindle.

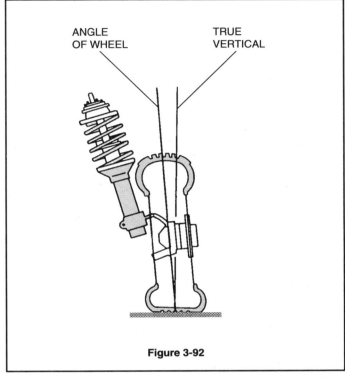

ANGLE OF WHEEL   TRUE VERTICAL

Figure 3-92

Thrust Angle   Thrust angle is basically the line of direction along which the rear wheels tend to steer a car. On cars with adjustable rear suspensions, wheels should be aligned to the thrust line, not the geometric centerline of the car. Thrust angle is depicted in Figure 3-85.

Toe-in   Toe-in is the difference in distance between the extreme front of the front tires (or the rear tires) and the extreme back of the front tires (or the rear tires). Toe-in is shown in Figure 3-88. Incorrect toe-in causes the tires to wear in a feathered-edge pattern.

Toe-out on Turns   In a turn, the outside wheel turns at less of an angle than does the inside wheel. The difference in the turning angles, called toe-out on turns, is illustrated in Figure 3-93.

Mistakes and Ripoffs

The following information will help you control the cost of wheel alignments. The topics covered are those most likely to be associated with errors commonly made by mechanics or deliberate attempts to defraud the consumer.

The Performance of a Wheel Alignment on a Car Having Worn or Damaged Steering Components

On a car that has been driven 75,000 miles or more, significant wear of steering components such as ball joints, tie rod ends, and control arm bushings is fairly common. Before a mechanic performs a wheel alignment, he must first verify that no excess wear is present in any steering parts and that no parts are bent or otherwise damaged. If an alignment is done on a car having one or more of these problems, the car may steer adequately for a short while, only to start to pull to one side or the other shortly thereafter or develop other steering difficulties.

The Performance of a Wheel Alignment on a Car Having Incorrect Riding Height

If a car sags to one side, it usually indicates a weak or broken spring. It is impossible to do a satisfactory wheel alignment on such a car. Before performing a wheel alignment, the mechanic must check the car's riding height. Depending on the make of car, the riding height may be measured from the

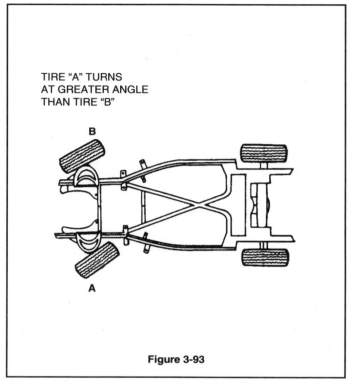

TIRE "A" TURNS AT GREATER ANGLE THAN TIRE "B"

B

A

Figure 3-93

inside fender well to the road, from the top of the front and rear bumpers to the road, from a suspension or chassis part to the road, or from other locations. The measuring points established by the car manufacturer must be observed by the mechanic to verify that the car is at riding level and at the proper height to ensure a correct wheel alignment.

Failure to Align Front Wheels to the Thrust Angle Instead of the Geometric Centerline

If a car with an adjustable rear suspension is aligned to the geometric centerline instead of the thrust line, it is very likely that the car will drift to one side of the road. Also, the steering wheel will probably not be centered while the car is moving straight ahead. Mechanics often fail to do a wheel alignment to the thrust line because it takes more time and requires special alignment equipment not available in all repair shops. See symptom one for more details about thrust angle and thrust line.

Failure to Check and Disable the Electronic System Controlling Ride Height Before Performing Wheel Alignment

Some high-priced cars are equipped with electronic control of the car's ride height. This system automatically levels the car in response to the weight placed in it and to road surface conditions. If this electronic system is not operating, there is no point in doing a wheel alignment. Furthermore, if the ride height is not properly calibrated, the alignment will not be satisfactory because the vehicle will not ride levelly.

When a vehicle with electronic control of ride height is aligned, the control system must be turned off. Failure to do so will likely result in improper camber and toe-in adjustment. If you have a car equipped with an electronic control system and it doesn't seem to steer properly after a wheel alignment, ask your mechanic to recheck the ride height and recheck alignment specifications with the system turned off.

Failure to Align Vehicle with a Full Gas Tank and Its Spare Tire in Trunk, or with Miscellaneous Heavy Objects Removed from Trunk

Wheel alignment specifications set by car manufacturers are based on the assumption that the alignment is checked with no passengers or extra weight in the car, a full gas tank, and nothing in the trunk except the spare tire and the jack. Mechanics often fail to check the trunk for heavy items that must be removed. They also fail to remind the customer that a full tank of gas is necessary to properly load the suspension.

Unnecessary Replacement of Ball Joints or Struts

Some auto repair shops advertise greatly discounted wheel alignments to lure customers. Although there are occasional sales in auto service, the motive behind continuously low prices is often the sale of expensive front suspension repairs that may not be needed. High on the list of parts unscrupulous shops try to sell customers are ball joints and struts. If you respond to an advertisement for a low-priced wheel alignment and the mechanic tries to sell you new ball joints and/or struts, get a second opinion unless you have been doing business with your mechanic for some time and trust his judgment and integrity.

Unnecessary Wheel Alignment to Correct Steering Wheel Vibration

A favorite tactic of dishonest mechanics involves selling a customer a wheel alignment to correct a vibration in the steering wheel. Improper wheel alignment does not cause vibration. Improper wheel balance does. If you have a problem with steering wheel vibration, the cheapest and usually most successful solution is wheel balancing. Sometimes worn steering parts can cause vibration; these parts can be checked when the wheel balancing is done.

Maintenance Tips

The following maintenance tips will help you ensure maximum suspension life and avoid costly wheel alignments, or obtain a better wheel alignment when one is necessary:

- Have your car's suspension greased at least as often as the manufacturer recommends. Check your owner's manual for the lubrication schedule. If your car does not have grease fittings, ask your mechanic to install them (on some cars there is no provision for the installation of grease fittings).

- If you have a problem involving steering wheel vibration, don't expect a wheel alignment to correct it—the two are not related.

- Have your car's front wheels balanced every 15,000 miles or sooner if you feel a vibration in the steering wheel. This step will greatly reduce wear of steering parts.

- If you have a car with an adjustable rear suspension, make sure your mechanic is familiar with the techniques for four-wheel alignment.

- Don't have an alignment done by a shop that uses portable equipment. The most accurate alignments are done on drive-on racks.

- Ask your mechanic when he last had his alignment equipment calibrated. Uncalibrated equipment can produce incorrect alignment and premature tire wear. If your mechanic has no idea when his alignment equipment was last calibrated, you might consider another shop.

Wheel Balancing

(See also Shock Absorbers,
and Wheel Alignment)

Symptoms

If you feel a vibration in your car's steering wheel at speeds over 30 mph, the most likely cause is an imbalanced wheel. Here are some of the symptoms you will notice that indicate the need for wheel balancing:

1. Vibration in steering wheel and/or front end shimmy at speeds over 30 mph. Vibration may disappear as velocity is increased.

2. Vibration in rear of car or vibration felt in driver's seat.

Typical Causes and Corrections

Here are some of the most common causes of the aforementioned symptoms listed in numerical order. If you see a term printed in *italics*, it means that a definition of that term (and possibly an illustration) is found in the section entitled Parts and Terms. If you see a triangle symbol (▲) next to the number of the symptom you are reading, it means that additional information is contained in Mistakes and Ripoffs.

Here are some of the topics covered in detail in Mistakes and Ripoffs:

- Unnecessary replacement of shock absorbers to correct steering wheel vibration.

- Unnecessary wheel alignment to correct steering wheel vibration.

- Failure to check for out-of-round tires or bent wheels when wheels are balanced.

- Failure to dynamically balance wheel and hub as an assembly.

Vibration in Steering Wheel and/or Front End Shimmy (1) ▲

Most cases of steering wheel vibration and front end shimmy are caused by improper *static* or *dynamic* imbalance of a wheel/tire assembly. Left unbalanced over thousands of miles of driving, the tire will wear unevenly, displaying scalloped depressions or cups on the tread (Figure 3-94). If these depressions get deep enough, the tire becomes so noisy that it can sound as though a wheel bearing were failing.

It is not uncommon for new cars to roll off the assembly line with improperly balanced tires. If you feel the steering wheel vibrate in a new car, make sure your dealer checks the wheel balance before cups begin to form. On older cars, you should always suspect incorrect wheel/tire balance as the cause of vibration and get this problem tended to before trying new shock absorbers or major front suspension repairs to fix the shimmy.

In some cases, vibration is not corrected by balancing the front wheels. This is sometimes the result of an improperly balanced *brake disc* and *hub assembly*.

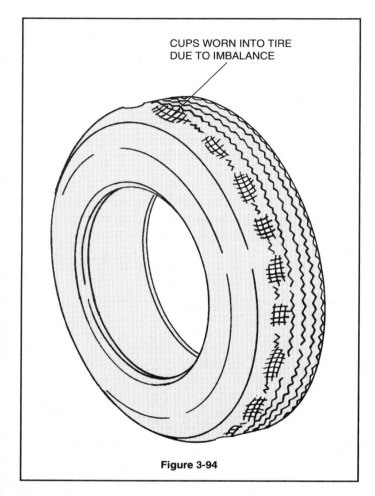

Figure 3-94

Vibration in Rear of Car or Vibration Felt in Driver's Seat (2)

On many cars, particularly those with independent rear suspensions, an imbalanced rear wheel can cause substantial vibration. The vibration can seem to emanate from the rear of the car, or it can be felt in the front seat. Usually, rear wheel imbalance must be relatively severe to cause a discernable vibration; however, even in cases of mild imbalance, premature tire wear can occur. Some cars with independent rear suspensions are very susceptible to tire cupping (Figure 3-94) due to incorrectly balanced rear wheels.

Parts and Terms

If your car needs wheel balancing, your mechanic might mention one or more of the following terms:

Brake Disc   A brake disc mounted on a hub is shown in Figure 3-95. The disc itself can be unbalanced, causing steering wheel vibration. If a disc or the hub it is mounted on is unbalanced, the entire wheel and tire assembly should be balanced on the car with an on-car wheel balancing machine. If such a machine is not available, it may be necessary to replace the disc. If one disc is replaced, both front discs must be replaced in matched sets.

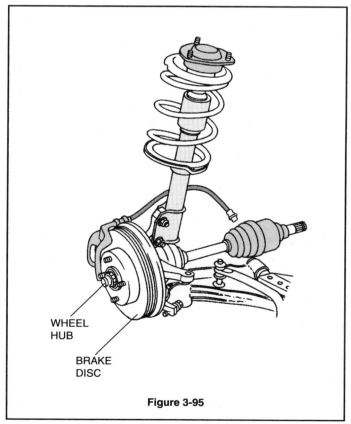

Figure 3-95

Dynamic Balance   A wheel is dynamically balanced when the centerline of the weight mass of the wheel is in the same plane as the geometric centerline of the wheel. Figure 3-96 shows a wheel that is dynamically imbalanced. Notice the heavy spots in the upper right and lower left corners of the tire. These heavy spots would cause the wheel to shimmy from side to side at high speed. To compensate for the heavy spots, weights are installed in the upper left and lower right corners. Dynamic balancing is achieved using a balancing machine that spins the wheel. Some machines are designed to balance the wheel with the wheel removed from the car. Other balancing machines can balance the wheel on the car.

Hub   Figure 3-97 shows a typical hub on which a wheel would be mounted. It is very rare for a hub to be imbalanced.

Static Balance   When a wheel is statically balanced, its weight mass is evenly distributed around its axis of rotation. Figure 3-98 shows a statically imbalanced tire having a

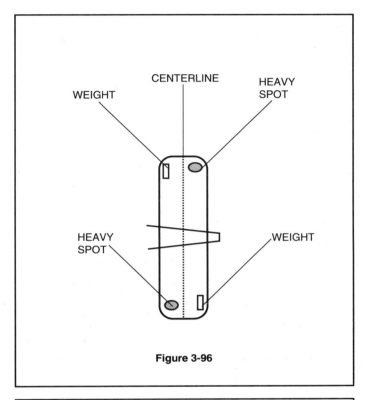

Figure 3-96

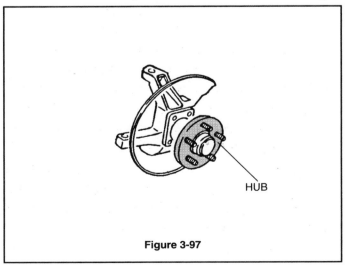

Figure 3-97

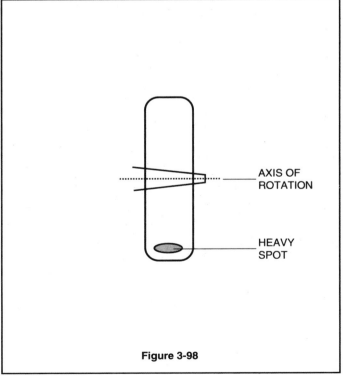

Figure 3-98

heavy spot. Although static balance can be achieved using a relatively inexpensive device called a bubble balancer, few repair shops still use these devices because they are inaccurate and do not ensure correct dynamic balance. When a wheel is dynamically balanced by a mechanic, static balancing is performed at the same time.

Mistakes and Ripoffs

The following information will help you control the cost of wheel balancing. The topics covered are those most likely to be associated with errors commonly made by mechanics or deliberate attempts to defraud the consumer.

Unnecessary Replacement of Shock Absorbers to Correct Steering Wheel Vibration

A favorite trick of some unscrupulous shops is the replacement of shock absorbers to correct a steering wheel vibration that could be repaired inexpensively by balancing the wheels. It is not uncommon for shock absorbers and struts to last 75,000 miles or more on late-model cars. If the shock absorbers or struts are not leaking, that is, if they don't show fluid stains, you should be suspicious of a recommendation to replace them. Ordinarily, worn or defective shock absorbers do not cause steering wheel vibration. Ask your mechanic to check wheel balance before he replaces your car's shocks or struts.

Unnecessary Wheel Alignment to Correct Steering Wheel Vibration

Incorrect wheel alignment does not cause steering wheel vibration or front end shim-

my. Do not allow your mechanic to sell you a wheel alignment job to correct a vibration problem. The source of the vibration is probably either improper wheel balance or worn front-end parts.

Failure to Check for Out-of-round Tires or Bent Wheels when Balancing Wheels

Sometimes, despite properly balanced wheels, a steering wheel vibration or wheel shimmy persists. The problem could be caused by out-of-round tires or wheels (rims). You can tell if a tire is out-of-round by raising it off the ground with a jack. Make sure the vehicle is adequately supported so that there is no danger that it might slip off the jack. Hold a pencil across the front of the tire about one-eighth of an inch away from the tread. Then spin the tire and observe whether it seems to move in and out toward the pencil. If it appears to move more than one-eighth of an inch, it may have excessive radial runout, a more technical term for the out-of-round condition. If the wheel on which the tire is mounted is somewhat out-of-round, sometimes repositioning the tire on the wheel and rebalancing the wheel and tire assembly will correct the steering wheel vibration. In other cases the only cure is a new tire.

Failure to Dynamically Balance Wheel and Hub as an Assembly

Most repair shops use off-the-car wheel balancers. These machines do an excellent job. Unfortunately, a front end or steering wheel vibration can persist after balancing has been done on one of these machines.

This problem happens when the *brake disc* and/or *hub* is not correctly balanced. If you are unable to obtain a satisfactory wheel balance using off-the-car balancers, there is a chance that an on-the-car balancer will solve the problem. This kind of machine does not require removal of the wheels from the car. The entire tire and wheel assembly, along with the brake disc and hub, are spin balanced. Any imbalance in the brake disc or hub is corrected while the wheel is on the car. One disadvantage of using this method is that an imbalance could occur if the wheel is removed from the car and reinstalled in a different position on the hub.

Maintenance Tips

The following maintenance tips will help extend tire life, reduce the need for frequent wheel balancing, and help control the cost of related repairs.

- Maintain proper tire pressure at all times.

- If you remove a wheel from your car, mark the position of the wheel relative to the studs or the hub so that it can be put back on the hub in exactly the same position.

- Don't pay for a wheel alignment to correct a vibration in the steering wheel or the front end. It won't work!

- Periodically check your car's tires for scalloping or cupping in the tread. This kind of wear usually indicates the need for wheel balancing.

Here's what you'll find in The People's Car Book

Index